The Investment Alternative

BOOKS BY BARRY KAYE

The Investment Alternative

BARRY KAYE

Forman Publishing

ISBN: 0-936614-16-1

Library of Congress Catalog Card Number: 97-60386

Printed in the United States of America

98 99   5   4   3   2

DEDICATION

Once again, I am dedicating my book to the professionals in America who serve a great cause in helping and guiding people down what should be a simple, but is often made complicated, road. A person's lifetime of work should not be decimated, nor possible guarantees against losses not implemented, nor diversification that could create and optimize assets overlooked.

Many have followed me into a new era totally different, unique and creative in solving these problems. They have dropped the complex, convoluted plans of tax avoidance for the simple Investment Alternative approaches that I have helped develop.

I hope this book will help many others to further understand and join my crusade to better serve the public, our professions, and America.

YOU DON'T HAVE TO SELL THE DODGERS, PETER O'MALLEY

Just as we were putting the finishing touches on this book and sending it off to press, the news and sports worlds exploded with the shocking story that Peter O'Malley, co-owner of the Los Angeles Dodgers, was going to sell the team because the estate tax burden of the illiquid asset was too heavy for his heirs to bear. Valued at between $300 million and $500 million, the taxes on the ownership could total as much as $275 million, an amount Mr. O'Malley's heirs would have to pay within nine months of his death. Afraid of the havoc this necessity could wreak on his family's fortunes, Mr. O'Malley had come to the conclusion that he had to sell the team now in order to make the asset liquid to ensure having the capital needed to meet the estate tax requirement.

But **YOU DON'T HAVE TO SELL THE DODGERS, MR. O'MALLEY**.

Mr. O'Malley's EXACT situation is covered by various Investment Alternative techniques discussed in this book. How to protect an illiquid asset and avoid forced liquidation, how to discount the estate tax costs and, most importantly for him, *how to effectively raise your exemptions so that no taxes are due on an asset value of up to $363 million*!

In Concept #24, I demonstrate a means for increasing your estate tax exemptions up to $363 million. If the Dodgers are worth $363 million, Mr. O'Malley could retain the team and leave his heirs free of any tax liability for them. And the cost for doing so would effectively be only $5 million. $5 million and he retains ownership of the team for the rest of his life and for his children without any further estate or gift tax burden. Or, he can sell now, lose the asset, pay capital gains tax and still be faced with $200 million of estate taxes. To me, it seems a simple choice.

Luckily for him, Mr. O'Malley still has that choice. Consider the case of a colleague of his, Joe Robbie, owner of the Miami Dolphins.

Mr. Robbie's unexpected death left his heirs and estate completely unprepared. His children had to sell both the Dolphins and the stadium which was named for their father because of the dire nature of the estate tax nightmare they were left with at his death. Peter O'Malley can completely avoid that situation by planning now and leave his heirs completely free of any estate tax depletion.

How can this financial miracle be possible? Through the amazing power of the Investment Alternative.

As is demonstrated by this timely story, the tragic effects of estate taxes on the wealthy families of America are happening every day around us. And this will only get worse as the richest generation in history, the parents of the baby boomers, age and die, passing on their estates to their children and charities. We saw it in the news about Jacqueline Kennedy Onassis' estate planning failure, we see it now with Peter O'Malley.

The concepts presented in this book offer an alternative to the decimation which occurs and allows families to retain the assets they worked so hard to amass. You don't have to sell the Dodgers, Peter O'Malley. No one needs to suffer that kind of loss anymore. Whether your asset is $363 million or $50 million or $2 million, whether you own the Dodgers, real estate or other substantial assets, the programs detailed here work the same.

Don't let your joy and desire be negated by estate taxes, Peter O'Malley. Read Concept #24, and learn how to fully exempt your interest in the Dodgers from the estate taxes you fear.

ACKNOWLEDGMENTS

This is my fifth book with Rhonda Morstein as my contributing editor. There are no words left to thank her and properly acknowledge her previous, current and ongoing assistance in my work and my quest. She is into my thoughts and work and therefore invaluable in the assistance she offers. Her dedication, abandonment of time, interpretation of my ideas and commitment to these concepts extend beyond anything I could have hoped for.

I also want to extend thanks to Adam Gilligan for his work on the outstanding charts which graphically depict my concepts throughout this book.

My gratitude is further extended to Arieh Krumkop for the compilation of tables and charts that appear in the back of this book. Furthermore I shall always be in debt to Arieh who sat me at a computer and, at my advanced age, taught me the impossible so that I have been able to write these last few books using this amazing contraption!

CONTENTS

12 CONTENTS

ESTATE TAX COST DISCOUNTING   131

PART TWO
Myths, Misconceptions and Misinformation

PART THREE
Incomparable Comparisons

PART FOUR
The Moment of Truth Or "How To Stay on The Forbes 400"

PART FIVE
Too Good To Be True

FROM THE AUTHOR

The development and implementation of the materials and procedures presented in this book represents the major focus of the last 35 years of my life. The wealth creation and preservation industry has been, throughout that time, not just my job, or even just my passion. It has been my life.

I live and breathe my work. I have authored six books including three previous books on this subject, one of which is the leading bestseller in the field; three of them have been reprinted in paperback. I travel the country and present approximately 100 seminars a year. I am a regular guest expert on the subject on radio and TV programs. I tell you this not for the sake of my ego, but to demonstrate the level at which what I do consumes my life.

So what is it I do that so consumes my passion? I SELL LIFE INSURANCE. It is that simple. And it is that complex.

I sell life insurance. But I sell so much more than that.

Life insurance, as I utilize it on behalf of my clients, becomes a funding mechanism which, as an alternative to any investment, can effectively increase your estate tax exemptions up to $363 million, turn any tax into an asset, protect the value of your investment portfolio, recapture a financial loss, double the proceeds from the sale of a business, optimize your municipal bond yields up to 25%, turn a $10 thousand tax free gift into a $1 million gift at no extra cost, increase your IRA or Pension 10–20 times. And much more!

That the vehicle which accomplishes these valuable financial feats is life insurance is irrelevant to the benefits my clients reap. The Investment Alternative of life insurance is a method, a concept, an approach, a vehicle, a design, an idea, a formula, a system, a program, a technique. It is a means to an end, an end that NOTHING else can achieve in the same way with the same results. And it is for these reasons that I sell life insurance with such a passion.

But I don't just sell life insurance; I live what I preach. I have used the methods presented to you here to increase my endowments to the charities and institutions which I support. I have used them to ensure the financial security of my wife, children and their children, the grandchildren I love with all my heart. Those who are skeptical might say I have done what I have done over the years only for money. To increase my own wealth. And it is true that I have done well and built a significant estate through my career. But can you imagine that at age 68 I would risk the welfare of my wife, children and grandchildren just to further some 'money making scheme' when I already have all that any of us will ever need? Of course not. I practice these techniques because I *believe* in them, because I *know* them to be true and because I realized long ago that nothing else will accomplish for the people I love what these plans will. Nothing.

Now, in this book, it is my desire to help you see the same truth. That nothing will do for your family what the Investment Alternative methods I am going to describe to you can do. Nothing. Because of the unique features and advantages of life insurance, the financial power of a portfolio which includes it is increased many times over. Increased and protected so that your posterity can realize the benefits of your hard work, wisdom and love.

The need for this fourth book lies in the fact that, due to the highly specialized and somewhat untraditional nature of the Investment Alternative concepts, most professional and lay people are not aware of, or do not comprehend, their power. Attorneys, accountants and other financial advisors who are not proficient in this arena all too often overlook this tool in structuring their clients' portfolios. Or they think the utilization of life insurance is secondary and so only include it as an afterthought. As a result, families needlessly lose millions of dollars every year. Even the financial media, trained in the more conventional methods and suspicious of that which is unfamiliar, so misunderstands these programs that they too, with alarming frequency, completely misrepresent them to the public. In answer to this I have included the chapter entitled <u>Myths, Misconceptions and Misrepresentations</u>. In it, I review the common misconceptions and errors made by the media and professionals in other fields and demonstrate where their problem lies. Too many people have been financially damaged as a result of bad advice to leave the matter unaddressed.

In the chapter entitled <u>The Moment of Truth Or "How To Stay on The Forbes 400,"</u> I demonstrate the amazing power of the Investment

Alternative system using as examples the estates of some very famous and rich people. I show you how their estates can be optimized and preserved so that they and you might better comprehend these applications and see for yourself exactly how they can impact an estate.

The methods themselves are presented in the chapter entitled The Investment Alternative and are broken down into two sections: Financial Optimizing and Estate Tax Cost Discounting. A few of the programs described in these chapters had their genesis in earlier materials of mine. However I have updated and revised them to reflect the new direction of the Investment Alternative system. I use, for each technique, a generic example designed to methodically walk you through the recommended procedure for saving or creating wealth. You can customize each example to your own exact situation by using the charts and tables at the back of this book which show the returns and yields you can expect and the financial liabilities your estate is facing.

Also included in this book is a chapter entitled Too Good To Be True. In it, I detail how to utilize life insurance to protect your estate for your heirs and create wealth for you and them to enjoy.

As always I include one caution that I can not emphasize enough. As part of a diversified portfolio, the life insurance policies described in these pages are an invaluable financial tool. However, you should not utilize ANY financial vehicle if doing so will negatively impact your lifestyle. Use ONLY funds that you do not require to support your current comfort level. Or reallocate existing funds from current investments that you have already determined as being available. Your well-being must always come first in any plan that you undertake. As much as you love your children and grandchildren, as much as you desire to support your preferred charities, you must provide for yourself and your spouse first and foremost.

If I could, I would go door-to-door throughout America and tell each and every one of you about the Investment Alternative. It is that important. I would ask you to have your attorney or advisor there so that I could answer his or her questions or concerns and you could listen to both sides at the same time before making your decision. I would suggest that you bring up questions and doubts that have been raised in your mind by the media so that I could methodically show you, step by step, exactly where their comprehension and logic breaks down. I would evaluate, one-on-one, your current situation and demonstrate how to avoid the liabilities it is facing or maximize the opportunities it affords. I would do this because I see all around me, every day, great tragedies of financial planning occurring. Tragedies I KNOW are avoidable just as I KNOW that I am not alone in my love of my family and my desire to protect them and preserve for them the financial legacy of security and well-being I have worked so hard to provide. And just as I KNOW that the Investment Alternative method is the single best method for achieving that goal. Frankly, it tears me apart. This needless waste, this wholly avoidable decimation, this tragic devaluation of people's life work. It doesn't have to be like that. The means exist to prevent the loss and to enjoy huge gains, safely, surely and affordably.

Obviously I can not go door-to-door throughout America. So I have written this book instead in the hopes that it will be my emissary. That you can use it to confront your advisors or better comprehend the media or envision your own potentials. And that, as a result, families all across our great nation will take advantage of the Investment Alternative system to secure a better life for themselves and their loved ones.

That the concepts and ideas expressed in this book utilize Life Insurance as the funding mechanism to accomplish their ends is due to the fact that IT IS THE ONLY WAY to achieve the desired goals. There is no alternative as efficient.

Over my 35-year career in this business I have created and implemented almost every one of these concepts and I was the catalyst in 1963 for creating the first last-to-die/survivorship policy.

BUT THIS BOOK IS NOT ABOUT LIFE INSURANCE. The purpose of the Investment Alternative is to show you methods of fully optimizing your assets for your family, heirs and favorite charities. It will also show you how to reduce your estate tax costs to a minimum and in many cases eliminate them completely. After all, the purpose of estate planning beyond the orderly disposition of your assets at your death is to reduce your estate taxes as much as legally possible and optimize what you leave your heirs. Life insurance, if you qualify, is the only proven method of accomplishing that dual goal.

LIFE INSURANCE IS NOT AN INVESTMENT. Yet it belongs in every investment portfolio. LIFE INSURANCE IS <u>NOT</u> AN EX-

PENSE SINCE IT <u>DOES</u> GAIN PROFIT AND INTEREST FOR FUTURE BENEFIT OR ADVANTAGE.

Webster's Dictionary defines Investment as: A possession, as property, acquired for future income or benefit. To commit money in order to gain profit or interest. To utilize for future benefit or advantage. It defines Alternative as: In place of another. Choice between two mutually exclusive possibilities. A choice between two things.

LIFE INSURANCE IS AN ALTERNATIVE TO INVESTING. This is the alternative for anyone over 60 who is worth more than $2 million. It reallocates funds beyond those they need to support their lifestyle and diversifies and optimizes their assets for the future benefit of their heirs or favorite charities.

The perception of an investment includes the potential for a future gain. The perception of an expense is money out of pocket which, once used is gone forever. If money used for real estate or stocks to provide a greater eventual gain is an investment then money used for insurance to provide a greater eventual gain must be called something other than an expense.

Estate planning is not a legal happening. It is an economic event. Estate taxes are a dollars and cents proposition. Mathematics and simple arithmetic producing a clear bottom line will indicate whether a complicated, convoluted estate plan is necessary to reduce and pay taxes or whether the use of a life insurance policy to effectively increase your $600,000 exemptions beyond your actual estate is more efficient and the least expensive method. No rhetoric from any attorney, adviser or insurance man is necessary. ONLY THE BOTTOM LINE!

Only after this determination is made should you incur legal fees beyond your normal wills, and Revocable and Irrevocable Trusts. Always consult your attorney for all legal documentation and tax ramifications as well as any special programs needed to cover your tax exposure beyond your exemptions.

Throughout the book you will see references to the phrase "based on current assumptions." This means that all insurance policies are based on the assumptions of expense, mortality and interest which are CURRENT at the time of purchase. Any change in the current assumptions could effect the death benefit, cash value, total premium or number of premium payments to be made. I have not found this to be a major concern to people unless it is not revealed to them at the time of purchase. More importantly, when an investment turns sour usually all is lost. When an insurance policy is effected, it can be salvaged by borrowing against the policy, cutting the death benefit, shortening the life of the policy depending on your health or paying additional or larger premiums. At least all is not lost, **the policy doesn't blow up**. There are options available to correct it.

All figures, policy premiums, and returns are based on the numbers and pricing available at the time of the writing of this book. They appear in the charts and tables at the back. They are also based on the current laws and regulations.

In this book I describe situations that are familiar to me. Without knowledge of your specific requirements, the author and the publisher disclaim any liability for loss incurred by the use of any direct or indirect application of the material contained herein. Certain ingredients to make these concepts totally work may have been omitted. My staff is ready to go into detail on any concept. We can not be responsible for any implementation of these ideas that we have not executed.

Guarantees of results are also limited by the assumed solvency of the company or consortium of companies participating in your program.

In all examples given in this book, I have taken the liberty of eliminating the cost of money from all proposals and projections. This eliminates lengthy and unnecessary discussion about the "internal rate of return." This rate cannot be accurately determined since we do not know your date of death. Furthermore in all cases cited as examples, I have diversified my clients' portfolios either by using, in almost all cases, less than 10% to 20% of their assets, or by reallocating funds from existing IRA's, Pensions, Municipal bonds, stocks, or other assets. More importantly, I have never proposed any course of financial action that would adversely affect my clients' lifestyle; therefore the internal rate of return is irrelevant in the context of the benefits that these programs provide.

This book has been written primarily for people who have more than $1 million and who can afford to reallocate funds from current investments or who have excess, surplus, discretionary money that they can afford to transfer to their children, grandchildren or trust in order to accomplish these concepts without impacting their current lifestyle. Some of these concepts can be used by people with less than $1 million to create a significantly optimized inheritance.

The true excitement and beauty of these concepts when used to cut your estate tax costs is that they benefit everyone and harm no one. Your money is optimized, your family's financial security is protected, Uncle Sam gets every dollar he has coming and the American people benefit from the increased funds available for investment. These are not loopholes, they are not plans for tax avoidance that will hurt our country. These concepts truly let you live rich knowing that you have done the best by your country, yourself and, most of all, for your heirs and future generations.

For any information on any aspect of this book or its concepts, updated tax changes, current insurance interest, premium pricing, new ideas and approaches or actual implementation, please call me personally at 1–800–343–7424.

PART ONE

The Investment Alternative

Wall Street. The New York Stock Exchange. Here, on the trading floor, a frenzy of investment occurs on a daily basis that is used on every edition of the nightly news around the country as an indicator of the nation's financial health. In a cacophony incomprehensible to an observer, the traders buy and sell the futures of public companies and the people who have invested in them. The big board, glowing with its own unique life force, scrolls the tally of win and loss.

The activity has gone on in this same spot virtually uninterrupted since 1792 when a group of 24 traders first met under a buttonwood tree to make a pact setting forth rules for trade in securities. In the two hundred years that have passed since then, the New York Stock Exchange has become the largest marketplace for securities in the world. Stocks, bonds, futures, options—all are commodities here, to be bought and sold in tiny portions or huge blocks, by multi-national corporations or by individual investors, all with the same hope and goal. To make more money. To invest earnings in the pursuit of higher yields then mere labor can produce.

For the vast majority of individual investors, investment represents, at its most fundamental, a path to the achievement of the American promise. A means to increase their personal financial value and thereby make life better for the next generation.

People rarely invest money they need to support their own lifestyles. Those funds are spoken for, promised to the mortgage bank and the phone company and the utilities that provide light and water and heat. They pay medical bills and college tuitions and are saved for vacations and new cars and occasional luxuries. But when there is some extra, some earnings beyond what are needed to provide a comfortable life on a daily basis, people's thoughts generally turn in the same direction. They seek to use that money to make more money to secure a better future for their families. They seek to invest.

Choosing the right investment is both science and art. Criteria include projected returns, safety, length of time needed to achieve maximum appreciation. Yet, of course, there are no guarantees; the vagaries of the marketplace create both the excitement of dreams exceeded and the despair of dreams destroyed.

The best hedge against the possibility of financial ruin is diversification. Don't put all your eggs in one basket. Take your risks in smaller portions, spread them out, meld potentials for safety and quick, high returns into an overall portfolio that is, like any hybrid, healthier and more sturdy. This may be the one piece of investment advice all the analysts agree on. Diversify.

Diversify. Include in your portfolio individual investment vehicles each intended to fulfill various aspects of your ultimate goal. Dollars in blue chips for security and steady, safe growth. Some bonds for smaller, yet guaranteed, yields. Some speculative investments for the thrilling possibility of high, rapid growth. This has been the valued and time-tested advice of all the best investment counselors.

Yet, for all of this, most people remain dreadfully unaware of an incredible alternative to investing that can protect all the rest. An alternative which provides a predetermined return based on certain defined and calculable variables, which has proven over time to be safer than almost any other, which can achieve the goal of increased financial position for your family free from all income and estate taxes and which can yield its promised return from the first day that you buy it.

No matter how well your investments do, most are subject to income taxes. *All*, as they become part of your estate, will be subject to the estate taxes that can claim up to 55% of their net value. This means your investments actually have to double just to stay even. In the lower tax brackets the estate taxes are not so dramatic, but neither then are the funds available to invest and so achieving maximum safe returns becomes even more important. Meanwhile, as world markets and national economic conditions swing and dance, investment values rise and fall with alarming unpredictability. Families work harder and harder these days just to support their lifestyles and the promise of the American Dream that brought most of our ancestors here, that goal of each generation leaving life a bit better and a bit easier for the next, becomes harder and harder to provide.

And the one Investment Alternative that can recover the equilibrium of the American Dream goes overlooked simply because people are unaccustomed to viewing its potentials in this way and uneducated into the truth of the incredible opportunity it affords.

If I announced the release of a new stock that offered a predetermined return of as much as 40 times its purchase price with that return being available the first day that you owned it and for as long as you owned it, the traders on the Stock Market floor would stampede in their rush to secure a portion of this treasure for their investors. If I sweetened my offer by constructing the purchase of the stock in such a way that it would come to the owner's estate income and estate tax free, thereby effectively increasing its value by an up to ADDITIONAL 100%, a madness of demand would ensue that would surely surpass anything even Wall Street has seen before. Yet, such a financial vehicle *does* exist and, even though it is not bought or sold on Wall Street, it has been quietly purchased and utilized by some of the wealthiest, most knowledgeable and most financially exposed families in America to further their own ability to make life better for their families.

"Why haven't I ever heard of this amazing financial vehicle?" you might be thinking. You have. It has been around even longer than the Stock Exchange. What you haven't done is heard of its incredible potentials within a healthy, diversified portfolio because this is not the common usage to which it has been put.

It often happens that a product or service is created or invented to serve a specific need, provide a focused benefit, solve a singular problem. The product does its job so well in its singular, specific niche that it becomes a part of the background of that niche, a piece of the environment no one gives a second consideration to anymore. Not being squeaky, it gets no grease. It can be years, even decades, before it serendipitously happens that someone *sees* the product anew and realizes there are even more far reaching applications for it than the successful but limited use to which it has been put. When that does happen, whole new vistas of opportunity can be opened up to the broad thinking visionaries capable of seeing and reaching beyond what has commonly been the conventional wisdom. Sadly, there are also always those people who fear to change their thinking, who do not dare to reconsider. For them, the opportunity goes unwelcomed and they find themselves passed by.

The Investment Alternative of which I speak works for big investors, or small. The guarantees it makes are available to everyone who qualifies. Its tax-free status is not a dodge or a loophole, it is a wholly legal aspect of the structure of this financial vehicle. And it is THE ONLY financial vehicle so endowed.

The Investment Alternative of which I speak uses life insurance and, when placed in an Irrevocable Trust for the good of your heirs, it is virtually: 1) the ONLY financial vehicle into which you can place money and have that money provide a predetermined return, based on the assumptions at the time that you purchase it; 2) the ONLY financial vehicle which makes that return available the very day it is secured should the need arise and; 3) the MOST EFFI-CIENT financial vehicle for passing its return on to your heirs income and estate tax free effectively doubling it actual value.

So why have you never thought of life insurance in this way before? For several reasons.

To begin with, many people have a seemingly-instinctive aversion to discussing life insurance beyond the absolute most bare necessity. Some have had bad experiences with insurance salespeople. Most just don't really want to spend their time dwelling on the uncomfortable fact of their own mortality. Yet, death occurs to each of us in our turn and all the denial in the world won't change that fact. All it will do is leave you and your family unprepared. Whether you utilize these concepts or not, you WILL die. Do you really want your fear of the inevitable to be the factor which decimated your family fortune, which deprived your heirs of up to 55% of what you had intended for them, and which devalued by as much as half everything you labored all your life to amass?

. Complementing this aversion perfectly is the fact that most financial advisors, accountants and attorneys know little or nothing about life insurance and its uses in capital optimizing and estate tax cost discounting. Since it is not an area they comprehend the far-reaching abilities and nuances of, they overlook it in their planning. And since their clients often want to avoid the issue anyway, it simply isn't pursued when a non-traditional thinker like myself suggests it.

Some financial professionals, in their quest to discredit life insurance as a fundamental necessity in a carefully constructed and well-diversified portfolio, will often point to two factors which they love to bandy about: internal rate of return and expense/investment.

The internal rate of return is a non-scientific unit of measurement used to compare the value of investments. Theoretically the net return is measured against the factor of the time it took for the investment to earn the return and a basis of comparison exists by which one investment's performance can be measured against another. All of which would be fine and good if it had any relevance at all to real life which, unfortunately, it does not.

NO ONE KNOWS HOW MUCH TIME IS LEFT THEM. Illness, accident, tragedy is all around us. If you are investing some portion of your estate in order to leave your heirs better off, how can you justify making only investments which require time you may not have in order to fully mature and reach their greatest potential? If you die tomorrow—and while no one likes to consider the grisly fact, it is, nonetheless, a fact that you could—will the stock you bought with the anticipated 25% or more growth potential have achieved even a fraction of that growth? Almost assuredly, it will not have. While, equally assuredly, the life insurance policy which you purchased will.

You raise this point to your financial advisor and he or she replies by telling you that, while that is true, the stocks are now part of your estate and your heirs will inherit them so they can continue to grow and earn that great internal rate of return within your heirs' estates. But remember, as they come to your heirs they will be subject to estate taxes of up to 55%. Right away, those stocks have lost as much as half their value. And, given the possibility of forced liquidation, the true loss could be substantially more. Now the stock needs to increase by 100% *just to stay even!* To reach the 25% or more net return you had hoped for, the stock now needs to increase even more.

Even bonds, T-bills and Munis, vehicles which do offer a promised amount of income, are subject to taxation which makes them worth less than half to your heirs. Point this out to your financial advisor the next time you are reviewing your portfolio. Ask that they provide the same guarantees that life insurance does; that they promise the amount of return available; that they promise to make it available in full the very next day, if needed; that they promise the return will gross enough to net the desired amount after taxes are paid and see what they say. Then, ask them again why they haven't advised you to include life insurance, the one financial vehicle which CAN make all those claims, in your portfolio.

The other nonsensical distinction which is made between life insurance and investments has to do with the comparison of "expense" versus "investment."

Turning again to the dictionary, we find that Webster's defines expense as "a laying out or expending; the disbursement of money." Disburse is further defined as "to pay out, as money; to spend or lay out; to expend." Meanwhile, invest is defined as "to put money into business, real estate, stocks, bonds, etc. for the purpose of obtaining an income or profit."

When you buy an insurance policy, are you not "putting money into (the policy) for the purpose of obtaining an income or profit?" In all ways, the policy performs similar to an investment with those notable and beneficial exceptions I just delineated above. Yet, I am forever told by people who opt not to purchase a policy that the expense of the policy is too much. Instead, they want to invest the same money.

IF YOU PUT MONEY INTO A FINANCIAL VEHICLE AND IT RETURNS MORE THAN YOU PUT IN FROM THE VERY FIRST DAY, ISN'T THE INITIAL OUTLAY BETTER THAN AN INVESTMENT? Of course, it is. Yet, the myth that the cost of life insurance is an expense you pay to purchase a commodity is perpetrated. And because you've been indoctrinated to think of it this way, you are missing out on a marvelous opportunity that surely surpasses any of the conventional investments which you think of as being worth the risk they entail. But the truth can not be obscured by attorneys, financial advisors, accountants or tax specialists. Life insurance is, for all intents and practical purposes in terms of how it functions, not an expense but as good as any investment. One which offers phenomenal returns.

Like an investment, you put in money, whether in a single lump sum or paid over time as you might pay off a loan you took to buy a particularly promising and exciting stock. Like an investment, you put the money in anticipating a greater return down the road. Here, however, there are departures from the analogy: With the stock, you can only *hope* it grows. There are chances it won't. But with life insurance you know exactly how much it will be worth, based on current assumptions. With the stock, you need to consider an internal rate of return to measure its value. Life insurance pays it full return the first day, if necessary. With the stock, a 20%–30% return would be considered significant even though that return will effectively be reduced to 10%–15% after estate taxes are assessed. Life insurance policies offer returns of as high as 40–50 times, the equivalent of 80–100 times due to the estate tax free nature of a properly structured policy.

It is, I think, quite clear. You put money in, you get more money out. That's how an investment works by *anyone's* definition. The Investment Alternative concepts work the same way. The policy is not an expense, not when it offers a return higher than the amount put in to get it. But again I stress, life insurance is NOT an investment. It's an *alternative* to investing that works in the same manner to create wealth and which must be evaluated fairly against any investment vehicle.

I am not suggesting that you should put all your excess money into life insurance. That would be as irresponsible as allowing you to have a portfolio that didn't contain any. Investing can be fun and exciting and it CAN yield great results. Just as there is no guarantee of time enough for your investments to grow, there is also no certainty that that time is not available. Perhaps you will live long enough to score big on some stock or piece of real estate that will yield additional funds to re-invest. You should pursue all your options. But you should definitely contain within your portfolio the one alternative to investing which offers the unique and extremely valuable benefits only life insurance can.

Throughout the pages of this book you will read example after example of how life insurance, as part of a diversified portfolio, can greatly optimize your assets. Plans and methods, all of which can easily be customized to your particular circumstances using the charts and tables at the back of the book or by calling for a proposal, depict the amazing variety of usages to which life insurance can be put to increase your assets, protect your estate, effectively discount your estate taxes, dramatically increase endowments to your favorite charity, and more. In just about each and every case the simple fact is that **NO INVEST-MENT VEHICLE** can accomplish what the Investment Alternative approach of life insurance in an Irrevocable Trust can with the same benefits and returns. Have your advisor try to plug any stock, bond, CD, T-Bill, business, collectible or piece of real estate he or she favors into the included equations and see for yourself how the performances compare when you take everything into account.

And try to avoid the tension and stigma you may experience when you hear the words "Life Insurance." They are just words, they can't hurt you. In fact, they can do you a great deal of good if you will just let them. Don't let your irrational fears rule your judgment. Would it make it easier to accept these concepts if they were being achieved with the use of a stock, or proceeds from a gold mine? If it helps, substitute a fictitious stock in a company we'll call American Dream Incorporated—ADI—everywhere you see the words life insurance throughout this book. Try this on just one sample and see if there isn't a significant difference in your acceptance of the concept. If there is, you will know that your previous resistance was not based on the facts but on your own pre-conceived intolerance for something the astonishing truth of which you had not been helped to fully understand before. Remember, no one ever needs to know where the source of your optimized, preserved and protected estate assets came from. If for some reason you are more comfortable attributing your financial acumen to the buying of stocks than to the purchasing of life insurance create a file folder labelled ADI Stock Purchase and put the insurance policy inside it. The results will be every bit as impressive, your financial goals every bit as accomplished, no matter what you call the process by which you achieved them. CD's, T-Bills, real estate, stocks, life insurance—in the end they are all money and they all spend the same.

FINANCIAL OPTIMIZING

Many investments are, quite frankly, a gamble. You risk the outcome and hope for the best. But life insurance is guaranteed to pay at death, based upon the assumptions of interest, earnings and mortality current at the time you purchase it, and its return is predetermined based upon those same assumptions which allows it to be used in ways conventional investments couldn't be. Planning for financial optimization becomes much more clear and direct when the outcome is known and available at its full value the very day it is purchased. In a diversified portfolio designed to enhance the value of an estate, the Investment Alternative can achieve unprecedented results of capital optimizing and financial planning. The following examples show ways to use the Investment Alternative system to create and preserve wealth. They are only a small sample of the myriad ways this amazing vehicle can be integrated into your portfolio to add a new dimension of options and possibilities. Your own specific situation will undoubtedly suggest many other ways of customizing these methods to best serve your own needs.

Included in the concepts that follow are plans to:

- Guarantee any financial portfolio
- Double the proceeds from the sale of an asset
- Avoid the fall of Wall Street
- Dramatically increase charitable donations
- Maximize Pension and IRAs
- Optimize Financial Gifts
- Create money out of thin air at older ages

Concept #1:

RECEIVE A $10 MILLION RETURN FOR A $75 THOUSAND ANNUAL OUTLAY

If, as we discussed earlier in this book, you are making some of your investments in order to provide a greater legacy to your heirs, you need to be acutely aware of the fact that each and every dollar you leave them in excess of your combined spousal $1.2 million exemption will be subject to estate taxes of up to 55%. That means that if your investments have a total value of $20 million at the time of your death, your heirs will only receive approximately $10 million. Right away, the day you die, your investments have become devalued by 50%. (In actuality, estate taxes on all assets over $3 million would be 55% and, in some instances, they can go as high as 60%. However, for the sake of simplicity in this and other sample concepts, we have elected to round them down to 50%. In truth, the liability of the estate in this example would be even greater than the $10 million we use.)

The Investment Alternative discussed throughout these pages uses **THE ONLY** financial vehicle which can provide a means to retain your assets' full value to your heirs. And *there is a way that you can utilize the already existing power of your current investments to borrow the cost of the insurance so that you can earn a return equal to the full $10 million which would otherwise be lost to taxes for only $75 thousand a year*!

Since the insurance's returns are based on solid, specified and calculated factors and are not dependent upon the vagaries of the real estate industry, the management of some company in which you hold stock, the whimsy of the collectibles market, or the uncontrollable element of chance, you can know at the time of purchase exactly how it will perform for you, based on the current assumptions at the time of your purchase. So, if you and your wife are average age sixty and in reasonably good health, there is every reason to believe that you can receive a firm 10-to-1 return on your insurance dollar. That means that it would cost you $1 million to replace the $10 million which will be lost to taxes at your deaths. This is a substantial return in a market that currently sees average returns of approximately 5%–6%. But it is an even more incredible return when you consider the fact that this return will be available to your heirs the very day the insurance purchase is completed should tragedy strike at that time and that it will not be subject to the 50% decimation of estate taxes if structured correctly.

It would seem that an outlay of 1/20 of your total estate valuation, $1 million from $20 million—5% of your total assets, a sum that would in no way appreciably affect your lifestyle—would be well worth it in order to protect $10 million of your heirs' legacy. Furthermore, in real dollars, that $1 million outlay only costs $500 thousand since it too would have been halved by taxes had it been left inside your estate. But you need not expend even this much in order to achieve the desired result. In fact, **you can provide your heirs with the entire $10 million for an outlay of approximately $75 thousand a year**!

With an estate valued at $20 million, assuming current LIBOR or broker call rates of 7-1/2% interest, you could easily borrow the $1 million cost needed to execute the Investment Alternative concept for $75 thousand a year.

In this way, **ONLY $75 THOUSAND A YEAR PROVIDES A RETURN OF $10 MILLION**, based on the current assumptions at the outset.

Now, I know what you are thinking. You are calculating in your head how much that could cost you in total over your average, expected lifespan. You are employing your skepticism and the skepticism of your other financial advisors who do not fully comprehend the almost unimaginable power of the Investment Alternative methods to find the hole in this seemingly too-good-to-be-true scenario. I invite you, in fact, I welcome you, to do so.

Supposing you were to live to be 80, a nice life expectancy in these days and times. You would wind up paying the $75 thousand interest for 20 years and the total cost would be $1.5 million. A $1.5 million outlay yielding a $10 million return would not be something you'd want to pass up if it were offered to you on the same basis as the Investment Alternative in some other, more conventional form, now is it?

But would the total cost REALLY be $1.5 million? Not if you are fairly assessing the costs and purposes of the purchase. Remember, if you did not pay that $1.5 million in interest for the insurance policy it would have remained within your estate and been subjected to the same 50% estate taxes that the rest of your estate will be assessed. So, to your heirs, the posterity whom are the point of your intentions to begin with, that $1.5 million was only worth $750 thousand. In effect, you actually purchased the $10 million for an accumulated net cost of $750 thousand. That becomes equivalent to a more than 13 times return.

Furthermore, and this is a critical point of consideration that your advisors CAN NOT get around no matter how hard they try, you have no guarantee that you will live to be 80. In fact, you have no guarantee that you will live past tomorrow. It is altogether possible that you might only pay one year of interest before tragedy strikes and your heirs receive the benefits of your planning. In that case, you would have purchased $10 million for one payment of $75 thousand. Imagine any of your investments yielding that sort of return! Challenge your advisors to put into writing a guarantee that they will pay your heirs $10 million out of their own pockets should you not live long enough for their plans to come to an equal fruition and see how they respond. Nothing else can do what life insurance can do in this regard.

But then, what if you don't die. Suppose you do live to be 80. Might you not do something else with that $1.5 million that would eventually yield the same $10 million? Are there stocks or bonds or real estate purchases or pieces of artwork which might be expected to appreciate from $1.5 million to $10 million over the next 20 years?

Perhaps there are but it's very unlikely. Consider this. **ANY IN-VESTMENT RETURN YOU ARE FORTUNATE ENOUGH TO EARN WILL BE SUBJECTED TO THE SAME 50% TAXES UPON YOUR DEATH**. Your investment would not have to increase from $1.5 million to $10 million in order to be considered of equal value to the insurance. It would have to increase to a value of $20 million in order to ultimately yield the same $10 million to your heirs.

From $1.5 million to $10 million might be possible. But from $1.5 million to $20 million? Do you really think so? And, more importantly, is it worth the gamble? You don't have to take the chance with the insurance since its return is structured from the first day to be worth $10 million. And, with the built-in advantage of having its return available IN FULL on the first day you make the purchase, what possible reason could you have for not including this amazing financial vehicle in a diversified portfolio of investments? Even at a cost of $75 thousand a year, the small outlay leaves you with plenty of other income—assuming your $20 million estate is yielding an average 7.5% return of $1.5 million a year—to pursue numerous other investment vehicles.

At this point, some clever attorney or accountant is probably pointing out to you that, in fact, the return of $10 million was NOT purchased only with the $75 thousand in loan interest payments you were making each year. There is still, they are cautioning you, the actual $1 million loan. The $75 thousand annual payments were just debt service on that $1 million amount. And they are right. But, only to a point.

Yes, when you die, your heirs will have to repay the $1 million loan amount from the $10 million they inherited from you thereby effectively raising the cost of implementing the Investment Alternative concept. But, even if you lived to be 80 and paid $1.5 million in loan payments in addition to the $1 million loan amount itself, the total cost would still only be $2.5 million. $2.5 million to produce $10 million is not a bad deal at all. Yet, again, the cost was not REALLY $2.5 million nor was the return REALLY $10 million.

The outstanding $1 million loan is a liability against your estate at the time of estate reckoning. This means that your estate is no longer valued at $10 million; the $1 million outstanding loan amount has reduced its value to $9 million. The estate taxes due on $9 million are not $5 million, but $4.5 million. Your net estate tax has been reduced from $5 million to $4.5 million! A difference of only $500 thousand, not $1 million. So, in effect, Uncle Sam has repaid 1/2 your loan!

Furthermore, in the same way, Uncle Sam also pays off 1/2 the loan interest paid over the life of the couple. Since every dollar left in their estate at the time of their deaths would be subject to a 50% estate tax, the loan interest, had it not been paid out and removed from the estate, would have been reduced by 1/2 when the estate passed on to the heirs.

Therefore, if left within your estate, the $2.5 million of combined principal and interest would have been worth only $1.25 million to your heirs after it had been subjected to the 50% estate taxes levied on the total value of your estate. So the loan principal was not in actuality $1 million, it was $500 thousand. And the loan interest was not $1.5 million, it was $750 thousand. Realistically, $1.25 million earned the $10 million return, IF AND ONLY IF, you actually live to be 80.

Furthermore, as you may recall, the effective amount of return on your life insurance policy, if compared fairly with the yield for any traditional investment you might make, is actually $20 million. It would take a $20 million pre-tax return from any investment to equal the tax-free return of my properly structured Investment Alternative utilizing life insurance.

Of course, at different ages, or different projected life spans, the numbers change. You can use the charts and tables at the back of this book to better determine what your own potentials are. But the key factors remain inarguably the same: 1) The return is predetermined, based on the assumptions current at the time of purchase; 2) The return is available from the first day you buy the policy; 3) Left within your estate the funds would be worth half to your heirs; 4) Any investment you might compare this to would have to yield double the return in order to equal the insurance's tax-free return. **NO INVESTMENT CAN LEGITIMATELY MAKE ALL THESE CLAIMS**.

If all of this is not persuasive enough or you are still crunching numbers convinced you can do better, consider this. For an additional approximate 1%, you can recover the cost of the insurance-funding loan itself!

The cost of the loan in the example above was $500 thousand ($1 million pre-tax, $500 thousand real value after tax.) For the same 60-year old (average age) couple, an additional outlay of $50 thousand would yield a 10 times return of $500 thousand to recover the cost of the loan. So they now pay $1.05 million and receive a return of $10.5 million. Now the numbers work this way:

The couple's $20 million estate is reduced to $19 by the $1 million loan against their assets which was taken to purchase the insurance policy. That $19 million was then reduced by half to $9.5 million by estate taxes. However, the policy yields a tax-free $10.5 million which, when added back into the remaining $9.5 million recreates the entire $20 million which was the intended legacy. Now the effective cost of the whole package becomes the $50 thousand plus $75 thousand a year in interest payments. Assuming the couple lives twenty years, that debt service would equal $1.5 million but that $1.5 million would only be worth $750 thousand if left in the estate and reduced 50% by taxes, so the total for ten years debt service is effectively $750 thousand making the cost of the $10 million death benefit really only $800 thousand. If the couple lives thirty years, the annual $75 thousand debt service would total $2.25 million which, when halved, is an effective cost to them of $1.1 million making the cost of the $10 million return $1.6 million. And if this 60-year-old couple is lucky enough to live 40 more years to the ripe old age of 100, they still will net $10 million for their heirs for only $2 million as the 40 years of debt service will cost $3 million gross but $1.5 million net in addition to the original $50 thousand outlay.

Now consider this. There is nothing which says you must utilize or limit these methods to the recovery of assets decimated by estate taxes. Imagine the wealth you could create for your heirs using this Investment Alternative technique as simply one more tool in your diversified portfolio. At younger ages, when the returns can soar as high as 40–1, the opportunities for wealth creation are almost staggering. The tables and charts included in this book will show you differing applications of these plans and how your individual situation can best benefit. But one thing should already be abundantly clear: The Investment Alternative method offers a means to achieve returns far in excess of any investment with benefits virtually NO OTHER financial planning tool can offer.

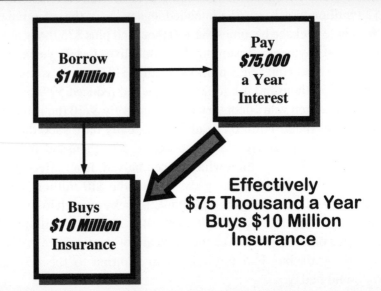

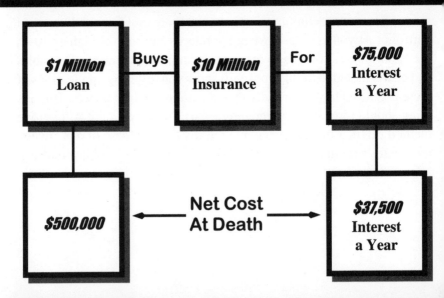

All figures are based on current assumptions. Charts are for illustrative purposes only.
This illustration used a last-to-die insurance policy for a male and female both age 60.
©1997 THE INVESTMENT ALTERNATIVE - Barry Kaye Associates

$1 Million Loan Principal

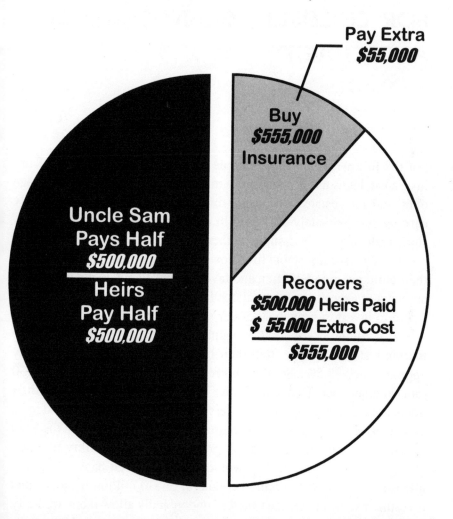

Pay Extra
$55,000

Buy
$555,000
Insurance

Uncle Sam
Pays Half
$500,000

Heirs
Pay Half
$500,000

Recovers
$500,000 Heirs Paid
$ 55,000 Extra Cost
$555,000

UNCLE SAM PAYS HALF
INSURANCE COMPANY PAYS OTHER HALF

All figures are based on current assumptions. Charts are for illustrative purposes only.
This illustration used a last-to-die insurance policy for a male and female both age 60.
©1997 THE INVESTMENT ALTERNATIVE - Barry Kaye Associates

Concept #2:

A YEARLY $150 THOUSAND OUTLAY YIELDS UP TO $86 MILLION FOR CHILDREN, GRANDCHILDREN AND CHARITY

For the following amazing example of the incredible leverage of life insurance, let us use for example a married couple with an average age of 60 and a net estate value of $10 million. Their $10 million, currently earning approximately $500,000 in tax free interest income at an assumed rate of 5% a year, supports them nicely and allows them to lead a comfortable, secure, stable life. However, they would like do more for their children, grandchildren and favorite charity but do not have large amounts of excess capital available from their yearly interest earnings to use to invest in growth stocks or speculative investments.

The substantial size of the couple's estate easily allows them to margin a sum of money from their broker at his call rates—currently approximately 7.5%. So they borrow $2 million at a cost of $150 thousand per year. This would leave them with $350 thousand of their interest income to support their lifestyle which they have deemed to be sufficient. However, if for some reason it were not enough and the $150 thousand loan interest would too greatly affect their ability to enjoy their lives to the fullest, they would really not even have to pay the interest amounts. With secured collateral of $10 million in stocks and investments, the brokerage firm will undoubtedly allow them to simply accrue the interest along with the principal loan amount. Upon their deaths, the brokerage firm will basically just subtract the original loan amount along with the total accrued interest from the total value of the estate and give the heirs the remainder.

In any event, the couple now has an extra $2 million to invest without having impacted their lifestyle in any appreciable manner. Using an amazing combination of financial vehicles and taking advantage of the unique power of life insurance and its tax-free status, that freed-up $2 million can be used to create and optimize huge amounts of money. In this example, you will see a dramatic account of how the $2 million creates $86 million! But keep in mind that this is just one of many courses that the couple could undertake using the power of the Investment Alternative technique included within their portfolio.

The couple makes a gift of the $2 million to their favorite charity with the provisions that $1 million be used for current projects and operations and the other $1 million be used to provide for a future endowment. In this case, the purchase to be made is a last-to-die insurance policy taken out on the lives of the couple which can be assumed, at their ages, to produce a return, based on current assumptions, of $10 million which will increase the couple's gift from $2 million to $11 million.

So far, the $150 thousand a year interest on the borrowed $2 million—which need not actually ever be paid—has yielded an eventual $11 million. But with the Investment Alternative concept, that same $150 thousand yearly interest payment accomplishes much, much more.

Having an estate of $10 million, it is fair to assume that this couple are in a close to 50% income tax bracket so the fully deductible charitable donation of $2 million would produce an approximate $1 million tax savings. (Check your accountant and tax attorney to verify your own tax bracket.)

Now, the $150 thousand they paid in annual loan interest on the $2 million loan amount that the couple gave to charity has earned them a $1 million tax savings! Wisely, they now opt to use this savings to purchase a policy for the benefit of their children and **ANOTHER $10 MILLION IS PRODUCED WHICH WILL COME TO THEIR HEIRS INCOME AND ESTATE TAX FREE**.

$150 thousand a year, a sum which could even be allowed to accrue and need not effect one single other dollar of investment capital or living expense, has now produced $11 million for charity and $10 million for the couple's children to receive income and

estate tax free. In real dollar terms, the gift to the children is actually worth $20 million since any other form of producing the same $10 million would be depreciated by half by estate taxes. But the monetary results of the Investment Alternative method comes into their estate income and estate tax free. That means that it is effectively $31 million that has been produced.

But the power of this incredible financial vehicle does not stop there. In fact, it's not even close to being tapped out.

Of course, by its very nature, life insurance produces a higher yield the younger you are when you purchase it. Greater life expectancy equals greater returns. The couple in this example cannot change how old they are. But that does not leave them without alternatives to maximize the yields their purchase can return. Thinking creatively, an additional $40–$50 million can be produced!

If, instead of purchasing a policy on themselves for the benefit of their children, the couple were to spend the extra $1 million created by the tax deduction for the charitable donation on a policy on *their children's lives for the sake of their grandchildren*, they could earn as much as a 40–50 times return. The couple's children are considerably younger than they are and they represent a different risk to the insurance company. Based on the current assumptions of interest and mortality, the insurers can afford to provide a significantly greater return, *in this case, as much as $40 or $50 million*!

Now, there is $11 million for the charity and $40–$50 million for the grandchildren. *A total of up to $61 million from the same $150 thousand yearly interest has been produced, based on current assumptions, and is available on the same day the purchase is made should the circumstances warrant.*

If you were to try to figure out how much money that same $150 thousand interest would have to produce in more common ways in order to ultimately yield the same amounts after two generations of income and estate taxation, the real truth of the insurance's power becomes known.

The $1 million tax savings on the $2 million charitable donation which was used to produce $10 million for the couple's children would, if invested, have had to yield $20 million to net the same $10 million after tax. If invested on behalf of the grandchildren, it would have to go to $200 million! The children inherit the $200 million but pay over 50% estate taxes on it so it is reduced to $100 million. Then, as the grandchildren inherit it, they pay over an additional 50% taxes thereby reducing it to the $50 million which the Investment Alternative method produced. Of course, there are some ways of structuring a generation-skipping gift utilizing trusts that might help avoid some of the dual taxation costs and I have rounded off the 55% estate tax cost to 50% for the sake of simplicity. But NO INVESTMENT will *EVER* allow for a complete avoidance of income and estate tax costs in the same manner. At some point, the return yielded by every investment in your portfolio, as it is transferred from one generation to the next, WILL BE SUB- JECTED TO UP TO 55% ESTATE TAXES.

All of this should be dramatic enough to make an impression upon you. We just used $150 thousand a year, a negligible sum to this estate and an amount which need not, in reality, even be repaid (surely the children will not mind so terribly much being "burdened" with the principal and interest repayment costs when they have just realized $10 million they would otherwise never have had) to produce up to $61 million. But we did claim at the beginning that a total return of $86 million was possible. Here's how:

If the couple used the $1 million in tax savings they earned for the original $2 million donation to purchase additional coverage on their children for the sake of the charity, the charity would receive an additional $40–$50 million gift. They'd get $1 million now, $10 million when the couple died, and $40–$50 million when the couple's children died for a total of up to $61 million.

But now the couple has donated back to charity the $1 million tax saving they received for their original $2 million donation and so they earn an additional $500 thousand tax saving. They could use that $500 thousand to make a purchase of life insurance on themselves for their children's sake and earn an additional $5 million bringing the total to $66 million—$1 million to charity now, $10 million to charity when the couple dies, up to $50 million to charity when the couple's children die and $5 million to the couple's children. **OR** the couple could utilize the additional $500 thousand for a purchase of insurance on their children for their grandchildren's sake and receive a return of up to $25 million jumping the total to $86 million . . . $61 million over the years to the charity and $25 million to the grandchildren. All achieved for $150 thousand a year, based on current assumptions, all available immediately if needed and all actually worth twice their stated yield amounts when compared with any investment which would be subjected to income and estate taxation.

The combinations and potentials are virtually unlimited and all are totally legal and available to anyone with the wisdom to want them. Upon death, the children will have to pay off the loan of $2 million (or the principal and accrued interest). But, in effect, Uncle Sam will actually pay off 1/2 the total cost since the removal of the $2 million from the couple's estate will reduce the total of their asset by $2 million and there will be $1 million less in estate taxes due.

I think it should become quite apparent that we are not talking about insurance here as you have ever understood it. This is truly the phenomenal concept of the Investment Alternative.

$150,000 YEARLY BUYS UP TO $86 MILLION FOR HEIRS AND CHARITY

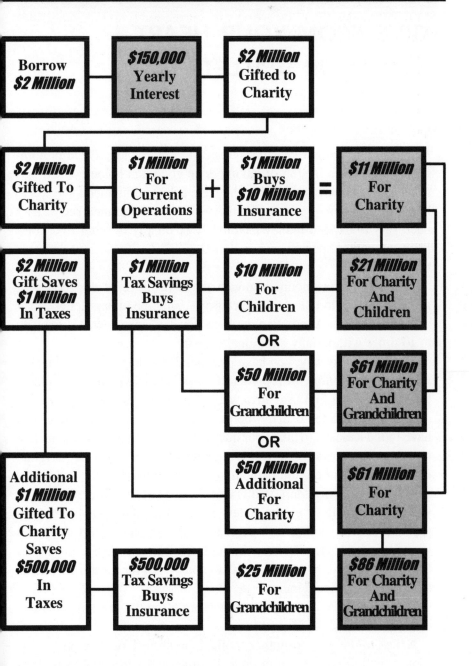

All figures are based on current assumptions. Charts are for illustrative purposes only. This
illustration used last-to-die insurance policies on parents both age 60, and children both age 30.
©1997 THE INVESTMENT ALTERNATIVE - Barry Kaye Associates

Concept #3:

GIVE FROM YOUR HEART, NOT YOUR WALLET

Supporting a favored charity is a special kind of joy. There is nothing quite like the feeling of having done good and helped out. It is, I think, the best way for people who have achieved financial success to demonstrate their gratitude for their own good fortune. Yet, it isn't necessary to expend money frivolously or blindly in order to accomplish the goal. Especially when donating _wisely_ can achieve so much more.

Think about the amount of money you have budgeted as a bequest or gift or donation to your favorite charity. Using the unparalleled power of the Investment Alternative methods you can increase that sum by up to 10 times without any additional cost.

Think of it this way, you have just found out about an amazing new financial opportunity with predetermined returns which are available the very day you first take advantage of the opportunity. Now, instead of simply giving the charity the lump sum you intend for them, you have found a means to take your intended donation amount and make it grow in such a way that you will now donate not just the original intended sum, but the total amount of the optimized yield.

You probably wouldn't do this with an investment. After all, though you may be willing to run a few risks with your own funds, you probably won't want to risk decreasing the amount you'd slated for your favorite charity. Plus the timing factor can prove quite detrimental. Frankly, it might take longer than you've got for most investments to return a significant increase.

But these concerns are not factors when using the Investment Alternative method of life insurance.

A last-to-die life insurance policy, purchased on you and your spouse, will yield a return of up to 10 times and will make that return fully available the very day you make the purchase should circumstances warrant. This makes your course of action safe and assured. You KNOW, without risk or doubt, that you are benefiting your chosen charity as much as ten times more than would have otherwise been the case.

At average age 60, a couple can receive a 10–1 return on a last-to-die policy. That means that if you've slated $3 million of your estate to go to charity and instead of giving it the cash you make this outlay on its behalf, the charity will ultimately receive $30 million! $30 million to your favorite charity for an outlay of $3 million you were going to give them anyway and the $3 million is deductible now. Wait until death and they get $3 million. Give them a $30 million policy now and you get $1.5 million income tax savings now and they get $30 million at death. You could even earmark $3 million back to your heirs (or more) and the charity would still receive $27 million, $24 million more than your original intended $3 million. Your heirs' inheritance wasn't effected.

At average age 70, the couple could expect to receive a 5–1 return so the same $3 million outlay would yield $15 million for their charity and at average age 80, with an expected 3–1 return, the charity would receive $9 million. Is there anywhere else that, at age 80, you and your spouse can put $3 million and have it grow to a sure and certain $9 million before you die, no matter when you die?

Remember also, you don't actually have to make the insurance purchase utilizing a lump sum of cash. If you had planned on making the donation as a bequest because you need the money during your lifetime to fund your lifestyle, you can borrow against your other assets to fund the purchase and have the premium and interest deducted from the life insurance proceeds upon your death while still leaving a more optimized total sum for the charity. In this way, you can make a wonderfully generous contribution without depleting your own resources in any way. Or, you can fund the policy purchase through the insurer, making yearly payments that you might find more accommodating to your financial situation. You could also hold the policy within your estate, thereby retaining access to its excellent cash values in case you should develop a need for the money down the line. Then the policy is transferred to the charity at your death without the concerns of estate tax decimation that make such a course unwise when planning money transfers within your family since charitable contributions are tax deductible and generational transfers of assets are not.

There is simply no investment that accomplishes all of this:

1) Provides a return of up to 10 times, allowing you to increase your charitable donations at no additional cost;
2) Provides that return the very day it is first purchased should circumstances require it to do so;
3) Develops cash values to which you can retain full access throughout your lifetime without having to sell off any of the asset and IN EXCESS of the initial payment.

Give from your heart . . . but give smart. Use the Investment Alternative technique to increase your bequests to charity with "soft" insurance company dollars and enjoy the special pleasure that comes from knowing you have done good for others who need it—ten times over!

Give From Your Heart

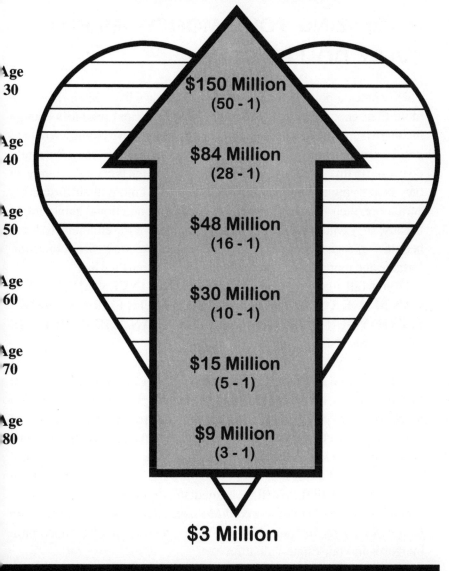

Age 30

$150 Million
(50 - 1)

Age 40

$84 Million
(28 - 1)

Age 50

$48 Million
(16 - 1)

Age 60

$30 Million
(10 - 1)

Age 70

$15 Million
(5 - 1)

Age 80

$9 Million
(3 - 1)

$3 Million

$3 MILLION DONATION INCREASES
TO AS MUCH AS $150 MILLION

All figures are based on current assumptions. Charts are for illustrative purposes only.
This illustration used last-to-die insurance policies for couples of various ages.
©1997 THE INVESTMENT ALTERNATIVE - Barry Kaye Associates

Concept #4:

THE INVESTMENT ALTERNATIVE

MAXIMIZING YOUR MONEY—MAKING EVERY DOLLAR COUNT

There comes a point in some successful people's lives when they have more than enough money to live on. Their principal produces enough income to support them in the style they desire and leaves some left over to provide the knowledge of security in the event of an emergency. But rarely do people in this position decide that having enough is enough. Rarely do they stop trying to make their investments yield more, their businesses earn more, their fortunes increase. Some pursue additional gains simply because they enjoy the "game." But most do it for the children. To leave behind as great a legacy as possible and help make life easier, more comfortable and more financially secure for the children they love.

If you fall into this category, there is **NO INVESTMENT YOU CAN MAKE TO MAXIMIZE YOUR ESTATE FOR THE BENEFIT OF YOUR CHILDREN BETTER THAN THE PURCHASE OF A LIFE INSURANCE POLICY**!

I have always called the money your principal earns in excess of that which you need to support your lifestyle "Junk Money." Some prefer to call it excess, discretionary or surplus funds, but I think "junk" is a much more apt description. This money sits around on the bottom of your pile of assets, accumulates in various stocks or savings accounts, gets invested in less than optimal manners. And what *really* 'junks up' those funds is the fact that after sitting around for all that time, at the time of your death they will be immediately reduced by up to 55% by estate taxes. Meanwhile, *you could be using that money to fund lasting financial security for your children*! You could use it to effect maximum increases in your estate valuation.

Imagine that you have an estate worth $30 million. Your principal earns 8% annually, or $2.4 million. But it only costs you $2 million a year to live the lifestyle you choose. $25 million, earning 8%, will yield $2 million. So, in effect, $5 million of your estate is earning $400 thousand of yearly "junk money" . . . money you don't really need and which you are simply accumulating for the sake of your children.

If you and your spouse are average age 60, you could use that extra $5 million to buy an insurance policy for the ultimate benefit of your children. Since you would use an Irrevocable Trust to hold the insurance purchase and keep it outside your estate, there would be gift taxes to pay. You would transfer $3.5 million to the trust and pay gift taxes of approximately $1.5 million. This would fund an insurance policy with a death benefit of $35 million. **$35 MILLION**! Is there any investment into which you could put that extra $5 million and have it become $35 million—tomorrow, if need be? It would take over 36 years of simply amassing the $400 thousand of interest the $5 million earns each year at compound interest before it increased to $80 million to net $35 million after taxes. You'd be 96 years old.

Maybe, just maybe, there is some stock or appreciating collectible which, if you put the same $5 million into would, given time, yield the same 7 times return. However, you have no guarantee that the investment will increase to that extent, no guarantee that you have time enough to get there even if it will. Furthermore, if the true purpose of this investment of your junk money is to increase your estate for your children, **YOU MUST TAKE INTO ACCOUNT THAT ANY INVESTMENT YIELD WILL BE SUBJECT TO ESTATE TAX AND VIRTUALLY HALVED IN ITS VALUE TO YOUR HEIRS**. The $5 million would have to increase to $80 million in order to be worth the same $35 million to your children.

Of course, this example is a bit extreme, made intentionally so in order to dramatize the point. In all likelihood, you are not going to want to utilize the full $5 million even though it is excess in that it produces income you do not need. But it is not necessary to involve that significant a percentage of your total estate in the Investment Alternative concepts in order to reap huge rewards.

Consider this usage of your "junk money":

With an estate of $30 million, your estate taxes will be approximately $16.5 million. At average age 60, it would take an outlay of $1.65 million on behalf of you and your spouse to earn a 10 times return of $16.5 million to recover the cost of the estate taxes for your heirs. With an estate of $30 million, already shown to be earning $400 thousand more annually than you need to live the life you desire and are accustomed to, you could technically afford to use up to $5 million for the ultimate good of your children. Now, for just $1.65 million, plus the gift tax of approximately $200 thousand on the $450 thousand you are transferring in excess of your combined $1.2 million exemption, you can achieve the same basic end. Using that junk money to fund the purchase of a life insurance policy for your heirs, you recover the $16.5 million of estate taxes which would have been lost and enable your children to inherit the full $30 million of your estate. Without this plan, they receive $13.5 million, less than half.

Remember, the $1.85 million of junk money ($1.65 million for the insurance purchase and $200 thousand in gift taxes), if left within your estate, would have also been subject to the decimation of estate taxation. Reduced by 55%, it would have been worth only about $850 thousand to your heirs. Therefore, it is really only $850 thousand which funds the Investment Alternative concept which yields the $16.5 million which keeps your estate intact for the good of your children.

There are an almost endless number of ways that you can use life insurance placed within an Irrevocable Trust to greatly increase the value of your estate and turn your "junk money" into significant wealth.

Maybe you don't want to expend any portion of your excess principal. Perhaps you want to keep it intact as a hedge against an uncertain future. Remember, in all cases of financial and estate planning you should put your own needs and comfort first. Still, significant optimization of the excess interest earned by that money can be achieved using the Investment Alternative approach.

The $5 million of excess money earns an 'unneeded' 6% after tax $300 thousand each year. Using that $300 thousand annual interest earned to enact this program, the couple would pay approximately $100 thousand in gift taxes (assuming their one-time $600 thousand exemption has already been utilized) leaving $200 thousand a year to be transferred to an Irrevocable Trust, for the purchase of insurance. $200 thousand in yearly premiums on a lifetime basis for a last-to-die policy on a couple averaging age 60 will yield about $22 million. Without touching the principal of $5 million so they have it for any use they may need it for, the couple has optimized their $300 thousand yearly accrual of excess interest earnings to produce an additional $22 million tax free for their heirs!

As part of a diversified portfolio, the insurance's unique, predetermined yield, guaranteed first-day return and tax free nature allow it to accomplish money magic that nothing else can come close to.

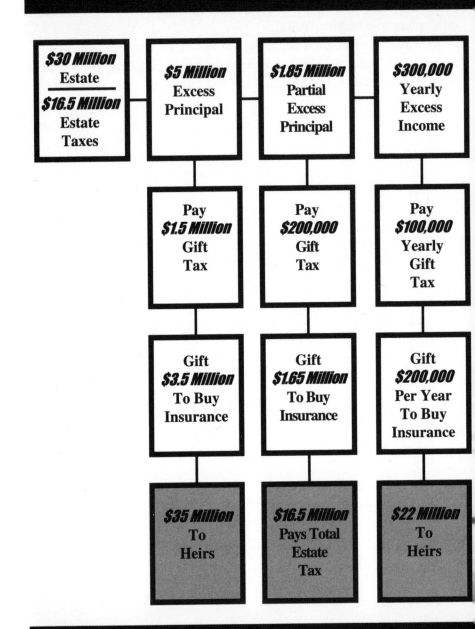

THE INVESTMENT ALTERNATIVE

| $30 Million Estate —— $16.5 Million Estate Taxes | $5 Million Excess Principal | $1.85 Million Partial Excess Principal | $300,000 Yearly Excess Income |

Pay $1.5 Million Gift Tax — Pay $200,000 Gift Tax — Pay $100,000 Yearly Gift Tax

Gift $3.5 Million To Buy Insurance — Gift $1.65 Million To Buy Insurance — Gift $200,000 Per Year To Buy Insurance

$35 Million To Heirs — $16.5 Million Pays Total Estate Tax — $22 Million To Heirs

TURN $5 MILLION JUNK MONEY

All figures are based on current assumptions. Charts are for illustrative purposes only.
This illustration used a last-to-die insurance policy for a male and female both age 60.
©1997 THE INVESTMENT ALTERNATIVE - Barry Kaye Associates

56

Concept #5:

AVOID THE FALL OF WALL STREET

Chances are that your portfolio carries a number of investments which are traded on Wall Street . . . stocks, bonds, securities, futures, options. All purchased as hopeful growth assets, all evaluated based upon sound investigation, thorough consideration and realistic potentials. You've consulted with your advisors, set out the goals you desire your investments to achieve for you and selected the vehicles which you all agree are most likely to accomplish those goals. Though you are aware that there's a risk involved in investing, it's a calculated risk deemed appropriate to the expected, potential rewards.

So the days go by, and the market fluctuates within tolerable limits, some days up, some days down, and you watch your investments and make adjustments where it seems necessary and feel safe that it is all well within projected parameters.

Then, one day, out of the blue, completely unexpectedly, the stock market crashes 3000 points and all your investments are devalued by as much as 55%!

Sounds ridiculous? Farfetched? It isn't. That day is coming as sure and certainly as the sun will rise tomorrow.

As far as you and your investments are concerned, the market will crash those 3000 points and your stocks will be devalued by that 55% the day you die. Nine months after you die, your estate value will be calculated by the government and up to 55% of your net worth will be assessed in estate taxes. The stocks and bonds and securities and options and futures which you so carefully nurtured, the plans you made and calculated and shaped, the goals you crafted and worked towards will all fall those 3000 points.

ANY MONEY WHICH YOU HAVE INVESTED FOR THE EVENTUAL BENEFIT OF YOUR HEIRS IS SUBJECT TO ESTATE TAXES OF UP TO 55% AND THEREFORE WORTH LESS THAN HALF OF ITS CURRENT VALUE.

Suppose you and your spouse, together averaging age 70, had

$3 million in investments above and beyond whatever other assets you have and need to maintain your lifestyle. This $3 million is for growth, primarily for the sake of your children.

But, as part of your total estate, the $3 million is subject to the same 55% estate taxes that will be assessed on your net value. That means it will really only be worth $1.3 million to your heirs. The market will crash and the investments you'd earmarked for your children's financial security will crash along with it.

But there is a way around this devastation.

If you had taken a small portion of the funds you'd invested, $330 thousand from the $3 million, and diversified your portfolio utilizing the Investment Alternative method, you could, even at age 70, receive a 5–1 return, based upon current assumptions. Your $330 thousand outlay would produce $1.6 million to replace what was lost in the estate tax "crash." This might be the best "hedge" you have ever made.

This did not involve any other expenditure of money than you were already making. It simply required that you diversify your investments and move some of the funds already earmarked for growth investments for the good of your children into the purchase of an insurance policy which, by virtue of its unique financial attributes, is able to protect all the rest.

If you had invested in shares of a $100 stock for the eventual benefit of your children, that stock will be worth only $45 per share at the time of your death when they receive it. It would have to double to over $200 per share just in order to net the same $100 at which you purchased it. That doesn't even allow for growth, and why do you purchase stocks if not in the hopes of growth? *ALL OF YOUR STOCKS MUST GROW TO DOUBLE THEIR CURRENT VALUE JUST TO STAY EVEN!*

Even more interesting, if you sold that $100 stock and put the money in a life insurance policy, at age 70 it could immediately be worth $500. Meanwhile each share of your $100 stock must increase to $1000 to net the same value. While the Investment Alternative approach is predetermined and fully available immediately, your stock is certainly not guaranteed to grow from $100 to $1000 and, unfortunately, you are given no guarantee that you will live long enough to see it happen even if it could.

Look at your investment portfolio. What's in there, what's it all worth? Consider the use you intend those funds to be put to. If there are principal assets included in your net which you do not need in order to preserve your lifestyle, there is no better diversification you can make then the one which protects all the others. Whatever totals you come up with, cut in half, or more, based upon your specific tax situation. Then calculate how much of an investment it would take to protect those assets for the welfare of your children. For general purposes, assume a 10–1 return if you and your spouse are average age 60; a 5–1 return if you average age 70; a 3–1 return at average age 80. For more specific calculations, see the tables and charts at the back of this book.

So, figure out how much you will lose when the market crashes for you: take your investment totals and, for the sake of simplicity, divide them in half. Now, based on your age, divide that number either by 10, 5 or 3. This will give you the amount, appropriate to your age, that you would need to divert and diversify from your existing portfolio into my Investment Alternative concept in order to replace the half lost to estate taxes for your heirs. Look at the numbers, and remember that any investment you might consider utilizing to replenish the tax drain must actually increase in value 200% in order to yield, after taxes, the same 100% recovery that the Investment Alternative approach inherently provides.

AVOID THE CRASH OF YOUR STOCK PORTFOLIO

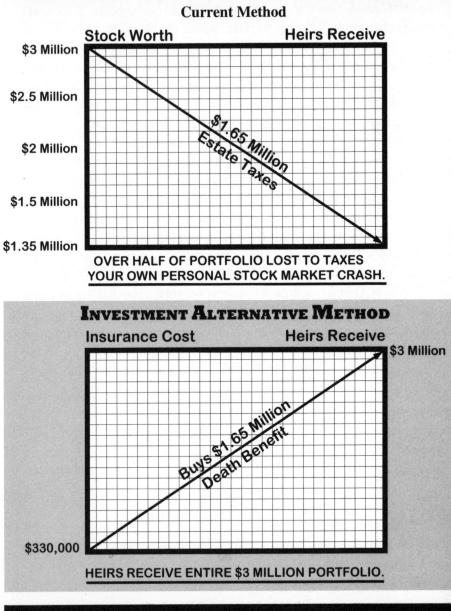

Current Method

Stock Worth   Heirs Receive

- $3 Million
- $2.5 Million
- $2 Million
- $1.5 Million
- $1.35 Million

$1.65 Million Estate Taxes

**OVER HALF OF PORTFOLIO LOST TO TAXES
YOUR OWN PERSONAL STOCK MARKET CRASH.**

INVESTMENT ALTERNATIVE METHOD

Insurance Cost   Heirs Receive

$3 Million

Buys $1.65 Million Death Benefit

$330,000

HEIRS RECEIVE ENTIRE $3 MILLION PORTFOLIO.

HEDGE THE MARKET AGAINST YOUR GUARANTEED TAX LOSS

All figures are based on current assumptions. Charts are for illustrative purposes only.
This illustration used a last-to-die insurance policy for a male and female both age 70.
©1997 THE INVESTMENT ALTERNATIVE - Barry Kaye Associates

Concept #6:

USE THE INVESTMENT ALTERNATIVE METHOD TO INCREASE YOUR PENSION AND IRA FUNDS UP TO 20 TIMES

A caution before reading this section: **IF YOU NEED THE INCOME FROM YOUR PENSION OR IRA TO FUND YOUR LIFE-STYLE, THIS PROGRAM IS NOT FOR YOU.**

For many people, pension funds and IRA's form a very necessary source of income after retirement. I have always maintained that no one should invest or utilize money they need to live on. Life is very short and providing for yourself and your spouse should, in my opinion, always be your first priority. Investment programs should only be undertaken with excess funds.

For that reason, I do not recommend the following program to anyone whose pension or IRA plays a major role in producing the income they need to support their lifestyle and protect themselves from a financial emergency.

There are a number of people, however, for whom pension, profit-sharing or IRA funds are excess principal and income. Their other principal earns enough interest to fully support their financial needs. For them, *using their IRA and Pension assets can be one of the most effective means of optimizing their funds, hedging the market, discounting their taxes and implementing any of the Investment Alternative concepts.*

Consider this example and then extrapolate how the same circumstances and planning might apply to you. Use the charts and tables in the back of the book to determine your specific costs and exposure.

Assume you have a pension or IRA worth $2 million. Further assume that your other assets bring your estate total to over $3 million putting you in a 55% estate tax bracket AND that they earn sufficient income so that you do not need the income from the $2 million pension or IRA principal to support your lifestyle.

When you die, the $2 million of pension principal which you have been planning to leave as part of your legacy to your heirs will be subject to income taxes of approximately $800 thousand. There may also be excise taxes of 15% to pay. But, even if not, the remaining $1.2 million will then be subject to estate taxes of $660 thousand. Ultimately, your children will inherit only $540 thousand or less of the $2 million pension which represents a lifetime of hard work and dedication.

But, you can avoid this loss and actually increase the amount your heirs will receive by almost a full 20 times through the purchase of a life insurance policy to be used as an alternative to investing.

Terminate the pension or IRA now. Though you will have to pay incomes taxes of approximately $800 thousand, it will be well worth it.

Use the remaining $1.2 million to purchase in an Irrevocable Trust a one-pay, last-to-die life insurance policy. Depending on your age and health, the insurance will yield an up to 10 times return of $12 million. Now, instead of $540 thousand, your heirs will inherit, income and estate tax free, $12 million. *Your $2 million pension or IRA has been fully maximized and instead of only receiving the $540 thousand which would have been left to them after taxes, or even only receiving the original $2 million you'd planned for them to have, they receive instead a greatly optimized $12 million!*

Now think about this, your $2 million IRA would have to increase in value an impossible thirty times to become worth $60 million, in order to produce the same ultimate net return for your children.

A $60 million IRA would be subject to a 15% excise tax of $9 million. Then the entire $60 million would also be subject to approximately 40% income taxes of $24 million. And the $27 million remaining after that would be subject to 55% estate taxes leaving approximately $12 million. $12 million from a $60 million IRA that had to increase a miraculous thirty times to be worth $60 million to begin with. OR, you could use an Investment Alternative approach, with its predetermined results, based on current assumptions, immediate returns when necessary and tax-free status to create $12 million. A miracle in its own way.

Don't forget, as an alternative you can use the income or asset increase from the IRA to purchase the insurance on a yearly basis. In this manner, your principal is kept intact for any future need. You can even utilize the income or asset increase to fund an Investment Alternative technique that will allow you to entirely replace the value of the IRA for your heirs while, at the same time, gifting the entire IRA principal to charity.

The yearly income or increase earned by the IRA's principal will fund an insurance policy which will provide a death benefit equal to the amount of the IRA itself or more. Then, instead of passing the IRA to your heirs and subjecting it to the decimation of the taxes which would be due, you gift the entire principal to charity. Now your heirs inherit the equivalent amount of the IRA's principal from the tax free life insurance benefit and the charity gets the full principal which, since it is a charitable donation, is also a completely tax free transfer. You've basically and effectively given away the whole principal amount twice without paying any estate, gift or other taxes. In the meantime, you have kept the principal of your IRA intact until your death and in your possession should a need for it arise. You have truly accomplished the best of all possible worlds, keeping your asset intact for your need, giving it away in its entirety to your children free from tax loss and also giving it away in its entirety to your favorite charity. Could you ask for anything more? And could any investment provide as much?

$540 THOUSAND OR $12 MILLION FROM YOUR $2 MILLION IRA OR PENSION

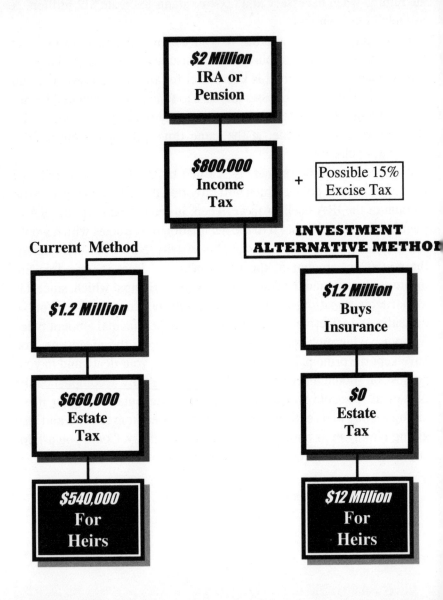

$11,460,000 MORE TO YOUR FAMILY

All figures are based on current assumptions. Charts are for illustrative purposes only.
This illustration used a last-to-die insurance policy for a male and female both age 60.
©1997 THE INVESTMENT ALTERNATIVE - Barry Kaye Associates

Concept #7:

OPTIMIZE MUNICIPAL BOND
YIELDS UP TO 25% YEARLY

Municipal Bonds Are <u>NOT</u> Tax Free.

They are *income tax* free. And that's valuable. But only to a point. While they allow you to save up to 40% of taxes assessed on the income they generate each year, they DO NOTHING to prevent the far greater decimation of the 55% estate tax they will be subject to at the time of your death.

$10 million in municipal bonds, earning 5% interest of $500 thousand yearly, will "save" their owner $200 thousand of income taxes annually. However, that same $10 million municipal bond will be subjected to approximately $5.5 million in estate taxes at the time the estate passes on to the heirs. Think about it. Your municipal bond will lose in one day to estate taxes what it would have taken 27.5 years of paying income tax to equal. In other words, 27.5 years of savings is thrown away at your death.

There is a way, however, of retaining the full income tax free potential of your municipal bonds and other similar investment vehicles' value undecimated by estate taxes.

Let us illustrate the program this way:

You are 75 years old and you have an estate worth $50 million of which $10 million resides in municipal bonds. Your net worth places you in a 40% tax bracket and you are receiving a return of 5% over the next 15 years.

The income tax savings of your Munis is considerable. 5% annual earnings equals $500 thousand a year. 40% of $500 thousand is $200 thousand. By avoiding the income tax on the $500 thousand of annual interest your receive, you save, over 15 years, $3 million!

But don't get overjoyed too quickly. Your heirs will still owe $5.5 million in estate taxes on the value of those bonds when you die. Your

$3 million savings is completely negated and an additional $2.5 million is lost.

Instead, consider the following alternative to municipal bonds.

Using a basic principal of reallocation, you sell the municipal bonds and purchase an immediate annuity. This is a vehicle which produces higher yields and promises to pay those yields for the rest of your lifetime at the end of which the principal "vanishes" or is forfeited.

Initially most people balk when I discuss the "vanishing principal" aspect of immediate annuities. But the structure of immediate annuities allows you to receive a greater yearly income than your municipal bonds and frees your heirs from having their inheritance drastically devalued by estate taxes. At older ages and in circumstances where retention of the principal is not important as long as the income generated remains constant, and where the ultimate estate planning goal is to provide the most fully maximized estate for the next generation, proper inclusion of an immediate annuity in a diversified portfolio can perform wondrous financial feats.

At average age 75, on $10 million, you and spouse could receive approximately $1 million annually AFTER income taxes. If you kept the same $500 thousand a year for yourself that your municipal bonds are currently producing, you would still have an additional $500 thousand a year remaining. Even at age 75, you could use that second annual $500 thousand to purchase $14 million of last-to-die life insurance for the benefit of your heirs. The insurance would cost $350 thousand a year and there would be $150 thousand of gift taxes each year. With proper use of an Irrevocable Trust to hold the insurance purchase, your children or grandchildren would inherit the $14 million income and estate tax free.

So even though they "lose" the entire $10 million of the immediate annuity principal, your heirs gain $14 million from this approach and, in the meantime, you have not lost a single dime of the investment income you were receiving from the municipal bonds. This is $14 million versus the $4.5 million your heirs would have received from the $10 million if it had not been used to purchase the immediate annuity.

Even at older ages this plan is still sensational. For example, a female, age 85 would receive yearly after tax income of $1.77 million on the same $10 million annuity. Using $500 thousand to support her lifestyle leaves $1.27 million. Assuming she has used up her exemptions, she gifts $800 thousand annually to a trust for the purchase of insurance paying $400 thousand a year in gift taxes on the transfer. The $800 thousand in annual premium payment will net $17 million for her heirs! The numbers are even better for a male but we're using a female because statistically women are more likely to live to 85 and therefore there are so many more widows than widowers.

Why would you leave your heirs $4.5 million when you could leave them $17 million without losing a dime of your income even at age 85? This is the ultimate optimization of reallocated assets. Meanwhile, you could also use the arbitrage—the difference between what you were receiving and what you are now getting—to meet your other financial obligations, pay premium commitments you have made on other policies, give more to charity, etc. This concept MUST but reviewed by every reader at older ages with substantial assets and conventional 5% yields.

$14 MILLION VS $4.5 MILLION TO HEIRS

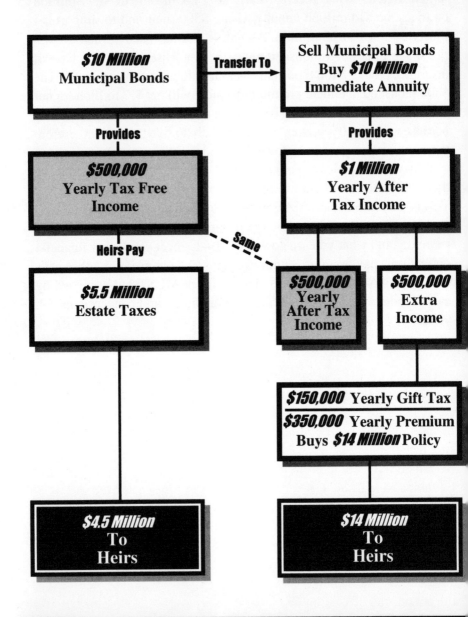

$10 Million
Municipal Bonds

Transfer To

Sell Municipal Bonds
Buy $10 Million
Immediate Annuity

Provides

Provides

$500,000
Yearly Tax Free
Income

$1 Million
Yearly After
Tax Income

Heirs Pay

- - - **Same**

$5.5 Million
Estate Taxes

$500,000
Yearly
After Tax
Income

$500,000
Extra
Income

$150,000 Yearly Gift Tax
$350,000 Yearly Premium
Buys $14 Million Policy

$4.5 Million
To
Heirs

$14 Million
To
Heirs

THE INVESTMENT ALTERNATIVE
METHOD MAXIMIZES YOUR MUNIS

All figures are based on current assumptions and life expectancies. Charts are for illustrative purposes
only. This illustration used an immediate annuity and a last-to-die policy for a couple age 75.
©1997 THE INVESTMENT ALTERNATIVE - Barry Kaye Associates

Concept #8:

USING THE INVESTMENT ALTERNATIVE CONCEPT TO OPTIMIZE YOUR ASSETS MANY TIMES OVER

We have discussed, throughout this part of the book, several different ways of diversifying your portfolio using the Investment Alternative techniques and seen how dramatic the results can be when this is done within a properly structured forum.

The following example reiterates various of these approaches to show the numerous options available in any given situation and demonstrate how each one is enhanced through the inclusion of insurance in the investment portfolio.

To begin with, let's examine the potential financial plight of a couple, average age 60, who have amassed enough money that they easily have an available $2.5 million of "junk" money languishing on the bottom of their pile of assets and available for use without in any way negatively affecting their lifestyle.

Undeterred from their present course, the couple's $2.5 million will be subjected to estate taxes of 55%—$1.3 million—and their children will realize only $1.2 million of it. While $1.2 million is, by anyone's standard, an appreciable sum of money, I don't know anyone who wouldn't rather leave their children as much as 400% more if it didn't cost them anything additional. Using the approaches developed to take advantage of the remarkable potentials of the Investment Alternative, the couple can do just that!

To begin with, while the couple is still alive, they could just gift their children $1.7 million and pay $833 thousand in gift tax. The children wind up with $500 thousand more from the same $2.5 million than if the money is not transferred until after death. This simple reallocation of funds, which does not hurt the couple in any way as we have already determined that they do not need the $2.5 million and have already earmarked it for their children's benefit, increases the children's inheritance by more than 40% from $1.2 million to $1.7 million. It reflects what can be accomplished simply by looking at the financial situation from a new angle and utilizing all the options available to you.

Now let us look at three increasingly optimized plans for generating huge returns using the same $1.7 million which is left after gift tax is paid on a transfer of $2.5 million total. Each plan builds upon the first and each presents a more dramatically maximized situation.

1) The parents gift the $1.7 million to the children now but instead of giving it all in cash, they reserve $700 thousand which they use to purchase an insurance policy on themselves. The policy will produce a return at age 60 of $7 million upon the couple's deaths. Instead of the $1.2 million they would have originally received, or even the optimized $1.7 million they could have received, the children now receive $1 million immediately and $7 million upon their parents' deaths for a total of $8 million! Even at age 70, the return would be $3.5 million and at age 80, it would be $2.1 million.

2) Further optimization occurs when the couple splits the $700 thousand into two lots of $350 thousand each, one for their children and one for the grandchildren, and use them both to purchase a last-to-die insurance policy. With one $350 thousand portion they procure a policy on themselves for the sake of their children earning an up to 10–1 return. With the other $350 thousand portion the couple funds the purchase of a policy on their children for the sake of the grandchildren. Given the youth of the couple's children, they can expect to receive a return of up to 50–1! Now, the same $2.5 million is producing HUGE money!

To begin with, the children still get $1 million immediately. They then receive up to $3.5 million when their parents die, which represents the 10–1 return on the $350 thousand insurance purchase. Furthermore, the grandchildren receive $17.5 million upon the death of their parents. In total, the program has now produced $22 million from the same $1.7 million left after gift taxes were paid on the original $2.5 million transfer.

3) The most dramatic results of all take into account that, if this couple has $2.5 million of "junk" money, they are probably worth considerably more than that in total and their children will most likely inherit additional sums not previously taken into account.

Therefore, the couple could just gift the children with the $1 million they want them to have now but not use any of the remaining $700 thousand on the children's behalf. Instead, the entire $700 thousand can be used to fund the purchase of a life insurance policy taken out on the children's lives with the grandchildren as beneficiaries. At a 50–1 return, the $700 thousand would yield an astonishing $35 million in addition to the $1 million gifted to the children for a total return of $36 million! Suddenly, $700 thousand has become $35 million and a $2.5 million gift has become a $36 million multi-generational legacy. All accomplished utilizing the principles of optimization as applied to the purchase of the life insurance using Investment Alternative methods.

Of course, you could always use the entire $1.7 million and create $17 million to $83 million using the same techniques.

TURN A $1.7 MILLION GIFT INTO $8 MILLION UP TO $83 MILLION

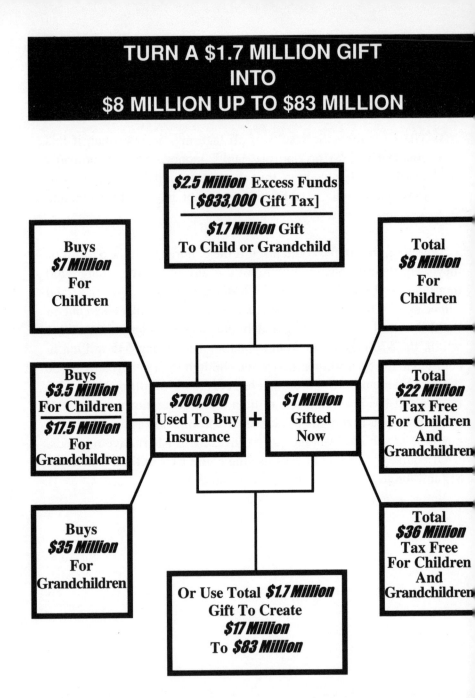

$2.5 Million Excess Funds
[**$833,000** Gift Tax]

$1.7 Million Gift
To Child or Grandchild

Buys
$7 Million
For
Children

Total
$8 Million
For
Children

Buys
$3.5 Million
For Children

$17.5 Million
For
Grandchildren

$700,000
Used To Buy
Insurance

+

$1 Million
Gifted
Now

Total
$22 Million
Tax Free
For Children
And
Grandchildren

Buys
$35 Million
For
Grandchildren

Total
$36 Million
Tax Free
For Children
And
Grandchildren

Or Use Total **$1.7 Million**
Gift To Create
$17 Million
To **$83 Million**

ALL FOR ONLY $833,000 OF GIFT TAX

All figures are based on current assumptions. Charts are for illustrative purposes only.
This illustration used last-to-die insurance policies on parents both age 60, and children both age 30.
©1997 THE INVESTMENT ALTERNATIVE - Barry Kaye Associates

72

Concept #9:

TURN A $10 THOUSAND TAX FREE GIFT INTO A $1 MILLION GIFT AT NO EXTRA COST!

Tax laws allow each unmarried or married person to gift anyone and everyone of their choosing up to $10 thousand per year without having to pay any gift or transfer tax. If you have an estate of $3 million or more, maybe even less, you undoubtedly are already aware of this as your accountants have probably advised you to make those gifts whenever your finances would allow. Their reasons for encouraging this practice are sound: by making the gift you are removing the money from your estate on a tax free basis. What you don't give away each year while you're alive will become automatically devalued by as much as 55% upon your death. For each $10 thousand that you DID NOT gift any year during your lifetime, your heirs could receive only $4.5 thousand. So giving away as much as you can in annual tax free gifts makes a great deal of sense. You can never recover a lost year.

In all likelihood, however, your accountant did not advise you of all the methods available for fully optimizing your annual $10 thousand tax free gifts so that they can become worth as much as $1 million for your children. *Using these Investment Alternative techniques, you don't merely save the $5 thousand of estate taxes your children might lose from each un-gifted $10 thousand, you increase the amount they receive 100 times still without any income, gift, or estate tax loss!*

In the beginning of this book we discussed the basic purpose of investment: to put money to work earning more money than mere labor could produce. We also examined the fact that in many instances funds used for investing are funds not needed to support your lifestyle. They are more discretionary funds and in many instances a large part of the desire to increase them has much more to do with leaving things better

73

for your heirs than it does with supplying additional means to support your own needs. We then looked at how perfectly life insurance fit into these definitions and desires. How it really is comparable to or better than most investments in the way it performs. This alternative can accomplish some of the goals of investing more safely, more certainly and much more dramatically than any investment. The method for turning annual $10 thousand tax free gifts into $1 million is one of the finest examples and culminations of the uses of life insurance as an Investment Alternative approach.

If you were to take the $10 thousand you intend to gift your child with every year and, instead of giving it to him or her directly, were to place it in an Irrevocable Trust and have the trust use it to purchase a life insurance policy on you and your spouse's lives, your child would receive a 3, 5 or even 10 times return at the time of your death. This could result in your annual $10 thousand gift becoming worth as much as $1 million to your heirs, all of it income, estate and gift tax free.

If your financial situation permits, you and your spouse can take further advantage of tax law by each gifting $10 thousand annually and using the combined $20 thousand to produce up to $2 million for your heirs. *That is a 100 times increase over the annual $20 thousand gift in any given year!*

You can utilize and combine these potentials to customize a solution to virtually any situation.

If your children need some financial help now but you still want to optimize your giving, one of you could make a direct gift of $10 thousand for their immediate benefit while the other used their $10 thousand to fund the insurance to still produce up to an additional $1 million. That would be $10 thousand a year direct to your child and another $1 million upon your death. Clearly, in this example, there is simply no investment you can name which can realize these achievements.

Even if you have to pay gift taxes of $5 thousand to give away an additional $10 thousand, this program still works to fully optimize your funds like no investment can. Think of it this way. Let's say you had earmarked that annual $10 thousand to invest in stocks or bonds or collectibles or real estate with the intended purpose that the investment's mature value would be a legacy for your heirs. Can you honestly think of a single investment opportunity that will be likely to yield a 100 times return if you met an unfortunate accident that year? Can your accountant or financial advisor suggest a single investment which will predetermine its return or which will make that return available the very day you purchase it if necessary? The answer is clearly: NO. Nothing else can perform like life insurance in circumstances where you have some excess, discretionary, "junk" money available to utilize on behalf of your children's ultimate welfare.

Let's assume that you have already made the maximum allowable tax free gifts to your children and do not want to pay gift taxes but would still like to help them further. *You can still maximize an extra $10 thousand gift more than 50 times*. Simply earmark an additional $7 thousand for your child. Yes, you will pay gift taxes of approximately $3 thousand. But if you don't make that gift that same $10 thousand, sitting within your estate, will be reduced by 55% upon your death to less than $5 thousand. You really have nothing to lose and up to $500 thousand to gain for your children!

After paying the $3 thousand in gift tax, you have $7 thousand from the allotted $10 thousand left. Placing that $7 thousand into an Irrevocable Trust and using it to fund the purchase of a life insurance policy will produce, at your deaths, up to $500 thousand which your heirs will receive gift, income and estate tax free. **Realistically, the $3 thousand gift tax you paid on the original transfers of $10 thousand yearly are the only taxes assessed on a $500 thousand gift. And that's one big effective tax discount**!

Keep in mind how much any investment you were to make with the same $5 thousand or $10 thousand would have to increase in order to equal, after taxes, the same $500 thousand or $1 million which this program will net your heirs. A highly unlikely proposition and one which does not carry any of the assurances that the insurance does.

Of course, if you are willing to pay the gift taxes—and there's no reason you shouldn't be since, in the end, you will still be saving estate tax costs and greatly optimizing your gift—there is no need to restrict the amount of your gift to $10 thousand. You could apply this program to any sum available for you to gift without negatively impacting your own lifestyle. And remember, in addition to annual $10 thousand gifts, both you and your spouse are permitted under federal tax law to gift anyone of your choosing with one lifetime gift of $600 thousand, the amount of the one-time estate tax exemption you are probably familiar with. You can apply the same $7 thousand/$3 thousand Investment Alternative gifting techniques to your $600 thousand one time exemption by giving $400 thousand to whoever you want and paying $200 in gift taxes. In other words, you can have as many $600 exemptions as you want as long as you don't use more than 2/3 of each one as a gift. But more about that later.

If you can afford to do so, rather than passing $600 thousand to your heirs tax free at your death, consider gifting it to them now. You still will not pay any estate or gift or transfer taxes—your exemption is available during your lifetime as well as at your death—but you will be able to greatly increase and optimize the gift through the shrewd usage of a one-pay, last-to-die insurance taken out on you and your spouse. *$600 thousand applied to this program would net a return for your children of up to $6 million!* You could even go one step further and utilize both $600 thousand exemptions to which you and your spouse are entitled for a combined investment total of $1.2 million. Utilized in the same way to purchase a last-to-die insurance policy, that $1.2 million will be worth $12 million to your heirs income and estate tax free.

What stock, bond, T-Bill, piece of property or other conventional investment will increase from $1.2 million to $12 million during the remainder of your lifetime? More on point, what stock will increase from $1.2 million to $24 million in order to equal the same $12 million for your heirs after estate taxes are assessed? Be honest. There simply isn't one.

YOU CAN ALSO USE THIS PROGRAM TO INCREASE YOUR INCOME TO YOUR SPOUSE UP TO 6 TIMES UPON YOUR DEATH.

$600 thousand, passed to your spouse at your death, will produce, annually, approximately $30,000 thousand income assuming a current 5% interest rate. But, if you were to use the $600 thousand during your lifetime, you still would not pay any taxes and could greatly optimize its value to your spouse.

By placing the $600 thousand into an Irrevocable Trust and using it to purchase a life insurance policy on yourself for his/her benefit, at death your $600 thousand exemption could be worth as much as $3.6 million, depending on your age and health at the time the life insurance policy is purchased. The trust is structured so the spouse can have the income during his/her lifetime while the principal remains for the heirs. $3.6 million will produce $180 thousand annually at the same assumed 5% interest rate. In this manner you have increased your spouse's income from $30 thousand to $180 thousand a year, every year, for the rest of your spouse's life without paying a single additional dime of tax. THAT is money management. THAT is sound financial planning. And THAT is the kind of return you should not settle for anything less than.

This is the Investment Alternative in its finest hour and when most needed. Why are people being advised to retain the $30 thousand income rather than turning it into $180 thousand? Does it make any sense to you? And if people aren't being advised to do this is it only making mistakes or is it omission? Where is the professional advice and what constitutes malpractice?

Increase Your

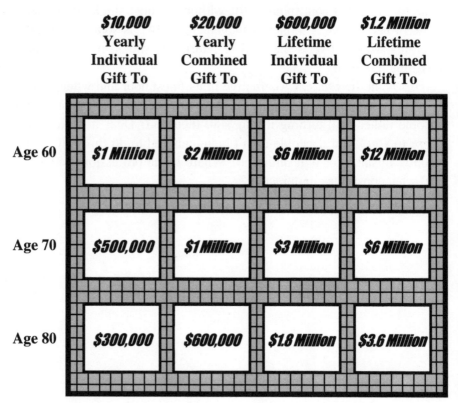

	$10,000 Yearly Individual Gift To	$20,000 Yearly Combined Gift To	$600,000 Lifetime Individual Gift To	$1.2 Million Lifetime Combined Gift To
Age 60	$1 Million	$2 Million	$6 Million	$12 Million
Age 70	$500,000	$1 Million	$3 Million	$6 Million
Age 80	$300,000	$600,000	$1.8 Million	$3.6 Million

INCREASE YOUR $600,000 EXEMPTIONS UP TO $12 MILLION

All figures are based on current assumptions. Charts are for illustrative purposes only.
This illustration uses last-to-die insurance policies for couples of various ages.
©1997 THE INVESTMENT ALTERNATIVE - Barry Kaye Associates

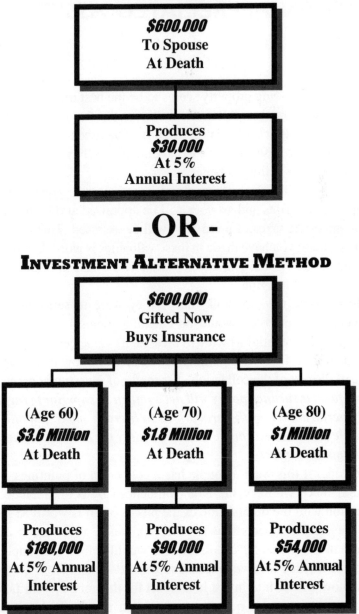

Current Method

$600,000
To Spouse
At Death

Produces
$30,000
At 5%
Annual Interest

- OR -

INVESTMENT ALTERNATIVE METHOD

$600,000
Gifted Now
Buys Insurance

(Age 60)	(Age 70)	(Age 80)
$3.6 Million At Death	**$1.8 Million** At Death	**$1 Million** At Death
Produces **$180,000** At 5% Annual Interest	Produces **$90,000** At 5% Annual Interest	Produces **$54,000** At 5% Annual Interest

All figures are based on current assumptions. Charts are for illustrative purposes only.
This illustration used individual insurance policies on males of various ages.
©1997 THE INVESTMENT ALTERNATIVE - Barry Kaye Associates

Concept #10:

TURN AN APPRECIABLE ASSET INTO AN APPRECIATED ASSET

Sometimes, amassing property seems to be the best means for increasing your estate's value. After all, the more you have, the more your heirs will get. Right? Afraid not. In truth, sometimes selling a piece of your estate is the best means for expanding it. Yes, buying is not always best. Sometimes selling is better.

Like everything else you own and have amassed, your rare coins, stamps, manuscripts and artwork will be appraised at the time of your death and estate taxes of up to 55% will be assessed. That means that the investment you have made in these valuables is worth less than half of their market value. Not exactly what you'd had in mind for your investment, I'd imagine.

Most people tend to think that if they were to sell one of their appreciable assets they would be cheating themselves out of some future growth potential which will escalate its value beyond the current market. But, in fact, selling one piece of artwork now can protect the value of the rest of the collection. *A transfer of investment assets from the art to an insurance policy will net a return so superior to the actual likely performance of the artwork as to literally make the one more valuable than the rest combined and possibly the art more beautiful in its bottom line effect*.

Consider it this way: a couple has a collection of paintings, each a singular piece whose value is not influenced by being included in a collection with the others. One of the pieces of art is worth $3 million and the couple expects that it could appreciate to as much as $4.5 million in time. That 50% gain in value would delight the couple, they would be thrilled to have invested so wisely!

Yet how wise is it to invest in an asset for the good of your posterity knowing that, without question or fail, that asset will depreciate by 55% the very day it comes to your heirs.

Should the couple then sell their entire collection in order to put the money 'more wisely' into life insurance? Of course not. The artwork gives them pleasure. And it *does* have some significant growth potential. More importantly, there is a difference between leaving behind a legacy of cash and leaving behind a more spiritually fulfilling gift that represents some aspect of yourself. Some reminder as to who you were as person, what you found beautiful or provocative, what you cherished, what moved you. Something tangible and poignant.

With a well thought-out diversification of your portfolio, you can do both and make sure the art remains in your family.

If the couple were to sell off just the one $3 million piece and use the money to fund the purchase of a life insurance policy, they could receive a return, based upon their age, health, and marital status, of 3–10 times. And though their policy will not be as lovely to look upon as their art, it will include benefits the fickle world of art collection never can and, more importantly, it will not be subjected to estate taxes as art work usually will be.

At a 3 times return at average age 80, the $3 million insurance policy will yield $9 million for the couple's heirs. The art would have to appreciate to $18 million to net that same amount after estate taxes were levied. At a 5 times return at age 70, the $3 million will yield $15 million, equal to a rise to $30 million pre-tax. Finally, were circumstances to produce a 10 times return as they could at age 60, the $3 million piece of art would have generated a staggering $30 million tax free, equivalent to $60 million pre tax. *The sale of the one $3 million painting, which would have only been worth $1.5 million upon their deaths, has funded a gain to the equivalent of $60 million!* Clearly there is no comparison. Most people just have not understood insurance and the power of these Investment Alternative techniques.

By making this one diversification within their portfolio, the couple is able to retain most of their treasured collection of art without having to worry about the massive devaluation that will occur upon their deaths. Their children can inherit the artwork AND the money needed to pay the taxes and protect the rest of the collection.

YOUR ART IS WORTH $7.5 MILLION

AFTER ESTATE TAXES IT IS WORTH $3.7 MILLION

SELL ONE PIECE NOW

				$3 Million **Art Buys** / *$30 Million* **Insurance Policy**
Value:	*$1 Million*	*$1.5 Million*	*$2 Million*	*$3 Million*
After Tax:	*$500,000*	*$750,000*	*$1 Million*	*$1.5 Million*
Net To Heirs:	*$500,000*	*$750,000*	*$1 Million*	*$30 Million*

AND IT CAN BE WORTH $30 MILLION

All figures are based on current assumptions and potential gift tax of $1.5 Million. Charts are for illustrative purposes only. This illustration used a last-to-die insurance policy for a male and female both age 60. ©1997 THE INVESTMENT ALTERNATIVE - Barry Kaye Associates

Concept #11:

A 10–1 RETURN THAT'S EQUAL TO A 20–1 RETURN

In your portfolio of stock, bonds, T-bills, real estate, etc. is there a single investment which can net you a 10–1 return, unrestricted by time and guaranteed to be available from the moment you make the purchase, based on the assumptions current at that time? If there isn't, there can be.

There is a saying in certain professional fields that of the three demands clients make—for service that is good, fast and inexpensive—they can have any two, but not all three. They can get what they need good and fast, but then it will not be inexpensive. They can get it fast and inexpensive but then it will not be good. Or they can get it inexpensive and good, but then it will not be fast. Conventional wisdom about investing seems to have a similar credo: If your investment is safe and sound, it will not produce dramatic returns. If it is likely to produce high returns it is more risky. This conventional wisdom, like most conventional wisdom, however, is not accurate. The fact is that there is an alternative to investments that is both safe and dramatic in the results it accomplishes.

Compare the features of these wonderful Investment Alternative concepts with investments. The facts will speak for themselves.

Let's say you invest $1 million in a stock your broker *raves* about. Do you think it likely that that stock will escalate 10 times in value to become worth $10 million? And if the possibility exists, what is the time factor involved? Is there any chance it's going to increase in value to $10 million *tomorrow*?

It must also be safe to assume that you have no need of the $1 million you invested since you seem content to have tied it up indefinitely awaiting the chance that the stock will rise. That being the case, the inference is that amongst your purposes in investing is the desire to pass on greater wealth to your heirs since it seems you don't need the money to fund your own current living expenses. You are anticipating the rise in the stocks value will help provide greater financial security for your heirs.

Unfortunately you have failed to take into account that the transfer of that asset from you to your heirs will be taxed at the rate of 55%. **The stock has to double in value just to stay even for your heirs**. Only if it goes to $2 million will they receive the originally intended $1 million principal left after the government takes its share.

ONLY THE INVESTMENT ALTERNATIVE CONCEPT OF USING LIFE INSURANCE, PLACED WITHIN AN IRREVOCABLE TRUST, OFFERS HUGE RETURNS OF UP TO 10–1, OR MORE IF YOU ARE YOUNGER. AND PROBABLY ONLY LIFE INSURANCE COMES TO YOUR HEIRS INCOME AND ESTATE TAX FREE THEREBY VIRTUALLY DOUBLING ITS VALUE AUTOMATICALLY! This is true because most people will not give money to their heirs while they are still alive. However, they are inclined to do so if it is for the purpose of purchasing life insurance.

Even if you and your wife's average age is 80, when the returns on the insurance purchase are about 3–1, the effective value of the tax exemption basically increases the yield to a 6 times return. So if you are going to diversify your portfolio to utilize an Investment Alternative approach and are going to use $1 million, at age 80 it will yield a return of $3 million. But that $3 million is effectively worth $6 million when comparing this program to any other since this $3 million will come to your heirs estate tax free thereby saving them the 55% tax cost loss.

At age 70, with a 5–1 return, your $1 million outlay would increase in value up to 5 times to $5 million. Any investment would have to increase to $10 million to net the same result.

For a couple with an average age of 60, it is possible to receive a 10 times return making the $1 million worth $10 million which compares to a $20 million yield from any stock or bond. Do you really think you know of a stock that will grow from $1 million to $20—and do so overnight, if necessary?

The return on the life insurance policy is available from the very first moment you buy it should it be required. THERE IS NOT A SINGLE INVESTMENT WHICH CAN MAKE THAT CLAIM. Yet it is a crucial aspect of estate planning. The very nature of estate planning takes into account that your assets will be passing on to your heirs and, as such, steps must be taken to protect and preserve as much of them intact as possible. How then can any responsible advisor overlook the very real, though distasteful, possibility of a tragedy occurring before your plans have all had a chance to come to fruition? Even if your stock could somehow magically go from $1 million to $20 million in order to net your children the same $10 million after taxes they would get using an Investment Alternative concept, what are the chances that it will do so *in time*? Think of Dan Blocker, Elvis Presley, Michael Landon, names we are all familiar with and sad examples of the hard, hard truth: death comes at its own time, not ours. Unfortunately the only guarantees you will get on this subject are the ones you provide for yourself by buying the time and being sure you are ready.

Compare any investment you are considering to the Investment Alternative system. Honestly evaluate its growth potential—can it produce an up to 20 times gross return needed to net a 10 time return after taxes? Carefully consider the timing—will it pay your heirs the return the day after you purchase it? Evaluate the financial ramifications—will it come to your heirs income and estate tax free? If you answered "No" to any of these questions (and you know that you did) then your intended investment may not be as good as you had imagined. Take another look of the attributes of the Investment Alternative methods and compare them to the goals you have set out for your estate. You will find that nothing accomplishes for capital optimization and wealth preservation what these Investment Alternative concepts can do. Isn't it worth having it in your portfolio? After all, isn't that what diversification is all about?

CONVENTIONAL INVESTMENTS MUST DOUBLE TO COMPARE WITH THE INVESTMENT ALTERNATIVE

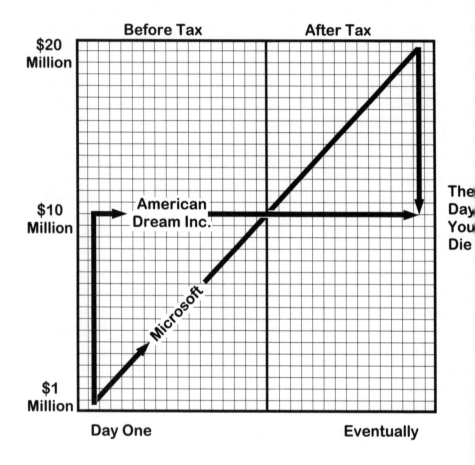

Before Tax

After Tax

$20 Million

$10 Million

American Dream Inc.

The Day You Die

Microsoft

$1 Million

Day One

Eventually

$10 MILLION TAX FREE AVAILABLE FIRST DAY OF PURCHASE

All figures are based on current assumptions. Charts are for illustrative purposes only.
This illustration used a last-to-die insurance policy for a male and female both age 60.
©1997 THE INVESTMENT ALTERNATIVE - Barry Kaye Associates

Concept #12:

ONE FINANCIAL VEHICLE OPTIMIZES ALL THE REST

Smart portfolios are diversified portfolios. No competent advisor would ever recommend that you put all your eggs in one basket and invest all your principal in one place. It's such an obvious thing that we often don't even really stop to consider WHY diversification is so critical to a well-constructed investment plan. But the reason is very important to acknowledge.

Diversification helps create balance between safety and maximized potentials.

Blue chip stocks are generally pretty safe, but they can grow at slower rates than some of the 'mavericks' out there. Speculative investments may produce greater yields, but you wouldn't want to risk everything you've got, your entire financial future, in them. So you diversify and your portfolio contains a blended balance of blue chips and mavericks, safety and risk. In this way, you hope to accomplish two goals which might otherwise seem at great odds with each other: To safely invest your money while earning the maximum returns available.

The use of the Investment Alternative concepts and the purchase of a life insurance policy is the one diversification which can protect and maximize all your investments.

There are a few things you have to remember as you review your current portfolio in terms of its accomplishment of your goals:

1) NOTHING is guaranteed. Stocks fluctuate, bonds are called, real estate dips and soars. Whatever the current assessed worth of your portfolio, it will almost certainly be different tomorrow. Better, maybe. Worse, possibly. The difference may not be great, or it could be monumental. Nothing is guaranteed.

2) Potential requires time and you also have no guarantee of that. It's a sad, drastic, brutal, dire truth, but a truth nonetheless. You have no guarantee of time enough for your investment to mature into its full potential. Internal rates of return are pure gibberish in the face of the wild, uncontrollable element of time.

3) Every dime your investments earn is subject to income tax when it comes into your estate and estate tax when it comes into your heirs'. That means a $100 thousand gain will be reduced approximately 1/3 to $66 thousand by income taxes when you sell it at its peak and will then be reduced up to an additional 55% to $33 thousand when your heirs inherit it as part of your total estate. Each and every gain you make will be similarly reduced by income and estate taxes. Nothing is worth what you think it is.

Given these realities, any financial planning course which does not include the one vehicle which can optimize the rest is irresponsible, possibly an example of malpractice and doomed to certain immense devaluation.

Going back to each of the three points regarding the shortcomings of investments, let's look at how things could be different if the investor utilized the Investment Alternative technique as a part of his diversified portfolio. See for yourself the optimization potentials this outstanding financial vehicle of life insurance can produce.

For the sake of the examples, we will utilize a married couple, average age 70. At that age, they can expect a return of 5–1 on their one-pay, last-to-die life insurance purchase, based on current assumptions. If younger, the couple could net as much as a 10–1 return; if older, a still beneficial 3–1. We will use the middle level 5–1 return just to not be 'gilding the lily'; the drama of these approaches will be revealed even without the full 10–1 possible return.

Please note, in the event that a last-to-die policy is not appropriate for your situation—perhaps you are a widow or widower, single, divorced, on a second marriage but protecting children from the first, or one of you simply does not qualify—you can still use these concepts by purchasing an individual policy. You will still earn wonderful benefits, it just may require that you put more money in.

Also, remember that there are numerous ways the life insurance policy can be structured so that the cost is borrowed or recovered. These examples are guidelines and can all be creatively customized to meet your needs and desires. See the charts and tables at the back of the book for the numbers that most specifically apply to you as you envision how these programs would benefit your portfolio and, more importantly, your heirs. Also, as needed add or subtract zeroes, half or double the figures used to more closely approximate your own situation.

1) Nothing in your current portfolio is guaranteed. It is all at risk from the vagaries of the marketplace. But the life insurance's returns are predetermined, depending on how much you pay and based upon current assumptions. You can use this fact to protect your other investments and optimize their potentials.

Assume our 70-year-old couple had an "extra" $50 thousand which they wanted to invest. Perhaps this money is excess interest from their other investments which they did not spend that year, or perhaps it represents the after-tax profit from some other wise investment they had made. However it came to them, it is there and they want to use it to earn more than the 5% which CD's, Municipal bonds and savings accounts are paying. As they do not need either the principal or the interest for themselves they are, in reality, investing for the sake of their children who will eventually inherit their estate.

They could, of course, purchase another stock or bond to complement their existing portfolio. Maybe that stock would increase 10%. Maybe 50%. Maybe even 100%. Given the reality of the markets, they'd probably be thrilled with that return. But maybe the stock will go down. That is also the reality of the market; there are no guarantees.

If the couple used the $50 thousand to fund the purchase of a life insurance policy, they could expect a 5–1 return of $250 thousand for their heirs, based on current assumptions. The stock they are considering would have to net more than $500 thousand to be worth the same to their heirs after estate taxes claimed up to 55%. That means the stock would have to increase 10 times in value in order to net the same return. It is the rare stock indeed which can be presumed, even hoped, to perform like that. More likely, one can almost guarantee that it simply won't happen.

The Investment Alternative method provides a return so high that their investment would have to increase in value 10 times to equal it. Surely there is room in a wisely diversified portfolio for a financial vehicle which can perform like that!

2) There is no guarantee of time enough to realize full potentials.

Our couple is making their investments on behalf of their children. They themselves do not need either the principal or the interest to protect their own lifestyle. So they are looking for an investment vehicle which will yield the best return for their heirs. Let's imagine that their stock broker found a company full of potential that he is CERTAIN will double if not triple in value in time. (Of course, he can not really be certain of any such thing; just ask him to put his certainty into writing in the form of a guarantee backed by his own resources.) The broker has a good reputation and a good history for producing returns for the couple and they believe him. They share his certainty and are primed to make the investment. But there is a fly in the ointment and it could be catastrophic.

Time. Time is the fly in the ointment. Even an exciting, promising opportunity like the one the broker has found requires time. And time will not let itself be 'required.' It operates entirely free of our control.

Distressing as it is to discuss, reality has a way of striking when we least expect it or can least afford it. Planning, in any sense and any forum, is about accommodating reality to the limits of our ability to do so, controlling what it is ours to control so that that which is not within our control need not have so devastating an effect. We write wills, we set up living trusts, we put money into IRA's, we budget and project all in an effort to be as prepared for reality as we can be. But stuff gets in the way as life happens.

A frayed wire somewhere inside a wall in the couple's house, a drunk driver who crosses into their lane as they go out to dinner, a trip on the wrong plane and all the plans stop. Everything freezes in the now. It is time.

And if the investment has not had the time it needs to mature, it is too late. Potential no longer exists. The estate is tabulated, the taxes due, the asset transferred and devalued. The children could keep it and create a new potential, but for the parents' desires for that money to have achieved greater financial protection for the children the time has come and gone.

The parents had hoped that the stock would double in value so their $50 thousand investment would become worth $100 thousand. Of course, after estate taxes, it would still be only worth $45 thousand to their heirs, sadly a loss of $5 thousand on a stock that did the remarkable and doubled in value. However, the $50 thousand, if it hadn't increased at all, would only have been worth $22.5 thousand after estate taxes so the children still would be ahead $22.5 thousand and that's not so bad.

But tragedy struck, by surprise, as it always does. The parents have died and the stock did not have time to reach its potential and the estate taxes are due so the heirs have to sell off half the stock to pay them. Now they have $22.5 thousand remaining invested in the stock and they still hope it will grow. The broker remains CERTAIN that it will. But now, instead of doubling to reach the $100 thousand their parents wanted for them, the stock has to quadruple! *The same $50 thousand, used to buy a life insurance policy, would have netted the couple's heirs $250 thousand the very day the purchase was completed had tragedy chosen that moment to strike*.

3) Income and estate taxes will decimate your investments' worth.

However successful your investments might be, they will lose a significant portion of any gain they earn as they pass to your heirs.

Even if time did accommodate our sample couple and their investment netted its desired $50 thousand return when they sold it, the gain would be subject to income tax. If they are in an approximate 30% tax bracket, that means they will pay about $15 thousand in income tax and have a remaining profit of $35 thousand. Now that $35 thousand becomes part of their estate. No matter what they do with it, it is theirs and, as part of their estate, it will be subject to estate taxation when they die and goes to their children. Estate taxes of 55% will take a little over $19 thousand leaving the couple's children $16 thousand. $16 thousand from a dramatic $50 thousand gain. Now the drama has become a tragedy.

If what the couple really wants is to create an additional $50 thousand for their children, they need to find an investment that will yield almost $150 thousand before taxes so that after paying $50 thousand in income tax the remaining $100 thousand will be worth $50 thousand to the heirs after the estate taxes are paid. It's a sobering scenario and hopefully one that should make you aware of the true extent of the frailty of your existing portfolio.

There were ways that the couple could have maximized the return without the decimation of taxes or at least recovered the lost amounts for their children.

They could have simply utilized the Investment Alternative technique by using the whole $50 thousand to buy a life insurance policy. They would have received a return, based on current assumptions, of $250 thousand for their heirs and that money would come to their heirs income and estate tax free if the policy were properly structured within an Irrevocable Trust. *Life insurance proceeds will PASS TO YOUR HEIRS INCOME TAX FREE*. And, having placed the policy into the Irrevocable Trust and removed it from their estates entirely during their lifetime, *it is not subject to estate taxes either.* The heirs get the $250 thousand in full. The stock the couple was so excited about would have had to grow from $50 thousand to $750 thousand before taxes to net the same $250 thousand. (From $750 thousand, 1/3—$250 thousand—is lost to income taxes and about half of the remaining $500 thousand— $250 thousand—is lost to estate taxes leaving $250 thousand.) **$250 thousand versus $16 thousand from the same original asset**.

However, there are those people who simply like to invest. There is definitely an excitement about picking a good stock and watching it grow. A sense of triumph at having beaten the odds, a feeling of accomplishment, a certain joy. They are after something more than just the financial gains, they like the game and they want to play. Though mindful of the tax loses and lack of guarantees associated with traditional forms of investment, they still want to pursue and challenge the market. Thankfully, there is a way for these people to have their cake and eat it too.

Our couple's stockbroker comes to them and tells them of this great, hot stock. It's the newest news, not generally known yet, an opportunity to get in at the exact right moment and hit big. The couple is excited.

Yes, they know any gains they make will be heavily hit by taxes, but they'll still have more than if they don't make the investment and if the kids inherit a few bucks less than they could they'll still be doing all right. So they make the investment and the broker is right. The stock takes off shortly after they buy and they watch with stunned delight as it keeps increasing and increasing. As the nightly news discusses what a coup the stock has become to those who got in early, the couple sits back in proud pleasure to know that, in a precarious world of uncertainties and risk, they bested the fates this once.

Finally the stock doubles and their broker advises the couple that it has maxed out; it's time to sell. Now the $50 thousand gain is reduced by income taxes of 1/3 to $33 thousand. And, as an asset within their total estate, that $33 thousand will be further reduced by 55% to just about $15 thousand. Not quite the windfall they'd hoped but still a significant return on a $50 thousand investment and they are content.

There is a way the couple can turn their $33 thousand net gain into $165 thousand.

Having had the fun of successfully playing the market, the couple can now turn their thoughts to maximizing the profits they earned. The $50 thousand they initially invested remains free to be invested over and over and over again as long as the couple lives and their broker keeps doing such a good job of recommending stocks. But the net return can be maximized many times over.

If the couple takes the $33 thousand of net, after-tax return they earned and reallocates it to the purchase of a life insurance policy yielding a tax free return of 5–1, their $33 thousand will become worth $165 thousand to their heirs. They have optimized their investment earnings five times over. This works the same with $500 thousand of investments or a $5 million portfolio. Just change the zeroes to your particular situation.

LIFE INSURANCE OUTPERFORMS YOUR INVESTMENT PORTFOLIO ... GUARANTEED

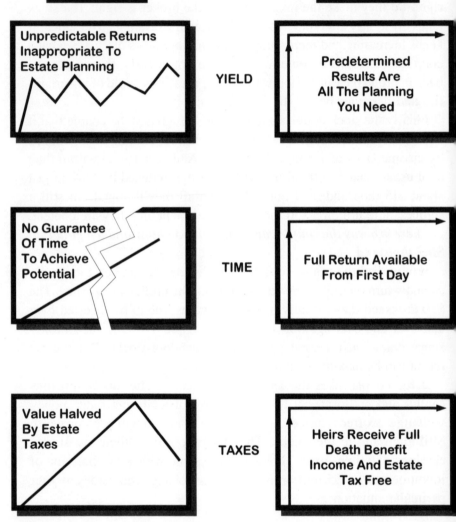

PORTFOLIO

INSURANCE

Unpredictable Returns
Inappropriate To
Estate Planning

YIELD

Predetermined
Results Are
All The Planning
You Need

No Guarantee
Of Time
To Achieve
Potential

TIME

Full Return Available
From First Day

Value Halved
By Estate
Taxes

TAXES

Heirs Receive Full
Death Benefit
Income And Estate
Tax Free

DIVERSIFY, REALLOCATE, OPTIMIZE USING THE INVESTMENT ALTERNATIVE

All figures are based on current assumptions. Charts are for illustrative purposes only.

©1997 THE INVESTMENT ALTERNATIVE - Barry Kaye Associates

94

Concept #13:

EXCISE TAX ADVANTAGE— GOVERNMENT 3-YEAR-ONLY SALE

Beginning on January 1, 1997, a new tax law went into effect regarding IRA's and Pensions. Intending to actually generate more taxes in its struggle to balance the budget, the government will "forgive" the excise tax on distributed funds from IRA's and Pensions during your lifetime. The thinking is that by encouraging people to take those funds now, they will enter the general economy and 'go to work.' The proceeds of those working funds will still be subject to income tax and it is this administration's belief that the aggregate income taxes generated as a result will justify the forgiveness of the excise tax. To this end, a program has been initiated and will run through 1997, 1998 and 1999 that forgives the 15% excise tax on IRA's and Pensions distributed during those years.

What this means to you is that you can now withdraw your money from your IRA or Pension without forfeiting 15% of it to the government in the form of the excise tax. HOWEVER, if you die in the next three years and your heirs inherit your IRA or Pension, the excise tax will still be assessed.

To put this into perspective, assume you have an IRA worth $5 million. Outside this special forgiveness, that $5 million would lose 15%—$750 thousand—to excise taxes and 40%—$2 million—to income taxes. The remaining $2.25 million would, as it passed to your heirs, be subject to an additional 55% estate tax of $1.2 million leaving only $1 million from the original $5 million for your children's benefit.

But this new, limited excise tax forgiveness, coupled with the amazing power of the Investment Alternative approach structured outside the estate tax situation, creates a powerful new wealth preservation and creation opportunity.

I'm assuming you know about the excise tax, assuming your financial consultants or tax attorney have made you aware of its existence and the impact it has on your IRA. I am therefore also assuming that you have reconciled yourself to the inevitability of this tax cost and are not counting on having that $750 thousand for your use in your life-time. Either you will not distribute your IRA while you live in order to avoid the excise tax or you will distribute it and fully expect to pay the 15%. In either event, the $750 thousand is money you have never figured into your plans. Now you have an amazing chance to use the unexpected financial boon of the excise tax forgiveness to create great wealth for your children!

Distribute your IRA now. You will have to pay the 40% income tax, but, one way or another, that's unavoidable. You have $3 million left. Take the $750 thousand that would have been forfeited to the excise tax and reallocate it to the purchase of a one-pay, last-to-die life insurance policy on the lives of you and your spouse. At average age 60, you can expect a 10–1 return; at age 70, a 5–1 return; at age 80, a 3–1 return.

Watch what the numbers do now!

Your $5 million IRA would have been worth only $1 million to your heirs as things were. Now, you paid 40% income tax reducing the $5 million to $3 million and used the forgiven excise tax equivalent of $750 thousand which you never had any expectation of having to purchase a life insurance policy. This reduces the $5 million to $2.25 million on which estate taxes of 55% will still be due. You are back to the $1 million total we arrived at before. With one very important difference. Now, the $750 thousand is working for you, instead of for the government.

At age 60, the $750 thousand alternative investment yields $7.5 million for your heirs income and estate tax free increasing the total they receive from your IRA to $8.5 million NET. At age 70, it returns $3.75 million for a total of $4.75 million and at age 80 it produces $2.25 million for a total of $3.25 million. **By using the forgiveness the government is offering to generate funds from money you never before expected to have, you have increased your children's legacy by as much as $7.5 million**! You have effectively turned a $750 thousand tax into a $7.5 million asset. Last year, if you took a distribu-tion, or at your death at any time, the $750 thousand would have been lost forever. Now it's up to a $7.5 million gain. What a difference a year made. Uncle Sam doesn't throw you such a bone often. What a tragedy if you were to let it rot.

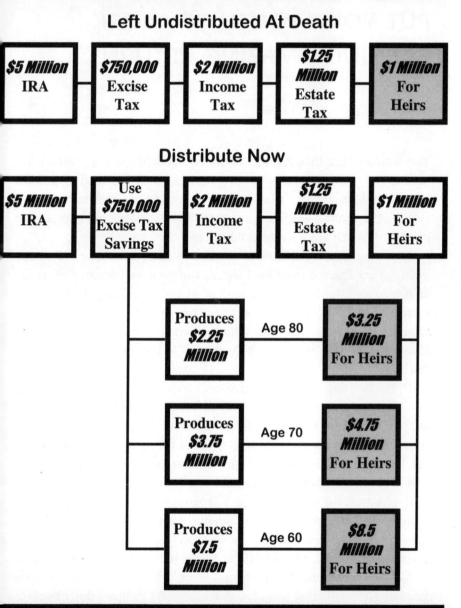

USE THE INVESTMENT ALTERNATIVE TO MAXIMIZE YOUR EXCISE TAX FORGIVENESS

Left Undistributed At Death

| $5 Million IRA | $750,000 Excise Tax | $2 Million Income Tax | $1.25 Million Estate Tax | $1 Million For Heirs |

Distribute Now

| $5 Million IRA | Use $750,000 Excise Tax Savings | $2 Million Income Tax | $1.25 Million Estate Tax | $1 Million For Heirs |

Produces $2.25 Million	Age 80	$3.25 Million For Heirs
Produces $3.75 Million	Age 70	$4.75 Million For Heirs
Produces $7.5 Million	Age 60	$8.5 Million For Heirs

INCREASE YOUR IRA'S VALUE FROM $1 MILLION UP TO $8.5 MILLION

All figures are based on current assumptions. Charts are for illustrative purposes only.
This illustration uses last-to-die insurance policies for couples of various ages.
©1997 THE INVESTMENT ALTERNATIVE - Barry Kaye Associates

Concept #14:

PUT YOUR YOUTH TO WORK EARNING AMAZING RETURNS

The nature of the Investment Alternative methods give a great advantage to the young. Returns at older ages are still outstanding against investments, especially when structured within an Irrevocable Trust. But, as the returns are based on current assumptions of interest and mortality, youth has a decided advantage.

At 60, a one-pay purchase of a last-to-die life insurance policy can net a remarkable return of 10–1. At 50, the same outlay can yield twice as much, an astonishing 16–1 return. At combined age 40, the return increases to 28–1, whereas, at age 30 it can increase to an almost unbelievable 50–1! That means that at average age 30, using a one-pay, last-to-die policy, it would only take $20 thousand to produce $1 million!

To put this into true perspective, let's look at it this way. If at age 30 you had achieved enough financial success that you had excess funds available to utilize on behalf of your children, you could purchase a life insurance policy and receive a 50–1 return for them, income and estate tax free. So, if you were to outlay a mere $10 thousand, your heirs would receive $500 thousand—half a million dollars!

If you were to put that same $10 thousand into an investment, it would have to grow to almost double what the insurance yields— specific comparisons would be based upon your total estate valuation at the time of your deaths—in order to net the same for your children. MAYBE you can find an investment that in the 40 or 50 years you hope you have left will grow from $10 thousand to $1 million. But, of course, to do so, it would have to consistently yield more than 10% a year. MAYBE you will live another 50 years. Unfortunately, maybe not. In contrast, life insurance WILL yield its promised return, based on current assumptions, and WILL do so regardless of how long remains for you. The whole subject is academic when you realize how little you are allocating from your assets to achieve this diversification.

If you do live to a nice ripe old age, you will surely earn more funds to invest and will be able to have a richly varied and diversified portfolio at work building a legacy of financial security for your children. But, don't you think it is simple and obvious that that portfolio should contain the only financial vehicle that will accomplish the goal irrespective of time and on a predetermined basis?

Think about some of the examples we have already examined, the remarkable things we have accomplished with a 10–1, 5–1 or 3–1 return. Now, consider how much greater their effectiveness would be with a 28–1 or even 50–1 return! Here are a few methods for optimizing the power of this aspect of the Investment Alternative concept:

1) CREATE INCREDIBLE PRINCIPAL FOR YOUR CHILDREN

We already covered the basics of this above. The process is simple, the results simply amazing.

At combined age 50, you and your spouse could realize a 16–1 return on the purchase of a last-to-die insurance policy. Most people at these younger ages think of insurance only as something they buy for the benefit of their spouse and family in the event of their untimely death. They want to make sure there are funds available for their loved ones' continued security. But given the remarkable returns available, the Investment Alternative funded with life insurance in an Irrevocable Trust goes far beyond the traditional thinking.

By placing the policy in an Irrevocable Trust and structuring it on a last-to-die basis, the return it yields would not be available to one spouse to use for raising the family in the event of the death of the other. There are other ways that this can, and should, be accomplished. However, structuring the Investment Alternative concept in the manner described CAN create a legacy of great wealth for your children.

If you are able to expend $15 thousand on a one pay basis at this time, your children can receive as much as $300 thousand at your deaths. If you can make a single payment of $50 thousand, they may receive as much as $800 thousand. And, if you are among the fortunate young who have inherited or built great wealth early on in your life and can afford to utilize $1 million, your heirs can realize an astonishing $16 million! **A virtual $16 million empire created from a single diversification of $1 million into an insurance policy**. And keep in mind, that $16 million will be available the day the policy is paid for, if necessary—it need not sit and grow and mature over years and years in order to reach its fullest potential—and, if structured properly, will come to your heirs income and estate tax free effectively making it worth more than double the same return on any investment. At younger ages, the results could be even more dramatic. At average age 40 or 30, the $16 million could become as much $28 million to $50 million!

2) CREATE A LEGACY OF
LASTING INCOME

Using the same parameters as in the example above, look at how you can use the Investment Alternative approach to provide a perpetuity of financial security for your loved ones.

You could simply name your children as beneficiaries to your policy and have the full return disbursed amongst them. But consider this. The $16 million which was generated by your implementation of the Investment Alternative technique can be expected, in today's world of approximate 5% interest, to earn $800 thousand a year. Your trust can hold the principal for your heirs and will pay this $800 thousand income to them and then, later, to their heirs, creating an estate-tax free family dynasty.

Structured properly, the Trustees can disburse the principal at any time. It might be that changes in interest rates make this a prudent thing to do. Or it is possible that a family business venture might require some of the capital to expand and grow. For whatever reason, the money is there and was created to support the best interests of the family. *In the meantime, your heirs will have $800 thousand every year, virtually in perpetuity, to provide for their financial security and* *well-being all from your single $1 million alternative investment purchase!*

3) THE ULTIMATE LOVING GIFT FROM GRANDPARENT TO GRANDCHILD

Money cannot buy love. Money cannot, in and of itself, express love. However, in the real world we inhabit today, money can help to secure those things we want for those we love. A good education, a nice home, a certain level of security and peace of mind. It is a tangible way of creating a lasting legacy of our feelings for one another. And no where is that bond and the desire to express it more prevalent than between grandparent and grandchild.

If you are in your sixties or seventies, a 10–1 or 5–1 return on a $50 thousand purchase of a life insurance policy on behalf of your grandchildren would net them between $500 thousand and $250 thousand. These are respectable sums and I doubt you could do any better with any investment given the realities of your age and the time you have left. However, if instead of purchasing the policy on your own lives, you were to purchase it on the lives of your children for the benefit of their children, you could receive returns more along the lines of 16 to 50 times, depending on your children's ages. Suddenly that same $50 thousand has become worth $800 thousand to $2.5 million, a significantly optimized return.

If you could afford to utilize $3 million for an Investment Alternative concept, you could insure the lives of your children for the sake of your grandchildren and produce a return of $48 million to $150 million! **Imagine that. $150 million to either be dispersed amongst your grandchildren or held in trust earning $7.5 million a year for your grandchildren and great-grandchildren, in perpetuity, all accomplished irrespective of time and free from income and estate taxes**.

4) OPTIMIZE GIFTS TO CHARITY
MANY TIMES OVER

If you are planning to slate some portion of your estate as a donation to your favorite charity, consider this: You can significantly optimize that gift by using the Investment Alternative method of a life insurance policy on your children's lives.

If you and your spouse are average age 70 and have come to a time in your lives were you are making plans for the ultimate disbursal of your estate, you may well have decided to leave some bequest to your favorite charity. We already showed you how to take that donation and increase it significantly by using the sum intended for the charity to purchase a one-pay, last-to-die insurance policy. The 5–1 return you would receive at age 70 would increase a $2 million donation to $10 million.

But, instead of making the insurance purchase based on your lives, you could optimize it even more by making it on your children's. At their combined age of 30 or 40, an insurance policy based on their lives could net a return of 28 to 50 times. **That means your same $2 million bequest becomes worth an absolutely astonishing $56 million to $100 million for your charity**. And the $2 million bequest will be tax deductible! Yes, the charity will have to wait a little longer to receive the money (so we all hope, although, of course, there is no guarantee) but good works will need to be done then as much as they are needed now. And think how much more can be accomplished with $100 million versus $2 million. You can also use a combination of your own lives and your children's lives for results sooner and later. What a marvelous way to start your own charitable foundation with salaried trustee positions for your grandchildren.

$1 MILLION CREATES UP TO $50 MILLION ASSET AND UP TO $2.5 MILLION YEARLY IN PERPETUITY

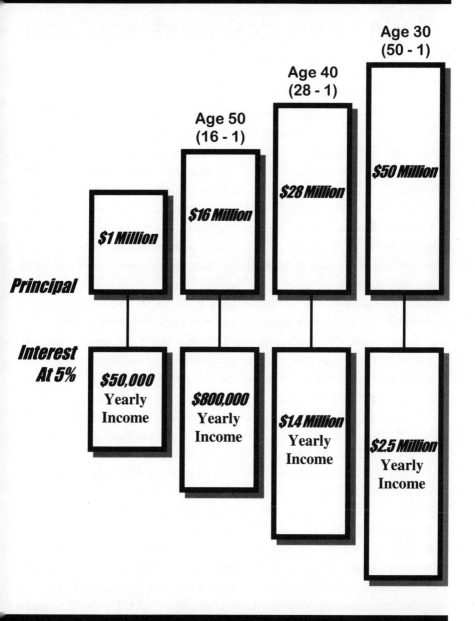

Principal

Age 30
(50 - 1)

Age 40
(28 - 1)

Age 50
(16 - 1)

$50 Million

$28 Million

$16 Million

$1 Million

Interest At 5%

$50,000
Yearly
Income

$800,000
Yearly
Income

$1.4 Million
Yearly
Income

$2.5 Million
Yearly
Income

PHENOMENAL RETURNS AT YOUNGER AGES OPTIMIZE PRINCIPAL AND INCOME

All figures are based on current assumptions. Charts are for illustrative purposes only.
This illustration used last-to-die insurance policies for couples of various ages.
©1997 THE INVESTMENT ALTERNATIVE - Barry Kaye Associates

Concept #15:

YOUR DEBTS CAN MAKE YOU RICH

Most of the rich people I know think that the best way to live is debt free. They believe, and often that belief is supported by the advice of their attorneys or accountants, that being unencumbered by debt is the best way to maintain their estates for themselves and their children. But often this is not the case. Often, retaining a debt so that you can use the money needed to pay it off for other things makes a lot more sense. The fact that this is often overlooked when undertaking financial and estate planning is a symptom of something I have always referred to as 'conventional wisdom.' Something has always been done a certain way, or common thinking has always held to a certain belief, so no one questions it anymore. Unfortunately, great harm is often perpetrated through this seemingly innocent adherence to obsolete thinking.

In my book, Live Rich, I devote a chapter to the dangers of "conventional wisdom." In that chapter, I examine some of history's greatest achievements, achievements which were only made possible by the courageous thwarting of the conventional wisdom of the day. For you, too, great achievements in financial planning may require the rethinking of some of the conventional wisdom you have been encouraged to believe by those who have not the courage or insight to reconsider.

Consider the case of a woman, widowed at age 65. Prior to his death, her husband had been a reasonably successful man and they had lived a comfortable life without any major debt except for the mortgage on their home which totaled $200 thousand. At the 6% rate they were paying on the note, the debt service was approximately $12 thousand a year, an amount they accommodated without distress prior to his death and which the widow would not have difficulty continuing to pay.

But the woman has received a life insurance benefit on her husband's death and, as a result, her estate has grown to $3 million, and now generates more than enough income to support her quite comfortably. Based on the conventional wisdom she has been accustomed to, and her accountant's advice, she decides the best course of action would be to use $200 thousand of the insurance money to pay off the mortgage so she can be entirely debt free. It doesn't matter to her that much—the $12 thousand annual mortgage payments do not negatively impact her lifestyle in any way—but she thinks this will be the best course of action for her children so that they can eventually inherit her estate free from debt.

Without examining the woman's decision more in depth, it might indeed seem the right and generous thing to do. But the truth of the matter is that her $200 thousand mortgage debt repayment is simply the transfer of a liquid and usable $200 thousand into a static and unusable mortgage document.

The woman's mortgage is costing her 6% a year. But her $200 thousand can earn much, much more!

At age 65 and in the good health this woman enjoys, she can expect to earn up to a 5–1 return on a life insurance policy. That means her $200 thousand could become worth as much as $1 million to her children. Given that she was prepared to part with the $200 by giving it to the mortgage bank which holds the note on her house, it is a fair assumption to say that she would be equally able, without harming her own lifestyle, to remove that same $200 thousand from her estate into an Irrevocable Trust instead for the purchase of life insurance.

By not paying off the debt and continuing to make the mortgage payments which had not negatively effected her before and using a portion of the insurance money she received on her husband's death to make the purchase of a life insurance policy, the woman increases her estate to her children by $1 million tax free at a net cost of only $9 thousand a year since her mortgage payment is deductible!

The conventional wisdom would have had her exchange the liquid $200 thousand for the $200 thousand note on her home and the children would not have benefited at all. In fact, given that the home is part of the woman's estate, it will be subject to estate taxes at the time of her death. With her estate totaling $3 million, those taxes will be approximately $1.1 million, or 1/3 of her total value. Basically then, 1/3 of the $200 thousand she used to pay off the mortgage will be forfeit to estate taxes. Her heirs lose $66 thousand instead of gaining $1 million. Put another way, her heirs receive $1 million after taxes instead of $133 thousand. Surely any conventional wisdom which would support such a course needs to be rethought.

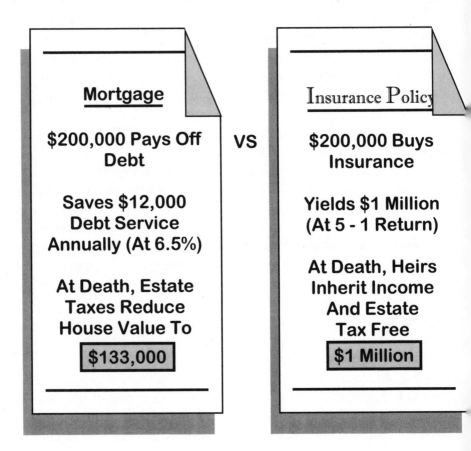

Mortgage VS **Insurance Policy**

Mortgage	Insurance Policy
$200,000 Pays Off Debt	$200,000 Buys Insurance
Saves $12,000 Debt Service Annually (At 6.5%)	Yields $1 Million (At 5 - 1 Return)
At Death, Estate Taxes Reduce House Value To	At Death, Heirs Inherit Income And Estate Tax Free
$133,000	**$1 Million**

FORGET THE "CONVENTIONAL WISDOM"
GO TO THE BOTTOM LINE

All figures are based on current assumptions. Charts are for illustrative purposes only.
This illustration used an insurance policy for a woman age 65.
©1997 THE INVESTMENT ALTERNATIVE - Barry Kaye Associates

Concept #16:

GREAT EARNING POTENTIALS AT OLDER AGES—CREATE MONEY VIRTUALLY OUT OF THIN AIR!

We talked in other chapters about life insurance's truly phenomenal returns at younger ages. In some instances when the initial purchase is made at age 30 to 50, couples can receive as much as a 50–1 return and create incredible wealth for their loved ones.

But the concerns of wealth creation and preservation are not limited to the young. In fact, it is generally at older ages that these concerns really present themselves. As we grow older we become more aware of the limits mortality places upon us. Our awareness of the finite nature of our time here increases. As we begin to feel the toll the years have taken on us, we recognize at last the truth we have been avoiding—that hideous, unrelenting, unavoidable fact of death. In addition, for many of us, after a certain age our earning potentials plateau and dip. We retire from our businesses, start looking at safer, less speculative investments, begin assessing our lives and what we have to show for them. In most cases, one of the things we focus on most is what legacy we will have to leave our children. But, at the same time, our need for expanded sources of income may grow as medical bills increase or simply because we now desire to enjoy some of the things we wanted to do before but didn't have the time or resources for.

It is difficult to balance these two seemingly conflicting desires: wanting to have more for ourselves and wanting to leave more for our heirs. Few financial vehicles can accomplish both goals. But one can.

One financial vehicle is available to people of older ages that can allow them to virtually pull money out of thin air without capital gains taxes, very little income taxes, with no loss of current income, no loss of future appreciation of their gross stock portfolio and no cash flow impairment AND, at the same time, provide for their heirs' well being without any gift or estate tax.

Sound too good to be true? Watch.

A man age 85, has an estate worth $6 million almost all of which is held in stocks and bonds. Taking advantage of the margin available through his stock brokerage firm, he borrows $1 million against those assets. By doing so, he pays no capital gains taxes on the newfound money, nor does it diminish his cash flow at this time. All assets are intact and in place to continue earning the same dividends or returns; all future growth potentials remain undisturbed.

The man takes the $1 million and uses it to purchase an immediate annuity which guarantees him an income for as long as he remains alive. Right away new income has been created from nowhere.

The income generated by the $1 million annuity is $192 thousand per year after tax, based on his life expectancy. From that, he pays the $75 thousand interest which is due on the margin loan from his stockbroker which leaves $117 thousand annually. From that annual $117 thousand, he takes $65 thousand each year for the purchase of a life insurance policy which will yield, at his death, $1 million for his heirs to use to pay off the $1 million principal from the loan from the stock brokerage firm. The man pays no gift tax on the transfer of the money and the heirs pay no income or estate tax on its receipt. Not a single dime of the children's inheritance is impacted and yet an extra $52 thousand annually has been created for the man to enjoy spending every year, even after paying the loan interest and even after purchasing the insurance policy. Furthermore, the heirs will actually come out ahead since the net cost of repaying the $1 million loan will only be $500 thousand; remember, Uncle Sam effectively pays off half of every loan at your death. **So the heirs actually come out more than $500 thousand ahead and the man enjoys the benefits of an additional $52 thousand per year, every year, based on his life expectancy**!

If the man wants to have even more newfound wealth, he could decide to only buy enough insurance to cover the *effective* cost of the estate taxes for his heirs. Since, without this program, his $1 million would only be worth $450 thousand to them after a 55% estate tax is assessed, the man could reason that replacing only the net loss of $550 thousand would be sufficient. In that case, the cost of the insurance policy would be about $32 thousand annually and the man would be left with $85 thousand a year in "found" money while the heirs would suffer no effective loss.

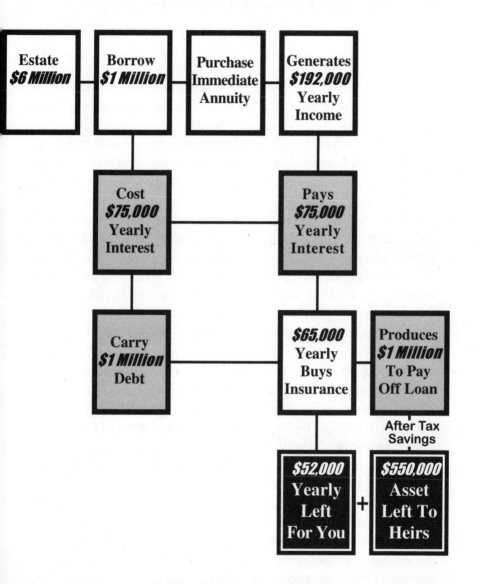

Concept #17:

HOME SWEET—FREE—HOME

There are few purchases any of us make as major, and expensive, as our homes. But what if your family could have the home of your dreams virtually for free?

Let's say you have found the perfect home. Its cost—$2.5 million—is high, but not prohibitive for you. Of course, there will be maintenance costs as well, gardeners and housekeepers, and other regular expenses such as utilities, the alarm system, taxes, and the sort of never-ending projects that homes always seem to entail: roofing, painting, repairs. In total, you figure out that those expenses will wind up costing you about $75 thousand a year or $1.5 million over 20 years.

Now, of course, you hope this purchase will not only be an investment in your family's happiness but a viable financial vehicle as well. But there are no guarantees. One need only travel through the major metropolitan areas of most of our country's biggest cities to see the numerous For Sale and Foreclosure signs to be reminded of how risky a venture real estate can be. Nonetheless you need a home for your family and are entitled to the best one you can afford. So how do you hedge the situation so that enjoying the lifestyle you desire today does not negatively impact your children's ongoing security later?

By transferring $1 million to an Irrevocable Trust and having the trust buy an insurance policy, a 5–1 return is realized and $5 million is secured for this couple's children (the couple averages age 70 and utilizes a one-pay, last-to-die policy, based on current assumptions). When the couple die, as inevitably they must, their children will recover the $1 million that was originally put into the policy as well as the full $2.5 million of the home purchase price. That leaves approximately $1.5 million to cover all other expenses.

Perhaps the couple will have invested wisely in the home they selected for their family. Perhaps the property will escalate greatly and significant profits will be available from its sale. If so, the children have been doubly, and triply, blessed. They lived in a lovely home and had a good life there. Then they recovered the full cost of the home so, in effect, they owned it free and clear. And, the heirs now can sell the property and earn significantly increased profits. Moreover, if they choose not to, they don't have to sell the house. The money is there to maintain it and for them to own it free and clear. The parents have provided for all possible contingencies. If property values decrease, the full price they paid is covered for their heirs. If property values increase, the heirs can make an even more substantial profit.

This Investment Alternative technique can be used to recover the cost of any investment made or tax or expense incurred. The insurance purchased can be a part of an increased mortgage if you finance the house.

OPEN THE DOOR
TO FINANCIAL SECURITY

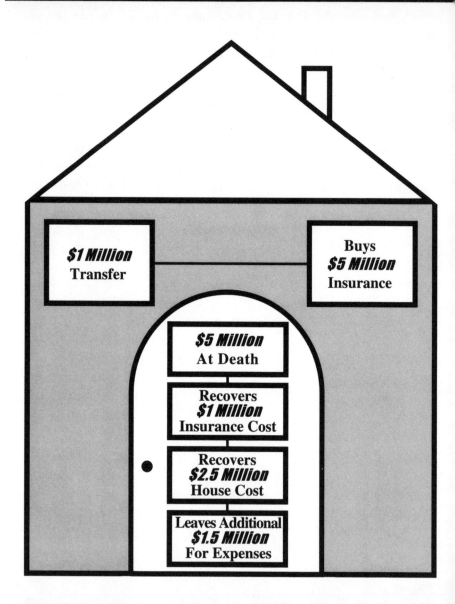

PROTECT THE VALUE OF YOUR HOME

All figures are based on current assumptions. Charts are for illustrative purposes only.
This illustration used a last-to-die insurance policy for a male and female both age 70.
©1997 THE INVESTMENT ALTERNATIVE - Barry Kaye Associates

Concept #18:

A LITTLE LESS NOW—
A *LOT* MORE LATER

When is a windfall not a windfall? When the crop lies in the field and rots. You may have bushels upon bushels of fruit, but, if a large percentage of it is inedible what good does it do?

This is often the case when it comes to windfall gains made on an investment. Consider the case of a 50 year old man who worked for several years to structure a buyout of the company he had inherited from his father. The business was sound and generated decent income, but it wasn't really the man's passion and none of his children had an interest in it. For years he courted buyers and finally an offer was made that fulfilled all his highest hopes. From the sale, he personally would net about $80 million. A windfall for his family!

Except for the inedible parts.

From the $80 million, the man would have to pay capital gains taxes of approximately $23 million leaving $57 million to provide for his family's welfare. Of course, $57 million can do nicely by a family; if it earned today's average 5% return, it would produce about $2.8 million yearly to secure the family's financial security. But this business was the family's legacy and it is the man's hope and desire that the proceeds from its sale will continue to assist his children, and theirs, to take care of their financial needs for many years and generations to come. But when his remaining $57 million passes to his children, it will be subjected to estate taxes of 55% which will claim almost $30 million. Only $27 million will remain. And, while $27 million is still a substantial amount of money, it represents a significant devaluation of the $80 million business he sold. A generation later, when his children pass the funds on to their children, estate taxes will claim ANOTHER 55% further reducing the $27 million by $14 million to $13 million. This was not the windfall he'd worked so hard to engineer.

But this could be avoided if the man were willing to settle for realizing a few dollars less now so that his family could retain every dime later.

If, instead of receiving $80 million from the sale of the business the man were to receive $75 million, the $5 million difference could be used to protect the rest. Used to fund the Investment Alternative technique, a policy could be taken out on the lives of him and his wife and they could expect to earn as much as a 16–1 return. There would be some gift taxes to be paid for the enactment of the program so the man would transfer $3.3 million to an Irrevocable Trust which would make the insurance purchase. The remaining $1.7 million would pay the gift tax on that transfer. At 16–1, the $3.3 million would produce a return of $53 million, which would cover the full expenses of the income and estate taxes which had so decimated his $80 million gain. By taking just a little less now—$5 million from $80 million left him a full $75 million—he ensured his family's financial well-being and got a full bushel of fruit from his tree.

Theoretically, the man could have taken the $57 million left to him after the capital gains taxes were assessed on the $80 million proceeds from the sale of the business and invested it in some other financial vehicle with the hope of growing it back into the full $80 million for the sake of his family. But remember, first of all the man has to hope that he will live long enough for his investment plans to come to fruition. The moment tragedy strikes and his estate passes to his heirs estate taxes will claim 55% of whatever total amount that $57 million has grown to. *IF* it has grown. He also has to hope that he invests wisely and realizes a profit instead of a loss. And it must be a significant profit. A HIGHLY significant profit because even if he does live long enough for his investment goals to be realized they will still be subject to the same 55% estate taxes. That means it is not sufficient for his $57 million to grow back into $80 million. It must grow to slightly more than $175 million to net the same $80 million to his heirs after estate taxes of 55% are paid.

Can he find such an investment? I'd say it's doubtful. And even if he did, would he have a guarantee of time enough left to him for it to mature to its fullest potential? No. There are no guarantees of that sort available for anyone. Also, does he want to go back into business or expose himself to risk again?

The man will have $52 million left even after he pays the capital gains taxes and executes this program. If he can locate an investment which will yield such a phenomenal return as the one detailed above, he has plenty of money left to put into it. Surely however, the wisest course is to diversify his portfolio to include the $3 million insurance policy which will protect the full price he received for the business even if tragedy strikes tomorrow.

SELL YOUR BUSINESS FOR $5 MILLION LESS
INCREASE ITS NET VALUE $50 MILLION MORE

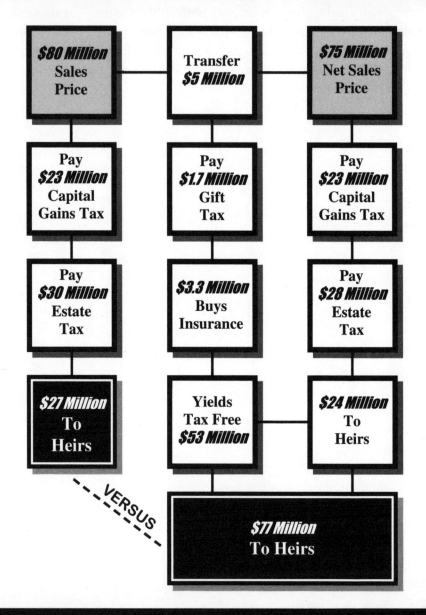

$80 Million Sales Price — Transfer **$5 Million** — **$75 Million** Net Sales Price

Pay **$23 Million** Capital Gains Tax — Pay **$1.7 Million** Gift Tax — Pay **$23 Million** Capital Gains Tax

Pay **$30 Million** Estate Tax — **$3.3 Million** Buys Insurance — Pay **$28 Million** Estate Tax

$27 Million To Heirs — Yields Tax Free **$53 Million** — **$24 Million** To Heirs

VERSUS

$77 Million To Heirs

$27 MILLION OR $77 MILLION
YOU DECIDE

All figures are based on current assumptions. Charts are for illustrative purposes only.
This illustration used a last-to-die insurance policy for a male and female both age 50.
©1997 THE INVESTMENT ALTERNATIVE - Barry Kaye Associates

Concept #19:

DOUBLE THE SALE PRICE OF YOUR BUSINESS OR REAL ESTATE

How would you like to double the sale price you receive for virtually any item of value you possess? You can. And more than that, you can effectively triple the price your heirs receive for it.

Let's assume you own a business that you have built and developed and run for years and years. Now, it's time to get out. Time to enjoy the fruits of your labor, to travel, to spend time with your grandchildren, to relax. So you put the business up for sale. Luckily for you there is no crisis driving the sale. It is not a forced liquidation situation and you can afford to wait for the right buyer and the right price rather than having to settle for less as your heirs might have had to if the need for the sale had been more urgent.

Finally the sale is consummated and you have received $25 million. Certainly a substantial amount of money and what you had determined to be a fair, equitable price for the asset. You are content with the result. But what if someone had come along before the sale was finished and offered you twice the asking price—$50 million. Would you have said, "Oh no. Thank you, but my business is only worth $25 million and I can't take anymore than that for it?" Of course you wouldn't. Value is determined by what someone is willing to pay for something and if someone were willing to give you $50 million then that would be the appropriate value for your business.

Well, unfortunately, no one came and made the $50 million offer. You settled for the $25 million which is still an equitable, valuable sum. However, you can now, after the sale is accomplished, double the sale price received for the asset. You would have jumped at the chance to make $50 million on the sale before it was consummated, why would you not leap with joy to achieve the same $50 million now?

Assuming that you and your spouse are age 60, you can take 10% of the proceeds from the sale of your business—$2.5 million from the $25 million proceeds—and use my Investment Alternative concept to purchase a life insurance policy that will yield, based on current assumptions, $25 million. This simple reallocation of a portion of your asset will basically double the amount the business sale netted from $25 million to $50 million.

Yes, that $50 million is actually reduced to $47.5 million by the outlay of the $2.5 which funded the additional $25 million death benefit. And yes, there would be some gift taxes to pay on the transfer of the $2.5 million from your estate to the Irrevocable Trust on behalf of your children. However, you and your spouse are together entitled to a one-time gift and transfer exemption of $1.2 million so taxes will only be assessed on the remaining $1.3 million. At approximately 40%, that gift tax would be $500 thousand. So, in fact, the $50 million would be reduced $2.5 million by the cost of the program and $500 thousand in gift taxes. Now, instead of $25 million from the sale, you 'only' receive $47 million. Is that close enough to double not to quibble? If the imaginary buyer had offered you $47 million instead of a pat $50 million would you have turned him away. Your children will not object to the increased value no matter where the $22 million came from?

Meanwhile, remember, when that original $25 million from the sale of the business before it was optimized to $47 million by this program came to your heirs, it would have been reduced by estate taxes of 55% to $11.25 million. If you undertake this program, that amount will be somewhat further reduced by the $2.5 million of the insurance purchase cost and the $500 thousand of gift taxes. The $25 million will become $22 million, which will be subject to $12 million in estate taxes leaving $10 million. So it might seem that your heirs have 'lost' 1.25 million. But with the additional, tax free $25 million which your heirs will receive from the insurance, the total value of the asset to them has jumped to $35 million and that's still over three times the net $11.25 million they would have received had you not undertaken the program and not incurred the costs of the insurance and gift tax.

In fact, Uncle Sam paid for half the insurance and half the gift tax because, had you left those sums in the asset the $2.5 million insurance premium would have only been worth about $1.25 million to your heirs after estate taxes and the $500 thousand you paid in gift taxes would have been worth a little less than $250 thousand. So, in truth, the real cost to your estate of the insurance purchase and gift tax was not $3 million ($2.5 million for the insurance and $500 thousand for the gift tax) but actually the $1.5 million that $3 million would have been worth to your heirs.

Of course, you could use any of the concepts I showed you earlier to borrow the $2.5 million insurance premium instead of paying cash from the newly sold asset. You could borrow the $2.5 million and pay the approximate 7% interest of $175 thousand each year or you could borrow it and let the interest accrue. In either case, you would not lose the use of the additional 10% of your asset and the total net cost of the loan, whether paid or accrued, would still be well worth the return of $25 million.

The same concept applies to increasing the value of any real estate or stock that did not perform as well as you had wished for. Your real estate is sold for $3 million. You pay capital gains tax of approximately $1 million leaving a net gain of $2 million. You ultimately die and your heirs pay approximately $1 million in estate taxes leaving a net value for your real estate sale of $1 million. If you followed my plan, you would have used $300 thousand (10% of $3 million) to purchase a last-to-die insurance policy with a return of $3 million (age 60), $1.5 million (age 70), or $1 million (age 79). In every case you have increased the net value of the sale of your real estate from $1 million net to $2 million, $2.5 million, or $4 million, from two to four times what your heirs would have received had you done nothing.

This same technique applies with the sale of any other asset. Since this money would not have been received by your heirs before the event of your death, for all practical purposes you can consider that you sold the business, real estate, or asset for double to quadruple its net sale value. Frankly, your children, grandchildren, other heirs or charity will not care whether the $2 to $4 million came from the asset sale or a combination of the sale and insurance. It all spends the same when your heirs make future purchases and no one will care nor will it make any difference. Obviously, this can be pro rated to a smaller or larger selling price.

These techniques can also be used to help you achieve a desired sale price that you couldn't receive instead of just maximizing a sale.

Let's say you felt your business was worth $25 million but you could only get $20 million for it. Now you are faced with a $5 million 'loss' of your business' expected value and you might be tempted to turn the $20 million offer down and wait and hope someone comes along and offers the full $25 million. You could wind up waiting a long time.

Or, you could take the offered $20 million and use the Investment Alternative techniques to create the 'lost' $5 million or more.

With the 10 times return on an insurance purchase you are earning at your average ages of 60, you and your spouse could take $500 thousand of the proceeds from the sale of the business and purchase a one-pay, last-to-die policy that would yield at death, $5 million income and estate tax free. For ten cents on the dollar you have recaptured the $5 million and sold the business effectively for the full $25 million you desired. You could use $1 million and buy $10 million thus raising the value of the sale from $20 million to $30 million, $5 million more than you originally wanted. In fact, you could double the value of the sale from $20 million to $40 million by using $2 million to buy the insurance.

You can apply this technique to the sale of any asset for which you can not now, and may not ever, receive what you desire or think it to be worth so that your heirs will benefit from the full value of the business, property or other asset you have spent a lifetime amassing for them. And you will not be left waiting and exposed to what may happen to the current value of your assets. More importantly, you won't have to stay in a business you no longer want the responsibility for as well as the inherent risks. The lower price you accept may be the best loss you ever take since it can be more than offset with the Investment Alternative.

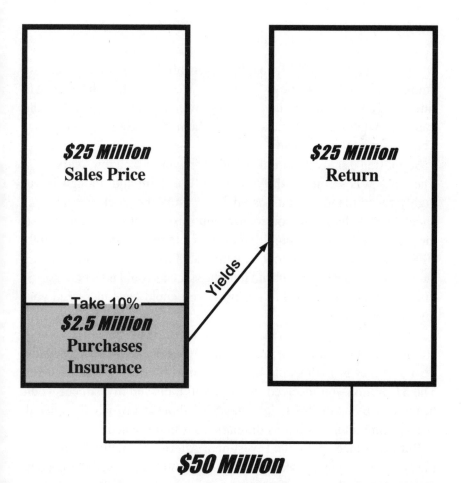

$25 Million
Sales Price

$25 Million
Return

Take 10%
$2.5 Million
Purchases
Insurance

Yields

$50 Million

ANY BUSINESS, STOCK OR REAL ESTATE
CAN BE WORTH TWICE
THE BEST OFFER YOU CAN GET FOR IT

All figures are based on current assumptions. Charts are for illustrative purposes only.
This illustration used a last-to-die insurance policy for a male and female both age 60.
©1997 THE INVESTMENT ALTERNATIVE - Barry Kaye Associates

Concept #20:

TURN BACK THE CLOCK ON MISSED STOCK OPPORTUNITIES

Do you ever wish you'd bought Microsoft back before it rose so dramatically? Or Netscape or Starbucks? Wouldn't it have been great to ride along and watch your investment grow and grow and grow? Would you like to turn the clock back and buy them at those early prices now? There's a way that you can.

Supposing a stock opportunity had come your way a few years back. The stock was selling at the time for $10 a share and, though it was highly recommended, you passed it up. Now the stock is trading at about $200 a share and you realize you missed out on a huge investment potential. Had you put $10 thousand into the $10 stock and bought 1000 shares, they would now be worth $200 thousand. More dramatically, if you'd put $50 thousand into the stock it would now be worth $1 million. What a bitter pill to swallow. You could have increased your investment 20 times over!

Of course, had you been making your investments on behalf of your children with the idea that the earnings would be part of their legacy, your 20 times growth would be cut in half to 10 times by estate taxes. The $1 million you received for your $50 thousand investment would be reduced by up to 55% to less than $500 thousand which, though still a significant return, is not as dramatic as it first seemed.

But here, once again, the Investment Alternative method can create the opportunity you passed up before if you no longer need these assets and are 60 or 70.

If you and your spouse are average age 60, you can reallocate some of your current investments into a last-to-die, one-pay insurance policy which will come to your heirs income and estate tax free, as long as it has been properly structured in an Irrevocable Trust, and can expect to receive a 10–1 return. By selling $100 thousand of stocks currently held in your portfolio and reallocating the funds to the insurance policy, you can produce the entire $1 million that represents the pre-tax value of the stock you are so sorry you missed out on. If you don't want to sell current investments, you can borrow the $100 thousand against them and pay or accrue the interest. In either event, you will have greatly optimized your portfolio and benefited the same as if you really had had the foresight to buy the $10 stock in the first place.

Your $10 stock would have had to go to $400 to net for your heirs the same $1 million. At $400 a share, the $50 thousand you used to purchase 5,000 shares would be worth $2 million which, after estate taxes, would be reduced to $1 million. So instead, you buy the life insurance and place it in a box or file labeled Microsoft, or Gold Mine, or the fictitious American Dream Incorporated stock I mentioned at the beginning of the book. The results are the same and no one ever needs to know where the money came from. If you don't want to admit how you will earn those great returns using life insurance, just tell them you were clever enough to get in on ADI or Microsoft when it was $10 a share and now it's at $400. They'll applaud your wisdom and wish *they'd* been smart and lucky enough to get in on the deal from its inception. You can do this with any stock or investment you missed.

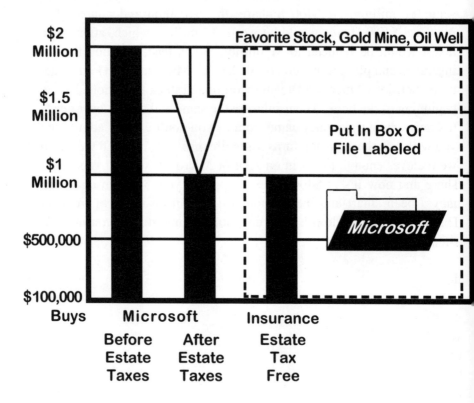

All figures are based on current assumptions. Charts are for illustrative purposes only.
This illustration used a last-to-die insurance policy for a male and female both age 60.
©1997 THE INVESTMENT ALTERNATIVE - Barry Kaye Associates

Concept #21:

THE MOST INCREDIBLE POLICY OF THEM ALL—WITH UNHEARD OF POTENTIALS OF UP TO $1 BILLION!

- Buy A Guaranteed $1 Million Policy
  With A Potential Death Benefit of $10 Million

- Buy A Guaranteed $10 Million Policy
  With A Potential Death Benefit of $100 Million

- **Buy A Guaranteed $100 Million Policy
  With A Potential Death Benefit of $1 Billion**

Throughout these concepts, I have reiterated that the predetermined nature of the life insurance return is based upon current assumptions. The assumptions reflect the interest and mortality rates that were in effect when you bought the policy. In the section of this book entitled "Too Good To Be True" I fully explain how those assumptions are determined and how they can affect you.

But there are those people who do not want their policy to be based upon current assumptions. Whether because they are extremely conservative or have been scared by unknowledgeable advisors into thinking that a policy based on current assumptions is financially dangerous, these people want an absolute guarantee. If they are willing to pay for it, there is a special program that, in addition to providing the absolute, unconditional guarantee they desire, can reap unbelievably huge death benefits and tax free returns for their heirs outside their estates.

When we structure policies, we use those that are based on current assumptions because they are much, much less expensive than those whose guarantees are unconditional. For most people, buying the most death benefit for the lowest premium is the preferred course of action. Of course, I wouldn't sell nor advise the purchase of a policy whose return was unrealistically inflated due to improperly calculated or promised returns. All the policies my firm recommends have their

125

premiums based on the interest and mortality that exist at the time of purchase. There is however, some risk of assumptions changing. But in exchange for assuming that risk, you get a much lower premium cost than if you require a risk-free policy.

With that said, there are policies that offer a total guarantee. They do this by using in their calculations the highest, or most costly for you, assumptions; the most extreme limits of interest and mortality. This drives the cost way up. For example, a couple age 40, buying a last-to-die, life-pay insurance policy to net a $10 million return **based on current assumptions** could expect to pay about $26 thousand a year. That same couple, buying a policy fully guaranteed to yield $10 million would have to pay $94 thousand a year. For some, the difference is worth it in terms of security and surety.

For most people, the difference in cost makes the policy both prohibitive and undesirable. Why expend $68 thousand more each year than is necessary to receive the same return? Even if assumptions change in a way that is unfavorable to you, the likelihood of them changing drastically enough to increase your policy cost from $26 thousand annually to $94 thousand annually is extremely improbable and practically impossible. Meanwhile, if you wanted to spend $94 thousand a year, you could purchase a policy that would produce, based on current assumptions, about $36 million.

There is however, one amazing benefit beyond the security of having a fully guaranteed policy premium that can make the extra expenditure worth it.

As you pay premiums significantly in excess of what the current assumptions require to fund the intended $10 million death benefit, you build up considerable cash values in the vastly over-funded policy. Those excess cash values will eventually create an increasing death benefit, based on the existing current assumptions through the years.

By age 70, the death benefit now totals $11 million. By 75, it's $13 million and by age 80, the death benefit has risen to $19 million. Then, at age 85, the death benefit reaches $27 million. By age 90 the death benefit is $38 million and by age 95 it's $51 million. And finally, should you live to be 100, the death benefit reaches over $72 million! In this way, the annual difference in expenditure from $26 thousand to $94 thousand—*$68 thousand*—completely guarantees the death benefit of $10 million and creates the potential for an additional *$62 million*!

If the couple had bought the policy on a one-pay basis, the premium needed to fund a $10 million death benefit, based on current assumptions, would be $356 thousand. To guarantee the $10 million death benefit, the one-pay cost would be $2 million. The difference of $1.6 million guarantees the $10 million return and creates the potential for the huge growth. And because the payment has been made in one, up-front sum, the increase happens more quickly and more dramatically.

Now, at age 70, the death benefit has risen to $16 million. At age 80, it has grown to $29 million. At age 90 it's $56 million and by the time the couple has reached age 100 their $2 million premium has come to fund a death benefit of $100 million. By paying the excessive $2 million premium, based on the current assumptions, the death benefit has increased from the guaranteed $10 million up to $100 million.

You can customize this program by adding or subtracting zeros. A policy to produce $1 million can be purchased based on current assumptions for $2600 annually and can be fully guaranteed for $9400 annually. As the death benefit increases, it can equal, in the 60th year as the couple reaches 100, $8.3 million.

For a $100 million death benefit, the policy could be purchased for $264 thousand a year based on current assumptions or $940 thousand fully guaranteed. At 100 years of age, the fully guaranteed policy, based on current assumptions, would have built up such vast cash values that the death benefit would now be an astonishing $730 million! And if the couple lived to be 110, the massive over-funding would yield a never-before imagined death benefit of $1 billion! And the return percentage is even better if the policy is purchased on a one-pay basis. Then, a policy purchased for $20 million to produce a guaranteed $100 million death benefit could increase to $1 billion as the couple became 100 years old!

And of course, once again, the cost of this program is really only half its paper expense since 55% of all the assets you hold in your estate at the time of your death will be forfeited to estate taxes. That means the annual $920 thousand in premium payments would only be worth $414 thousand to your heirs. In this way, it is really only $414 thousand annually that funds the potential $1 billion return!

It has been said that life insurance is of maximum value only if you die early. That the longer you live, the less value it has. There might be some statistical truth in that opinion, but there is absolutely no relevance to reality since statistics don't apply to individuals and there is no way you can know how long you will live. But now with the advent of these guaranteed policies and the remarkable growth they experience the whole issue is moot. Clearly insurance can become a source of ever-increasing value the longer you live.

The more you pay, the more the guarantee. The more the guarantee, the more the overpayment. The more the overpayment, the more the potential growth of the death benefit. The more the death benefit, the more tax free money out of your estate *for the same gift tax*!

GUARANTEED PREMIUMS CAN MAKE YOUR INSURANCE GROW UP TO $1 BILLION

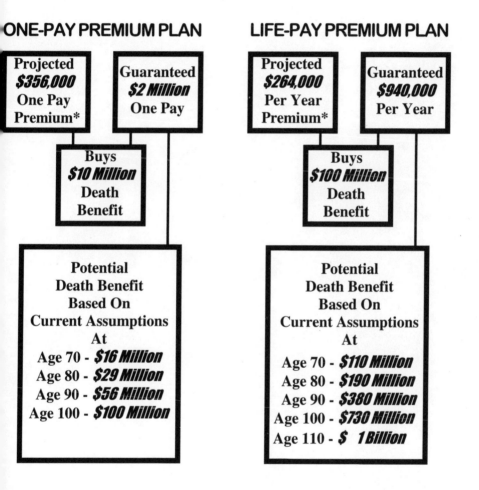

ONE-PAY PREMIUM PLAN

Projected **$356,000** One Pay Premium*

Guaranteed **$2 Million** One Pay

Buys **$10 Million** Death Benefit

Potential
Death Benefit
Based On
Current Assumptions
At
Age 70 - **$16 Million**
Age 80 - **$29 Million**
Age 90 - **$56 Million**
Age 100 - **$100 Million**

LIFE-PAY PREMIUM PLAN

Projected **$264,000** Per Year Premium*

Guaranteed **$940,000** Per Year

Buys **$100 Million** Death Benefit

Potential
Death Benefit
Based On
Current Assumptions
At
Age 70 - **$110 Million**
Age 80 - **$190 Million**
Age 90 - **$380 Million**
Age 100 - **$730 Million**
Age 110 - **$ 1 Billion**

*All figures are based on current assumptions. Charts are for illustrative purposes only.
This illustration used a last-to-die insurance policy for a male and female both age 40.
©1997 THE INVESTMENT ALTERNATIVE - Barry Kaye Associates

ESTATE TAX COST DISCOUNTING

I believe estate planning in America is done totally incorrectly. I never heard a doctor say, "After I've done surgery on you, I'll perform an examination to find out what's wrong." Clearly, the examination must come first. You must know your condition before you can determine a course of treatment. However, it is the conventional wisdom around estate planning that the surgery should come first before the accurate determination of your condition. Practitioners think that you make all sorts of expensive legal plans and machinations and THEN, afterwards, consider life insurance to cover the rest. I disagree completely with this thinking; it is, in my belief, totally backwards. If you are insurable you will be able to increase your exemptions and discount your estate tax costs and utilize the other incredible programs outlined in this book. However if you are not, an entirely different tact will have to be used. In spite of the fact that you can still buy insurance even if you are not insurable using my surrogate technique, the actual estate plan may require a totally different approach.

Estate planning is NOT a legal happening. It is an economic event.

How can you plan an estate properly until you know whether you can buy insurance or not and at what price? Obviously, if you can qualify and then purchase the insurance, you will utilize one approach in protecting your estate whereas if you can't buy insurance to cover the estate tax costs you must totally plan the estate differently. With this understanding, I believe you must see if you qualify for insurance **before** you go into costly legal estate planning. A medical examination should be the first requirement of any properly executed estate plan.

In my opinion, estate taxes are simply dollars and cents. Plain arithmetic and mathematics. My subject at seminars and in this book is a mathematical one and not a legal one.

Insurance is absolutely irrelevant to this discussion as well as to the entire book. It is strictly the funding mechanism that we use to initiate, implement and accomplish all of the concepts contained herein. If I had a choice between 10 legal documents and 1 insurance policy that produced money at my death, I would certainly take the insurance policy every time. However, this does not preclude the fact that once you know that you can qualify for the insurance, then you should have all of the legal documentation consummated and some of the exciting and unique cookie cutter concepts, including the GRITS, GRATS, GRUTS, Charitable Lead Trusts, Charitable Remainder Trusts, and Family Limited Partnerships, when appropriate to your situation and objectives. These things will certainly complement and enhance the insurance. But while documents alone, with no enhancement from insurance, can produce a lot of good reading when you die, they don't produce a dime's worth of extra money.

At its most simple, estate planning is, or should be, a method of reducing estate taxes to the minimum and maximizing your assets to their optimum for your heirs. No amount of legal documents can accomplish this as well or as surely as a single insurance policy.

I believe that the bottom line is the only thing that counts. What goes to the bottom line? What do the heirs or favorite charities actually receive?

Too often I hear inappropriate and unprofessional remarks by attorneys furthering an unreasonable bias against insurance salespeople. They suggest that our advice and programs are somehow diminished in their viability and value because we are "selling" them; that the fact that we make our livings selling products we believe in detracts from the value of those products. Do they make the same inference about the products your business sells? That somehow because you sell them your belief in them is tainted and no one should buy them because you are unreasonably biased towards them? Accountants sell protection against audits, doctors sell operations, insurance salespeople sell insurance and attorneys sell Revocable Trusts, Irrevocable Trusts, Family Limited Partnerships, Generation Skipping Trusts etc. No ethical professional would recommend any of the above unless necessary. The fact that each of these groups make their living selling the aforementioned products does not indicate that they have a bias or they are less professional than any other group. I do not denigrate any attorney for making his living selling and preparing documents. I do not believe a professional would recommend anything not in the best interest of the client. Is there any reason to feel that the man selling insurance is any less professional than the attorney who also makes his living with his recommendation? And if the attorney is dissuading his client from undertaking a program which would be of great value simply on the basis that the insurance salesperson will earn a commission for their labor, then a grave injustice has been done to that client who, in the meantime, will almost assuredly be charged at the attorney's hourly rate for the advice.

It is the attorney's part of the equation to maintain the legality of any methodology and implement any needed legal documentation. But you must ask yourself, "Is the attorney really qualified to speak out of his purview on insurance?" Only you can and should make the final decision based on the business sense which allowed you to make your fortune in the first place. Your logic, common sense, heart and the bottom line will direct you correctly. Don't listen to the insurance man's words OR to the attorney or advisor's rhetoric. Go to the bottom line. The numbers will tell you what's best for you.

It is my opinion, based on 35 years of experience, that the insurance must be implemented first. Then and only then can you know what your remaining exposure will be. And then and only then can you complement the insurance's incredible power with the various legal approaches that will certainly aid the overall program and achieve additional goals but which WILL NOT produce a single additional dollar for your heirs and WILL NOT produce the funds to pay the estate taxes.

Go to the bottom line. You know how, you've been doing it for years running your business, your home, your life. You get advice but you know that your advisors are only expert in one aspect of what you do. It is and always has been up to you to put the pieces together into a clear picture of your best course of action. And you're savvy enough to realize that each of your advisors has some personal professional stake in your following their advice. Each makes his or her living from the field of specialty they practice. Your lawyer sells trust and documents; I sell insurance. We both believe in what we are doing, we both earn through our labor and conviction and knowledge and wisdom the money that we make. But it is up to you to decide where your money is better put for the ultimate good of your bottom line, your family and your heirs.

Go to the bottom line. Estate taxes can claim as much as 55% of your estate. If you spent a lifetime amassing a legacy for your children or your favorite charity, more than half your sweat and labor will benefit one greedy relative—your Uncle Sam. But it doesn't have to be this way. Using the amazing power of the Investment Alternative concepts described in this book, you can effectively discount your estate tax by a full 90%—without taking one dime away from the government and country that has made your wealth possible. You can increase your exemptions to the point where you have virtually no tax exposure. Isn't THAT the bottom line you desire?

There are basically only four ways to pay your estate taxes and EVERYONE with an estate MUST utilize one. Your heirs can: 1) Pay in cash; 2) Take out a loan; 3) Liquidate assets; or, 4) Utilize the insurance you have included outside your portfolio to pay the full tax amount for as little as 10 cents on the dollar.

As you will clearly see from the following examples and applications, using life insurance proceeds to pay the taxes is the only way which leaves your estate intact for the benefit of your heirs and the only way to be sure that your intentions are realized. There is not a single legal document, trust, partnership or plan which will accomplish this in the same way.

Go to the bottom line. On the following pages I will demonstrate ways that you can:

- Turn any tax into an asset
- Effectively exempt your entire estate from estate taxes
- Reduce your estate tax cost up to 90%
- Eliminate your estate tax cost completely
- Double your gross estate and triple your net estate

These plans and accomplishments are real. They are legal. But they can not be accomplished only with legal documents nor can they be accomplished utilizing traditional investments. Only the Investment

Alternative concept of using life insurance properly structured in an Irrevocable Trust or owned by your heirs can achieve the optimization of your bottom line in these ways.

Remember every legal plan prepared by your attorney is a method of tax avoidance. Only life insurance pays the tax at a great discount, optimizes your assets and completely benefits your family and the country better than any other approach. Look to the bottom line.

Concept #22:

GIVE AWAY YOUR FULL ESTATE VALUE TWICE WITHOUT PAYING ANY ESTATE TAXES

The purpose of estate planning is to arrange your assets in such a way as to maximize the amounts of money you leave your heirs and minimize the amount of taxes you pay in the process. Without planning of this sort estate taxes, which can reach as high as 55%, devalue your estate and dramatically reduce the inheritance you leave behind for your heirs. If these things were not your concern you would do away with estate planning altogether, hand over more than half your assets to the government and leave behind a simple will detailing your intentions for the disbursal of what was left. But you go through the processes and jump through the hoops and draw up the documents and establish the trusts and consult with all manner of consultants in order to avoid that decimation as much as is possible. Yet none of those tactics will replace a single dime of the inevitable taxes. At best, they can help avoid some of the loss. This is a negative approach, a defensive tactic. I prefer a positive approach on the offensive in the battle against decimating estate taxes. Don't retreat and try to hold a fallback position. Attack! Don't just minimize your losses. Maximize your gains.

But only life insurance in an Irrevocable Trust CAN actually create money where none was before. It CAN actually replace tax losses and recreate the wealth that would otherwise be gone for good.

Despite anything your lawyer or advisor might tell you, there are only two ways to avoid all estate taxes on any sum of money beyond the combined $1.2 million exemption allowed to you and your spouse. One is to remove the entire sum from your estate prior to your death in which case you will pay gift taxes that are almost as decimating as estate taxes. The other is to leave the entire sum to charity. Charitable contributions are tax deductible, so if you leave the whole amount to charity it will be deducted from your taxable assets and there will be nothing left on which to pay taxes. Of course, there will also be nothing left for your heirs to inherit.

I will show you, in subsequent concepts, various means for minimizing the estate tax costs on any portion of your assets not gifted to charity, how to discount the cost of those taxes for your heirs, how to recover the estate tax loss they face. But even those concepts do not avoid the paying of estate taxes. They simply reduce and replace the amounts paid.

However, there is a way to leave everything you have to charity and therefore pay no estate taxes while still also leaving the entire current value of your estate to your heirs and paying no estate taxes. It's simple, it's legal, it requires no fancy, expensive cookie cutter legal transactions and it absolutely works.

Let's say you and your spouse are average age 60 and have an estate worth $8 million. If you do nothing, estate taxes will claim about $4 million leaving your heirs $4 million. But, if you follow this plan, you can leave your heirs the entire $8 million while at the same time leaving $7.2 million to charity and all without a single dime of estate tax liability.

It works like this: At average age sixty, you and your spouse can expect to receive a 10–1 return, based on current assumptions, on a last-to-die life insurance policy. Armed with that simple, yet powerful, knowledge, you transfer $800 thousand to an Irrevocable Trust which uses the funds to purchase a last-to-die policy on your lives. Since together you and your spouse are entitled to a total combined exemption of $1.2 million, you would pay no gift tax on this transfer.

At your deaths, the insurance policy will return a death benefit of $8 million to your heirs. Because of the unique nature of life insurance proceeds, the death benefit will come to your heirs income tax free. And because the policy was held in an Irrevocable Trust outside your estate, they will not have to pay any estate taxes on it either.

After making the one-time expenditure of $800 thousand, your estate was reduced from $8 million to $7.2 million. For the rest of your lives, you had the use of this principal and the income it produced to support your lifestyle. Then, when you die, you leave the entire sum to charity and, in so doing, avoid all estate taxes on the total asset. The charity gets a tax free $7.2 million while your heirs get a tax free $8 million all from the same original $8 million.

You have accomplished both goals of estate planning. You have maximized the legacy your children receive by eliminating the loss of 55% of your estate valuation from estate taxes and you have completely eliminated all estate taxes. You have given your entire estate away to charity. And you have left your entire estate to your heirs. And not a single dime of your asset was lost to taxes. In many ways, this is the epitome of estate tax planning and it was all accomplished in the most simple, direct manner possible using my most simplistic Investment Alternative concept of life insurance in an Irrevocable Trust.

And don't forget, your heirs can recover the $800 thousand you spent to implement this concept or you can leave them even more and give even more to charity based on the actual amount of insurance you purchase. My apologies to all my fellow professionals for making estate planning so simple. But it really is! It may sound too good to be true. But it really is true!

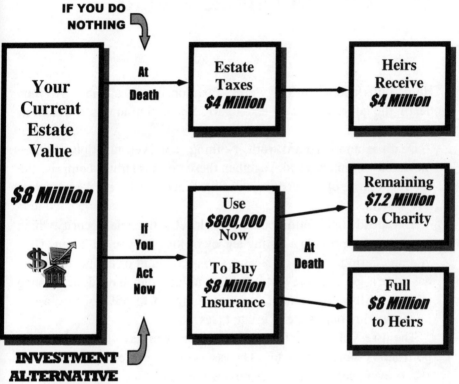

IF YOU DO NOTHING

Your Current Estate Value

$8 Million

At Death → Estate Taxes **$4 Million** → Heirs Receive **$4 Million**

If You Act Now → Use **$800,000** Now To Buy **$8 Million** Insurance

At Death → Remaining **$7.2 Million** to Charity

Full **$8 Million** to Heirs

INVESTMENT ALTERNATIVE METHOD

FAMILY GETS $8 MILLION
CHARITY GETS $7.2 MILLION
UNCLE SAM GETS $0

All figures are based on current assumptions. Charts are for illustrative purposes only.
This illustration used a last-to-die insurance policy for a male and female both age 60.

Concept #23:

DISCOUNT ESTATE TAX COSTS, INCREASE YOUR CHILDREN'S LEGACY TWO TIMES OVER!

Hard truths abound in our world. Taxation is one of them. At your death, the government will take up to 55% of your amassed wealth in estate taxes.

Death is another hard truth. Nothing, not even taxation, is more inevitable or more certain. Together, these two hard truths comprise the central premise of an outstanding utilization of the Investment Alternative system.

You spend your lifetime achieving a level of financial security which you hope will provide a lasting legacy of love for your children. Then you die. Period. Nothing your lawyer, accountant or financial advisor has done is going to prevent it. Just as nothing they have done is going to prevent the government from claiming up to 55% of any assets remaining in your estate in estate taxes.

The assessed value of every investment you have left within your portfolio is subject to the tax. The assessed value of every piece of real estate, every collectible, every possession you own is subject to the tax. Every cent received from your bonds, IRA's, Keogh's and pension is subject to the tax. Even those things which are income tax free are still subject to estate taxes when they pass from you to your heirs. Period. These are the hard truths.

Your Living Will can help ease the cost and burden of probate. Your trusts can shelter certain funds. But **EVERY DIME THAT IS YOURS AT THE TIME OF YOUR DEATH**, every penny you have not already given away or donated to charity, every dollar you use to live on and provide for your own comfort and well-being, **WILL BE SUBJECT TO ESTATE TAXES OF UP TO 55%**. And that means that every dollar of yours may be worth less than 50 cents to your heirs.

There is no one and nothing which can change these hard truths unless, perhaps, an act of congress reduces or abolishes the estate tax. But the likelihood of that, in the current political and economic climate, is not great. A reduction of taxes on the rich would not serve the interests of partisan politics no matter how unfair the tax may be— certainly no other tax would ever be permitted to reach as high as 55% —or how much the country would benefit by having those funds stay in circulation. Meanwhile, not even an act of congress can keep you alive forever.

So death and estate taxes remain inevitabilities. Not even the miraculous Investment Alternative method can change that.

But the Investment Alternative technique can achieve something no investment can. It can allow you to dramatically reduce the cost of estate taxes to your heirs—in many cases by as much as 90%!

You die. Nothing can change that. The government gets its due. Nothing can change that. BUT YOUR HEIRS DO NOT SUFFER THE UP TO 55% DECIMATION OF THEIR INHERITANCE. This is simply the best you can do in an imperfect world of hard, harsh truths.

Let's assume that you and your spouse are average age 70 with an estate worth $30 million. This program will work at virtually all ages and with any estate in excess of $3 million. Rates of return on the insurance change as do the estate tax costs and discounts, but the principles remain the same. For specific applications that better fit your own situation, see the charts and tables at the back of this book.

On an estate of $30 million, 55% estate tax equals $16.5 million which would leave your heirs $13.5 million. But, at average age 70 and based upon current assumptions, you can use the Investment Alternative technique of purchasing a last-to-die life insurance policy to yield a return of 5–1. That means that $3.3 million will yield a $16.5 million return upon your death whether it occurs a year from now, ten years from now or tomorrow.

Follow it through. You die. Nine months after your death or the death of your surviving spouse, the government assesses your net worth at $30 million and requires your heirs to pay $16.5 million in estate taxes leaving them $13.5 million of your original legacy. BUT . . . having reallocated $3.3 million during your lifetime to a last-to-die insurance policy yielding a 5–1 return and which you placed into an

Irrevocable Trust, the life insurance company now presents your assigned heirs with the return on your insurance—$16.5 million completely tax free. Your wisdom and foresight not only created the $30 million legacy during your lifetime, it protected it after your death. In effect, the entire 55% estate tax of $16.5 million was paid for by a single $3.3 million insurance payment, based on current assumptions, thereby significantly discounting the taxes and doubling your children's inheritance.

At younger ages, as spry and lithe as 60, the return on the insurance purchase can be more like 10 times. This means your estate taxes effectively get paid for as little as 10 cents on the dollar!

In truth, of course, the numbers work out in a bit more complex a manner. If your estate was valued at $30 million and you put $3.3 million into an insurance policy, it would reduce your estate to $26.7 million. Now your taxes are $14.6 million and your children would be left with $12.1 million. But they will still receive the full $16.5 million insurance return and will therefore inherit $28.6 million. This makes the effective cost of your estate taxes $1.4 million on a $30 million estate.

Furthermore, taking reality another step deeper into the financial process, the $3.3 million which you reallocated would have been subjected to the same estate taxes as the rest of your amassed wealth had it been left within your estate. Subjected to the same 55% estate taxes, the $3.3 million would have been worth only $1.5 million to your heirs ... $1.8 million would have gone to the government. It could fairly be said then that the amount required to produce the $16.5 million was not $3.3 million but, in effect, $1.4 million.

A single effective $1.4 million net expenditure yields $16.5 million, even at age 70, and allows your heirs to significantly discount or reduce the toll estate taxes take upon their legacy.

There is simply no investment, other financial maneuver or legal document which can do this within the parameters effected here. When your financial advisors express their skepticism or out and out distrust of this method—and, in all likelihood, some will because of their own agendas—verify that what they are suggesting as an alternative will accomplish ALL of the following:

1) The return on whatever investment they recommend is predetermined, based on current assumptions, to produce the needed amount;

2) That amount will be available from the very first day the investment is made, if necessary;

3) The return from the investment will come to your heirs income and estate tax free.

4) The advise and investment they use will both minimize taxes and maximize assets.

If their suggestions do not accomplish all of these goals, they are not effective means of discounting estate tax costs and assuring that your heirs inherit the full value of the legacy you spent a lifetime building.

REMEMBER, and this is **ABSOLUTELY CRITICAL** when it comes to estate tax planning: any investment which yields its return into your estate will have that return become subjected to the same estate taxes you are trying to reduce or discount. So, if your accountant tells you about some other investment which he believes will yield a greater average internal yield or rate of return or higher net or any of the other irrelevant terms they might bandy about, consider that *ANY INVESTMENT RETURN MUST ACTUALLY ACHIEVE DOUBLE WHAT YOU NEED TO ACCOMMODATE ESTATE TAXES OF 55%.* If he says he feels your portfolio should easily appreciate to the same $16.5 million over your lifetime that you need to replace the estate tax costs, remember that when your heirs inherit it, they will have to pay 55% of its net worth in estate taxes too, so it will be reduced $9 million to about $7 million. That investment your stock broker or accountant is so keen on would have to provide a return of more than $37 million in order to be worth the same $16.5 million to your heirs. Can you think of any financial vehicle that will grow from a $3.3 million initial investment to $37 million . . . overnight if need be?

Now you can think of one, and only one. The miraculous Investment Alternative system. Softening the blow of the hard truths like nothing else can.

You have $30 million. Plenty of extra money to experiment with, to invest in more traditional manners. Anyone who is smart, and the assumption is that you are if you made or kept $30 million intact, has a portfolio that is diversified and holds a variety of investments which represent some significant portion of their net worth. Anyone who is REALLY smart, will include the one financial vehicle which can preserve all the rest for their heirs.

$10 Million Estate

$5 Million Estate Tax Costs

$5 Million To Heirs

$500,000 Buys $5 Million Insurance To Pay Taxes

$10 Million To Heirs

TAXES PAID AT 90% DISCOUNT

All figures are based on current assumptions. Charts are for illustrative purposes only.
This illustration used a last-to-die insurance policy for a male and female both age 60.
©1997 THE INVESTMENT ALTERNATIVE - Barry Kaye Associates

Concept #24:

EFFECTIVELY EXEMPT YOUR ENTIRE ESTATE FROM ESTATE TAXES

When you undertake your estate planning, you know you don't need to make any special plans to shelter the first $600 thousand individually or, if you are married, $1.2 million combined assets of your estate. These funds are "exempt" from estate taxation and come to your heirs free from any estate tax loss. When you meet with your lawyer to go over the rest of your planning, you write down the amount of your estate and then automatically subtract that $600 thousand to $1.2 million. No taxes to be paid, no need to 'plan' how to protect that money.

Well then, if you could effectively exempt your entire estate from estate taxes wouldn't your planning be as simple and straightforward as that? Write down how much your estate is worth, subtract the amount that is exempt from tax costs—in this case, ALL of it—and that leaves nothing over which you must agonize and plan.

There is a way to effectively do exactly that.

The power of life insurance in estate tax planning is so great that it can virtually **transform your $600 thousand exemption into a $12 million exemption and your $1.2 million combined exemptions into an astonishing $24 million exemption**! That means you could have no estate tax loss on the first $24 million of your estate.

If you and your spouse are average age 60, you can receive a 10–1 return on your insurance purchase. Therefore, a single $600 thousand exemption could be transferred to an Irrevocable Trust, there would be no gift taxes to be paid as this one-time $600 thousand transfer is exempt, and the trust could use it to purchase a one-pay, last-to-die policy on the lives of both of you. That policy would yield $6 million, based on current assumptions, for your heirs income and estate tax free and $6 million will cover all estate taxes on an estate of about $12 million. You will have effectively exempted $12 million of your estate from suffering any loss due to estate taxes. Your original $12 million of

146

assets passes to your heirs virtually unreduced by estate taxes since the insurance proceeds pay the necessary $6 million in taxes. Isn't THAT the bottom line? You are worth $12 million. The taxes are paid and your heirs still inherit the whole $12 million. Could it be more simple? Is there any goal of all your planning and legal machinations that can accomplish more, or even as much?

The same plan, if implemented utilizing both $600 thousand exemptions—yours and your spouse's—can increase the combined $1.2 million exemptions effectively to $24 million!

$1.2 million used by the same 60 year old couple during their lifetimes to purchase a one-pay, last-to-die insurance policy will produce $12 million in death benefit, based on current assumptions. $12 million will pay all estate taxes on an estate of about $24 million. Therefore, using simple arithmetic, the $1.2 million exemption has been used to effectively exempt an entire $24 million from estate taxes. Instead of your heirs paying no tax on the first $1.2 million, they effectively will pay no taxes on the first $24 million. You could say the insurance company paid the tax for you. What planning is necessary when you have no tax? Clearly, none. And when your exemptions exceed your total assets you clearly have no tax.

Do you know of any traditional investment which will grow from $1.2 million to $12 million, tomorrow if need be? More importantly, do you know of any traditional investment which will grow from $1.2 million to $24 million, tomorrow if need be, so that after estate taxes reduce it by half it will be worth the same $12 million to your heirs? Do you know of any trust without funding that will produce $12 million to pay the estate taxes on your $24 million estate? Look at the bottom line. It's all just simple mathematics.

Of course, you can use this same program to exempt estates even larger than $24 million, however to do so there will be gift taxes to be paid. If, for example, your estate was worth $50 million and you needed approximately $25 million to pay the estate taxes, a one-pay, last-to-die policy on you and your spouse if you are both 60 years old would cost about $2.5 million. In transferring the $2.5 million, the first $1.2 million would be exempt from gift taxes as long as you had not already utilized that exemption. The remaining $1.3 million would be a taxable gift and the tax would be approximately $520 thousand. Even so, for

$2.5 million plus a $520 thousand gift tax you would have effectively exempted your entire $50 million estate from estate taxes! Would you let the $520 thousand stand in your way of effectively saving you $25 million in estate taxes?

One last note: Remember, even if there is some cost involved in effectively exempting your entire estate, every dollar you use to achieve this program would only be worth half if left in your estate. The $520 thousand of gift tax required to accomplish the example used above would only be worth $260 thousand to your heirs if left in your estate and not utilized in this manner.

It is only simple arithmetic and mathematics, but the results it achieves could not be more dramatic. In this way, you can effectively exempt up to the first $363 million of your estate using this Investment Alternative technique!

The maximum insurance allowable for any one to buy at this time is $200 million. $200 million pays all the estate taxes on an estate of $363 million. The cost for a policy which would yield $200 million would be $20 million for a couple of average age 60, based on current assumptions. Yet they cannot transfer $20 million to an Irrevocable Trust for the purpose of purchasing life insurance without paying gift tax as $20 million is in excess of their combined $1.2 million exemption. The gift tax on the $20 million transfer would be about $11 million. The $20 million premium can not fairly be considered an expense since it will fund a return of $200 million. Therefore, the only real expense associated with this technique is the $11 million gift tax. Meanwhile, had the couple not implemented this program, the $11 million would have remained in their estate and, at the time the estate passed to their heirs, it would have been more than halved by estate taxes from $11 million down to $5 million. So, effectively, it is a cost of only $5 million which provides the entire $200 million which effectively exempts $363 million from estate taxes! Would you rather your heirs pay $200 million in estate taxes or you pay a net $5 million of gift taxes—quite a difference! This is the exact situation outlined at the beginning of the book relative to Peter O'Malley and his decision to sell the Dodgers. Whether he sells or not, the tax situation and solution remain the same.

At combined age 70, the outlay, based on current assumptions, for the maximum allowable $200 million of insurance would be $40 million. Gift taxes on the $40 million transfer would be $22 million which, if left in the estate, would be reduced by estate taxes to $10 million. Now, effectively, $10 million cost has provided the $200 million which exempts the $363 million estate and makes any further estate planning, legal maneuvering or documents unnecessary.

Even at average age 80, this Investment Alternative method works to effectively exempt huge estates from estate taxes at very little cost.

The outlay for $200 million of insurance at average age 80 is about $66 million and the gift taxes due on the transfer are about $36 million. $36 million left in the estate is reduced by estate taxes to about $16 million so now it is only $16 million which effectively exempts $363 million from estate taxes. Even at such an advanced age, still a highly optimized program.

You can customize this program to achieve fantastic results for an estate of virtually any size up to $363 million. Then it is only on sums in excess of $363 million that any complicated estate planning is justified.

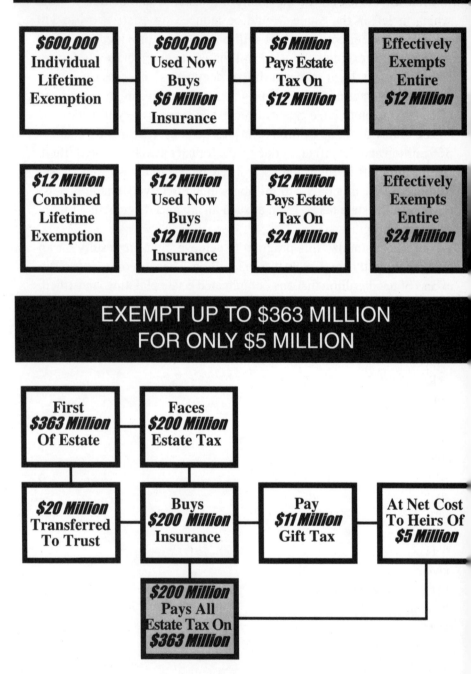

TRANSFORM YOUR $600,000 EXEMPTIONS INTO $12 MILLION TO $24 MILLION EXEMPTION

| *$600,000* Individual Lifetime Exemption | *$600,000* Used Now Buys *$6 Million* Insurance | *$6 Million* Pays Estate Tax On *$12 Million* | Effectively Exempts Entire *$12 Million* |

| *$1.2 Million* Combined Lifetime Exemption | *$1.2 Million* Used Now Buys *$12 Million* Insurance | *$12 Million* Pays Estate Tax On *$24 Million* | Effectively Exempts Entire *$24 Million* |

EXEMPT UP TO $363 MILLION FOR ONLY $5 MILLION

| First *$363 Million* Of Estate | Faces *$200 Million* Estate Tax |

| *$20 Million* Transferred To Trust | Buys *$200 Million* Insurance | Pay *$11 Million* Gift Tax | At Net Cost To Heirs Of *$5 Million* |

$200 Million Pays All Estate Tax On *$363 Million*

All figures are based on current assumptions. Charts are for illustrative purposes only.
This illustration used a last-to-die insurance policy on a male and female both age 60.

©1997 THE INVESTMENT ALTERNATIVE - Barry Kaye Associates

Concept #25:

MAKE YOUR LIQUIDS SOLID

Often, when I speak to people about the need to diversify their port-folios to include life insurance as a means of protecting their wealth for their children, they respond that they don't need the protection of insurance because their assets are liquid. Freed from the concern that their heirs will be faced with a tax bill they can only pay by liquidating assets or borrowing funds, they seem to think they are well prepared for what the future will bring.

They could not be further from the truth.

In financial planning, particularly as it pertains to estate taxes, the idea is not to have on hand the money you need to pay. The idea is to lose as little as possible of your heirs' legacy to taxes, period. Just having the cash or liquid assets available to pay the bill does not solve the problem of estate decimation through taxation.

Remember, in this section, we are dealing with the particularly potent uses of the Investment Alternative concepts as they apply to estate tax planning. We make the assumption, therefore, that a primary financial focus of the estate holders is to leave as much of a legacy as possible for their children. To think that the best one can do towards achieving this goal is to leave a liquid estate that won't be further ravaged by forced liquidation (which we will look at later) is old, narrow thinking which will lead to the loss of up to 55% of your total estate.

The mistake people make is to equate liquidity with safety. They have, for so long, been taught to look out for the dangers of illiquidity that they have forgotten to consider the other dangers which lurk out in the financial jungle. And estate taxation is a far more dangerous preda-tor than illiquidity.

No matter how prepared they are to do so, your heirs will have to pay up to 55% in estate taxes. If your estate is worth $15 million, they will pay approximately $8.2 million. If your assets are not liquid, it might even cost them more due to the need to liquidate. But, even if your assets are liquid, it will still cost them $8.2 million.

However, if you and your spouse are average age 60, you could purchase a life insurance policy for one payment of $820 thousand that would yield $8.2 million. More important than protecting the sums lost to illiquidity, you could, in this way, protect the entire value of your estate so that your heirs could inherit it intact.

There is a lot of old thinking which plagues the insurance and financial planning industries. Professionals who have either been in the field forever, or have been trained by someone who has been, too frequently do not look beyond the accepted, standardized ways of thinking about these topics. In the past, the need for liquidity was seen as a critical aspect of estate planning. This thinking has passed to many long-practicing and older attorneys. But thinking has progressed way beyond that and we can now see that the real issue is not about liquidity at all. It is not about having the means to pay the tax. It is about having the means to discount the tax, recover the tax costs and retain the estate intact.

Why would you throw away $8.2 million of your heirs' inheritance when the insurance company can pay the tax for you? You are taking nothing away from your country since the IRS still gets every dime it has determined it is due. The only difference is that your heirs do not suffer the depletion. This is not complex, expensive, legal tax avoidance. It's your choice and, to me, it seems a simple one: $8.2 million in estate taxes when you die leaving your heirs $6.8 million or $200 thousand net in gift taxes now and leaving your heirs the full $15 million. Do you want to pay your taxes retail or wholesale?

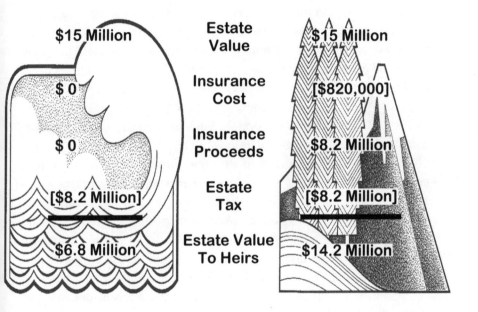

Liquid Asset		Non-Liquid Asset
$15 Million	Estate Value	$15 Million
$ 0	Insurance Cost	[$820,000]
$ 0	Insurance Proceeds	$8.2 Million
[$8.2 Million]	Estate Tax	[$8.2 Million]
$6.8 Million	Estate Value To Heirs	$14.2 Million

Liquid Asset

Non-Liquid Asset

THE INVESTMENT ALTERNATIVE METHOD MAKES YOUR ASSETS SOLID

All figures are based on current assumptions. Charts are for illustrative purposes only.
This illustration used a last-to-die insurance policy for a male and female both age 60.
©1997 THE INVESTMENT ALTERNATIVE - Barry Kaye Associates

Concept #26:

TURN ANY TAX INTO AN ASSET

Taxes, as you well know, are an expense. Or are they?

Most of us bow to the inevitably of estate taxes. In some cases, they can be minimized or maybe avoided or stretched out over time so they appear less onerous. But eventually the tax man gets his due. The funds are handed over, the estate depleted the requisite amount. I have shown you, in previous years, how to discount your taxes, how to effectively increase your exemptions so you lose less to taxes, how to Die Rich and Tax Free. But in all cases the bottom line has been the same: taxes are an inevitable expense your estate must face.

No more. *With the advent of the new thinking I espouse in this book—the utilization of the amazing Investment Alternative techniques—a way becomes clear and obvious for you to actually turn the inevitable expense of estate taxes into a highly valuable asset!*

Consider this: you and your spouse are worth $3 million on which $1.1 million of estate taxes will be due nine months after your deaths. Your heirs will HAVE TO pay this $1.1 million and no one, not your accountant, not your lawyer, not your financial advisor, not me, can change that fact. You can decrease the amount by giving away more money during your lifetime and removing it from your estate but then you won't have it to enjoy. You can discount the tax by using a life insurance policy in an Irrevocable Trust to generate the needed funds. But, one way or another, your heirs WILL pay estate taxes unless you give *everything* away during your lifetime or leave your entire estate to charity. And that makes that $1 million, fully 1/3 of your estate, a tax expense. And an expensive expense at that.

Using a life insurance policy, you can turn that same $1 million into an asset!

One way or another, the $1 million is forfeit. Your estate is worth $3 million and the government will not be denied its due. But what if you 'spent' that $1 million now?

Knowing that your heirs will never see that $1 million, you might realize that using it during your lifetime to increase your total net value would be one way to help your heirs inherit more. You could "pay the taxes" while you're alive by removing that $1 million from your estate and investing it. Of course, there are some problems with this program if enacted in traditional ways.

To begin with, if you invest your $1.1 million in something ill-fated, you could lose it altogether. In that event, your estate is now reduced to $1.9 million without even having paid your taxes. Your heirs inherit even less.

Or, you could die. Not a pleasant thought to consider but a realistic one. Not having had a chance to grow, your $1.1 million investment remains worth $1.1 million and your tax situation has not been improved at all; your estate is still worth $3 million and the taxes are still $1.1 million.

Of course, there is always the hope and potential that your investment will grow. Maybe even significantly. Would you be happy with a 20% growth? Probably. It's a good return on money these days. If it were to earn 50%, you would no doubt be ecstatic.

But not even a 50% return of $500 thousand would leave your heirs whole.

Earnings of 50% would increase your estate to $3.5 million. However, if you sold it while you were alive, income taxes on the $500 thousand gain would claim about 1/3, or $166 thousand reducing the gain to $334 thousand and your net estate to approximately $3.3 million. Estate taxes on the $3.3 million would be approximately $1.2 million. Now your $3.3 million is worth $2.1 million. Your 50% gain on your investment has netted your children $200 thousand more than they would have received otherwise.

If the profit wasn't realized until your death, your heirs would receive a stepped up basis and receive the entire $500 thousand income tax free. The estate tax would be $275 thousand, thus leaving a net gain to your heirs of $225 thousand.

If you had bought the stock and given it away to your children during your lifetime, or given them the cash and they had bought it, there would not be estate taxes due upon any profit that was earned but there would be capital gains taxes of approximately 28% to 33% on it at the time that it was sold.

If you were to use one of the Investment Alternative techniques and put that same forfeited $1 million into the purchase of a life insurance policy, you could increase what your heirs receive to MORE THAN YOUR ORIGINAL $3 MILLION! This is not just discounting your estate tax costs, or increasing your exemptions in order to leave your heirs whole. This is wealth creation of a whole new sort. Turning a forfeited tax expense into an asset of unparalleled power.

The $1 million, if used to purchase a life insurance policy can produce a return of 3, 5 even 10 times!

You can make the purchase on behalf of your heirs without paying any gift tax for the transfer of funds assuming that your $1 million falls into your combined $1.2 million unified gift and estate tax exemption. At age 70, you and your spouse could expect to receive a 5–1 return of $5 million. *Now your heirs inherit the $3 million remaining of your estate minus the estate taxes of $1.1 million—$1.9 million—PLUS $5 MILLION which they receive income and estate tax free for a total of $6.9 million! You have turned your tax into an asset that has effectively more than tripled your whole estate AFTER TAXES and irrespective of how long after you make the purchase you die.*

If you pay the government $1.1 million, your heirs get back nothing. But give the same $1.1 million to the insurance company and they get back over $5 million. The insurance effectively pays the $1.1 million estate tax PLUS leaves an optimized asset for your heirs.

If you are age sixty, the $1 million last-to-die policy could yield $10 million—now you've turned your tax into an asset that increased your NET estate value to your heirs to $11.9 million. And you accomplished this utilizing forfeited money, funds your heirs would have lost to estate taxes anyway.

Even at age 80, the program works to increase the net value of your estate.

At age 80, you can expect your insurance policy to yield an approximate 3–1 return. Your $1 million becomes $3 million and your NET, AFTER TAX estate increases to $4.9 million!

Of course, using your entire $1.1 million tax liability during your lifetime to fund this program may be a financial burden for you. But you can accomplish the same goal, though to a slightly lesser degree, for a "discounted" tax cost of 50%. In this model, we assume that you are entitled to a tax discount for paying early—if only the government saw it that way!

At age 60, for $500 thousand the Investment Alternative method would yield $5 million. Now it is as if you have received a 50% discount on your $1.1 million of estate taxes. The 'discounted' tax liability of $500 thousand nets a return of $5 million, based on current assumptions, and that $5 million pays the tax while still leaving $3.9 million. Once again, your tax has become a asset. Wait until death and $1.1 million will go to the government in taxes and your heirs will get $1.9 million. 'Discount' your tax now and outlay only $500 thousand and the government will still get its full $1.1 million leaving $3.9 million additional for your heirs.

At age 70, with a 5–1 return, your $500 thousand policy yields $2.5 million. Your net estate increases from $1.9 million to $4.4 million.

At age 80, realizing a 3–1 return, the $500 thousand becomes $1.5 million and your net estate increases from $2 million to $3.4 million— even at this advanced age still slightly more, after taxes, than the $3 million gross you started with.

And all of this is accomplished on a predetermined basis and irrespective of the wild card factor of time that virtually every conventional investment is bound by. Furthermore, given the fact that stocks and real estate and businesses and other investments fail every day while all life insurance policy death benefits have always been paid, the safety of this Investment Alternative technique remains incontrovertible and incomparable.

To find out exactly how you can turn your inevitable tax costs into the one asset best able to increase your estate and create new wealth for your heirs, check the tables at the back of this book. Use them to customize your approach and the returns you can expect.

And remember, if even the 50% "discounted' tax forfeiture is more than you can afford to expend at this time, there are alternatives. I can not impress upon you enough my belief that no mater how greatly you desire to preserve or increase your estate, no matter how much you want to leave your children with as much financial security as possible, you should never undertake ANY investment or expense which will detract from your ability to provide for your own desired lifestyle first and foremost.

However, as we discuss in great detail in other chapters of this book, there are numerous ways that you can enact this program using borrowed funds or by paying annually. The added interest costs of either of these alternatives will, of course, impact the net result, however that result will still be far superior to the one you are currently facing. Doing nothing does not make the tax go away. Stop procrastinating. You will never be younger, healthier or more eligible for better rates than you are right now. Meanwhile, you can increase your heirs' inheritance without interrupting your own lifestyle in any way—all by turning your tax into an asset and using the Investment Alternative method to maximize your returns!

TURN ANY TAX INTO AN ASSET

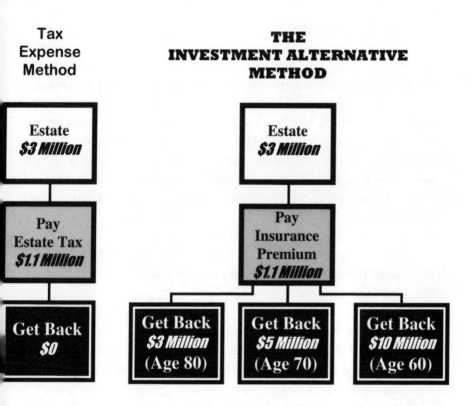

Tax Expense Method

THE INVESTMENT ALTERNATIVE METHOD

Estate
$3 Million

Estate
$3 Million

Pay Estate Tax
$1.1 Million

Pay Insurance Premium
$1.1 Million

Get Back
$0

Get Back
$3 Million
(Age 80)

Get Back
$5 Million
(Age 70)

Get Back
$10 Million
(Age 60)

PAY TAX - GET BACK $0
PAY PREMIUM - GET BACK UP TO $10 MILLION

All figures are based on current assumptions. Charts are for illustrative purposes only.
This illustration used last-to-die insurance policies for couples of various ages.
©1997 THE INVESTMENT ALTERNATIVE - Barry Kaye Associates

Concept #27:

PROTECT YOUR FAMILY FROM THE BIG LOSS OF A SWEEPSTAKES WIN

Most people think that a big sweepstakes win, or the unexpected receipt of any other large sum of money such as a bequest or taxable legal settlement or lottery win, is the most wonderful thing that could happen to them, the answer to many of their problems. Suddenly, and from out of the blue, a fortune has come their way and they won't ever have to worry about money and making ends meet again.

Unfortunately, as we learn over and over again on our journey through life, nothing is ever that simple. Winning a large amount of money can present equally large financial burdens.

There is a tax law having to do with "Income In Respect Of A Decedent" that can turn that wonderful sweepstakes win into a horrible financial nightmare for your family.

This section of the tax code assesses taxes on sums of money promised but not yet received. It does not apply to the original winner or recipient of the promised funds, but, should that person die before the full sum has been received, it would apply to the way taxes were assessed on his/her heirs.

Many large prizes are paid out over time. Though you might win $10 million in a sweepstakes, it may very well be structured so that you are paid $500 thousand for 20 years. But what happens if you die before that 20 years is up? It might seem that someone so lucky as to have won the sweepstakes to begin with couldn't possibly be the victim of such a terrible tragedy but life, and death, are equally indiscriminate and there are no guarantees about anything—except, of course, death and taxes.

Sweepstakes prizes, bequests, lottery winnings and some legal settlements are the legal property of the winner. They are transferable assets fully assignable to one's heirs which means that, in the event the prize winner dies, the prize payments will be made, for however long the stated term, to the heirs. But, there's a hitch.

The IRS code section having to do with "Income In Respect Of A Decedent" would levy estate taxes based on the current value of the promised stream of income. That means that the government would assess the estate taxes due based on its present value. And that could leave your heirs with a huge problem. This also applies to authors, songwriters, inventors and others who have a promise of any future stream of income.

If the sweepstakes prize was $10 million to be made in 20 yearly installments of $500 thousand each and the winner were to die after the first year, the heirs would owe estate taxes on the present value of the entire remaining $9.5 million worth of promised payments in addition to any other estate taxes due on the rest of the estate. Estate taxes on the future value could be up to 55%. But the winner only received $500 thousand of the prize at that time and, in all likelihood, has spent at least some of it. Unless he or she was quite wealthy before winning the sweepstakes, where will the heirs come up with the needed millions to pay the taxes on money they have not yet received?

Of course, they can borrow the tax money. Their $10 million sweepstakes prize is valuable collateral and getting a loan won't be too difficult with it as security. But the loan will cost them interest and that interest and principal payment will have to come from the yearly $500 thousand they receive. Suddenly their win isn't such a wonderful thing anymore.

So what is the winner to do to protect his family? He has only two choices. One, don't die. Two, be prepared for the reality that you have no control over number one.

Using only a fraction of his prize money, the winner can protect the entire amount from the ravages of estate taxes and secure his family's financial future. Depending on his age and that of his wife, he can use a life insurance policy to generate the funds needed to pay the taxes. At average age 80, a single sum would provide a 3–1 return. At age 70, it would return approximately 5–1, and at age 60, 10–1. Meanwhile, at younger ages, with the more dramatic 16–1, 28–1, and even 50–1 returns, it could take significantly less to secure the needed return. Then, should the winner die, the estate taxes can be paid and the family can continue to receive the yearly $500 thousand unencumbered by debt.

Of course, though it requires a slightly higher aggregate expense, the policy can be secured in a yearly fashion also, allowing the man to utilize only a fraction of the income his $500 thousand can be expected to earn each year to produce the needed return.

In the happy event that the man does not die prematurely, he will continue to receive the $500 thousand each year for the next 20 and, hopefully, retain enough of it by spending only the interest it generates to amass a sizable estate. In that case, the sum the heirs will receive will still help pay the estate taxes that will eventually be assessed on the prize moneys which came into his estate during his lifetime. And if he does spend all or most of the $10 million and estate taxes are no longer an issue, the policy will still provide his heirs with a significant return, income and estate tax free, and regenerate the sweepstakes or lottery win for them.

YOUR BIG WIN CAN BE
YOUR FAMILY'S BIG LOSS

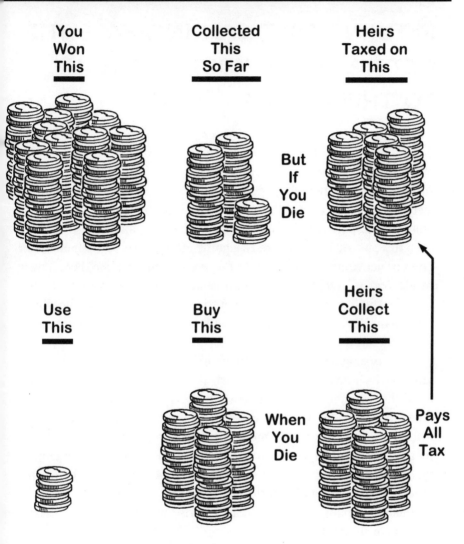

You
Won
This

Collected
This
So Far

Heirs
Taxed on
This

But
If
You
Die

Use
This

Buy
This

Heirs
Collect
This

When
You
Die

Pays
All
Tax

THE INVESTMENT ALTERNATIVE METHOD
TURNS A WIN INTO A WIN-WIN

All figures are based on current assumptions. Charts are for illustrative purposes only.

163

Concept #28:

RETURNS THAT CAN INCREASE THE NET VALUE OF YOUR ESTATE UP TO THREE TIMES

At its most basic, the whole purpose of investing is to make money to increase your net worth. Particularly after you no longer require the money to support your lifestyle. Most of the time, an increase of 20%, even 10%, would be considered a significant success. A 50% increase in gross or net value would be cause for celebration. Imagine then, how it would feel if you were to make that one amazing investment, that soared so high it virtually doubled or tripled the value of your holdings. One financial vehicle so potent as to effectively increase your entire net worth by 300%!

There is such a vehicle. This amazing Investment Alternative idea— yes, life insurance—can accomplish this goal of financial wizardry. Read the example below and consider the import. Then ask yourself, does it really matter what you call the tool used to achieve the end? Life insurance, blue chip stocks, municipal bonds, real estate . . . it's all just money management, none carrying any higher degree of acceptability than the others except by virtue of how well they perform. And, in this case, almost nothing else performs as well as the Investment Alternative technique designed to recreate the rise of a missed stock or any other investment that got away.

For this example, let's use a couple, average age 60 with an estate valued at $8 million. They transfer $800 thousand to an Irrevocable Trust and the trust uses the money to buy a life insurance policy which, given their ages, produces a return, based on current assumptions, of 10–1. Upon the death of the couple, their heirs receive the tax free proceeds of $8 million. That, of course, is in addition to the $7.2 million that remained in the couple's estate after they removed the $800 thousand to purchase the insurance. So now their children receive a $15.2

million gross estate—and that's virtually **DOUBLE THEIR ORIGI-NAL ESTATE!**

Of course, the government will not be left out of the equation. Estate taxes will still claim 55% of the couple's gross estate. On $7.2 million that's $3.6 million. So, in actuality, the heirs only receive the remaining $3.6 million plus the $8 million tax free from the return on the insurance policy purchase for a total of 11.6 million. Had the purchase not been made, the estate would have been worth the entire $8 million at the time of the couple's deaths. Assessed taxes would have been $4 million, leaving the children $4 million. Without the remarkable returns from the insurance policy, the children would net $4 million from the estate. With them, they net $11.6 million. *THE COUPLE'S NET ESTATE HAS VIRTUALLY TRIPLED AS IT PASSES FROM THEM TO THEIR HEIRS!*

Remember, any investment utilizing the same $800 thousand would have to yield a return of more than $16 million in order to be worth the same $8 million to the children at the time that they inherit the estate and pay the taxes. AND, any investment would have to be positioned so that it could produce that $16 million return one day after it was purchased, if need be. The fact is, nothing else out there even comes close!

INCREASE YOUR ESTATE'S VALUE
UP TO THREE TIMES AFTER ESTATE TAX

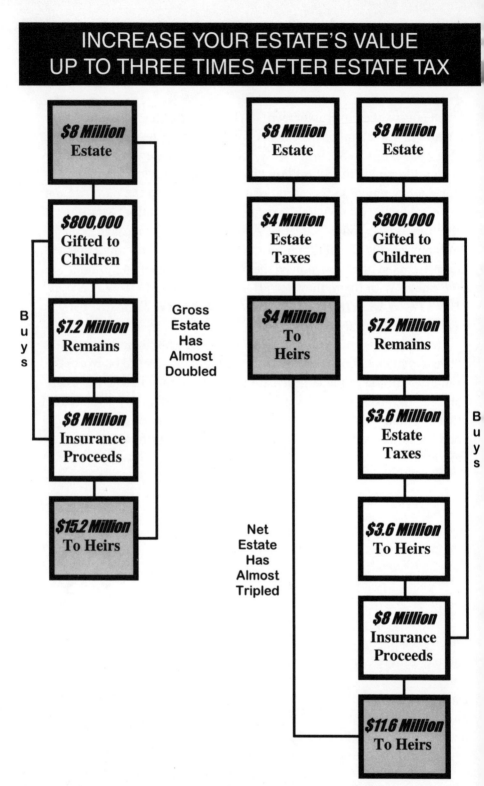

All figures are based on current assumptions. Charts are for illustrative purposes only.
This illustration used a last-to-die insurance policy for a male and female both age 60.

©1997 THE INVESTMENT ALTERNATIVE - Barry Kaye Associates

Concept #29:

STOP THE CLOCK
ON ESTATE DEVALUATION

Estate taxes are due nine months after you die or, if everything is left to your spouse, nine months after his or her death.

It is a simply stated fact, clear and concise, yet it has created more financial devastation than its nine words would seem able to contain. Here's why:

You have an estate. It's worth $15 million and composed largely of illiquid investments such as real estate, a business, art or other collectibles. When you die, the value of those assets will be appraised and 55% of that amount will be assessed in estate taxes. Your heirs owe the government $8 million. How are they going to pay it? The government will not accept a trust deed or a Rembrandt. They want cash. Where will your heirs get that much money? You left them very well off—on paper. But in the world of cold, hard, liquid cash, they are lacking and needy. And the government doesn't care. They KNOW your heirs are worth the full amount and they want their share.

So, your heirs have a couple of choices. Unfortunately, none of them are good. First, they could borrow the money against your other assets. Of course, at 7.5% interest rates, a loan of $8 million would cost them $600 thousand annually. Even if the assets you have left them earn the same 7.5% interest, that would only be about $1.1 million. More than half their yearly income from your estate would go to servicing the loan debt.

As a second alternative, they could borrow the money from the government under Internal Revenue Code Section 6166 if they qualify, and pay off the taxes over a 14 year period. But they would basically wind up paying, with principal and interest, about double your total estate tax liability. And double the estate tax liability is equivalent almost exactly to the total value of your estate. In simple terms, everything you'd built would be forfeit to the taxes.

As a third possible course of action you heirs could elect to sell off some of your property to raise the needed funds. Of course, first, while still grieving your loss, they would be faced with the burden of selecting which of the assets you'd cherished and built and labored to afford they would get rid of. Then they are faced with the horrors of forced liquidation.

If the business world were a kind and benevolent place, perhaps someone would take pity on your heirs and, seeing how dire and unfair their need, would, on general humanitarian principles, pay them the full market value of the asset they have selected for sale. Unfortunately, there are bottom lines to be met and competition to be fought and each person out there in the marketplace has their own exigencies they need to protect for the good of their own shareholders, families and posterity. The law of supply and demand is ruthless and unrelenting.

In all likelihood, your heirs will be faced with a forced liquidation sale where, in order to meet the ticking of the IRS clock, they will have to drastically reduce the price of the asset in order to sell it quickly enough to raise the needed cash on time. Historically, forced liquidation sales of this type have been known to devalue property by as much as 1/3 or even more. A sad, sad circumstance and one which can, with only minor diversification of your existing portfolio, be completely avoided so that your children not only don't suffer financial damage in excess of the assessed $8 million due to forced liquidation or the debt service on an $8 million loan, they can emerge completely whole with the entire $15 million of your estate intact.

As you know by now, at age 60, a return of 10–1, based on current assumptions and qualifying factors, can be earned on a last-to-die, one-pay life insurance policy. That means that $8 million can be produced for $800 thousand. Now the scenario goes very differently. You die. Your estate is appraised, valued at $15 million and $8 million of estate taxes are assessed. The insurer hands a check to your heirs for $8 million and they use it to pay the whole estate tax while retaining your $15 million estate intact. Of course, in truth, the estate has been reduced by the $800 thousand cost of the policy but considering the nightmare of the other options available, $800 thousand is a wondrously optimized amount. And, in fact, the cost is not really $800 thousand anyway because, if it had been left in your estate, that $800 thousand would have been subject to the same 55% estate taxes and lost $440 thousand of its value. In reality, what would have been the remaining $360 thousand has truly funded the insurance purchase which yielded the $8 million which paid the estate taxes and avoided forced liquidation for your heirs. Can there be any question that THIS IS THE ONLY WAY TO GO?

Even at older ages, the value of the program is incontrovertible. At age 70, when you might be able to expect a 5–1 return, the hard cost of producing an $8 million yield would only be $1.6 million. Far less than the up to $12 million it could cost your heirs. Plus, remember, that $1.6 million is only worth $720 thousand to your heirs if left within your estate where it will be subject to estate taxes.

At age 80, receiving a possible 3–1 return, the cost goes up to $2.6 million. But that is still only about 1/5 the $12 million the heirs might well have to liquidate.

Now, while you are doing your estate planning, is the time to select an asset from your portfolio and diversify it into the Investment Alternative method of avoiding the expense of forced liquidation. You have the time now to sell your asset aggressively and see to it that you get the best price. You also are now as young, fit and healthy as you are ever likely to be again and so will receive the best return on your purchase. How could anything be better? You have simply used an insurance policy that will outperform any investment in your portfolio by paying your estate taxes at a discount, avoiding forced liquidation, providing a means to retain your assets intact, avoiding the family dissension that occurs when money becomes an issue and, finally, diversifies your portfolio. Don't wait for the clock to run out on your heirs, take the time to examine your options and add a purchase of life insurance to your portfolio for the protection of your estate. Remember this simple axiom: You Buy, You Die, It Pays. Estate planning can really be that simple when you reduce it down to its most basic components. You Buy. You Die. It Pays. And because it pays, your heirs don't have to.

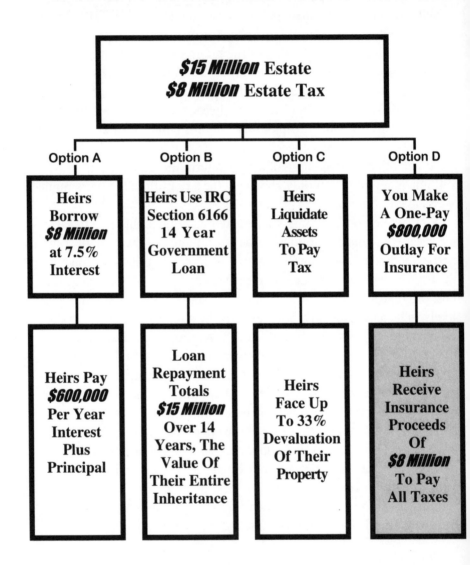

ONLY THE INVESTMENT ALTERNATIVE SYSTEM PROTECTS AN ILLIQUID ESTATE FROM FINANCIAL DEVASTATION

$15 Million Estate
$8 Million Estate Tax

Option A	Option B	Option C	Option D
Heirs Borrow **$8 Million** at 7.5% Interest	Heirs Use IRC Section 6166 14 Year Government Loan	Heirs Liquidate Assets To Pay Tax	You Make A One-Pay **$800,000** Outlay For Insurance
Heirs Pay **$600,000** Per Year Interest Plus Principal	Loan Repayment Totals **$15 Million** Over 14 Years, The Value Of Their Entire Inheritance	Heirs Face Up To 33% Devaluation Of Their Property	Heirs Receive Insurance Proceeds Of **$8 Million** To Pay All Taxes

YOU BUY. YOU DIE. IT PAYS.

All figures are based on current assumptions. Charts are for illustrative purposes only.
This illustration used a last-to-die insurance policy for a male and female both age 60.
©1997 THE INVESTMENT ALTERNATIVE - Barry Kaye Associates

Concept #30:

MAKING EVERY DOLLAR COUNT—
TWICE

All of the concepts in this book are based on the ideas of optimizing and maximizing your funds. Too often, the big picture is not fully considered and financial losses occur or opportunities are not realized to their fullest extent. Simple awareness of all the nuances and diversification of planning, however, can avoid the damage and make every dollar count—twice. What do I mean by making it count twice? First of all, I am referring to the consequences of poor estate tax planning. Allowing your estate to be depleted by up to 55% of its full net worth virtually halves each dollar you have amassed. By avoiding that depletion, you effectively make your money worth twice the value it would otherwise have had. Secondly, as you will see in the following example, by reassessing your options and reallocating some of your funds, you can take a singular financial situation and more than double the result it yields. That's making your money work twice!

Consider this: you have an estate worth $80 million which provides extremely well for the needs of you and your spouse and leaves significant funds not required for either their principal or the interest they yield each year. Those earnings are just going back into the overall estate balance.

When you die and your estate passes on to the children you have amassed it for, they will be faced with an estate tax bill for 55% of your estate's total valuation—$44 million. Your heirs actually have to sit down and write a check to the IRS for $44 million. Just imagine that for one minute. Having absolutely no choice but to pay the bill—and you can only hope the estate is liquid enough to raise the funds without your children having to borrow the tax money or liquidate real assets to raise it, either one of which options will cause significant further devaluation—your children will be left with $36 million.

But think of this: Since you have more money than you need to support your lifestyle, you could transfer $10 million to an Irrevocable Trust on behalf on your children. You would have to pay gift taxes on the transfer of approximately $5 million for a total tax of $5 million. Now, $5 million may seem like a lot to pay in gift taxes but it is a mere fraction of the $44 million in estate taxes your heirs will have to pay. In terms of its effect on your estate it is certainly better to utilize $15 million than to lose $44 million.

You use the $10 million which you transferred to the Irrevocable Trust to purchase an insurance policy which, at your combined ages of 70 nets a 5–1 return yielding $50 million for your heirs, income and estate tax free. The $10 million can not be considered to be an expense or cost since it netted $50 million. So the only cost involved was the $5 million of gift taxes. In effect, $5 million netted $50 million for your heirs.

Meanwhile, in actuality, the cost was not even $5 million. If you do not implement this Investment Alternative technique and therefore are not faced with the $5 million gift tax, that $5 million will remain in your estate and, as it passes to your heirs, be reduced by taxes to less than $2.5 million. So it isn't really a net cost of $5 million to implement this program but $2.5 million.

And it doesn't stop there. The transfer of the $10 million and the gift tax expense of the $5 million have reduced your estate from $80 million to $65 million which reduces the estate taxes from $44 million to about $36 million. Instead of $36 million remaining from $80 million, your heirs now have $29 million remaining from $65 million. A 'gain' of $7 million.

Had you not undertaken this program your $80 million estate would have been reduced to $36 million for your heirs. **Now, the Investment Alternative way, they receive $29 million from your estate after all estate taxes have been paid on the remaining $65 million PLUS the $50 million return from your insurance 'gain' for a total of $79 million and that is more than double what they would have received otherwise**. THAT is making your money work twice! Why would you pay $44 million in estate taxes and leave your heirs $36 million when you can pay $5 million, effectively $2.5 million net after taxes, in gift taxes and leave them $79 million? And yet some people say the insurance is too expensive. Where did all the thinking, common sense and logic go?

IF YOU DO NOTHING

INVESTMENT ALTERNATIVE METHOD

$80 Million
Estate

$44 Million
Estate
Tax

$36 Million
To
Heirs

$80 Million
Estate

$10 Million
Gift — Buys — **$50 Million**
Insurance
Proceeds

$5 Million
Gift
Tax

$65 Million
Remaining

$36 Million
Estate
Tax

$29 Million
To
Heirs

$79 Million
To
Heirs

IS THIS A DIFFICULT CHOICE?

All figures are based on current assumptions. Charts are for illustrative purposes only.
This illustration used a last-to-die insurance policy for a male and female both age 70.
©1997 THE INVESTMENT ALTERNATIVE - Barry Kaye Associates

PART TWO

Myths, Misconceptions and Misinformation

One of the frustrations which has plagued me throughout my career comes from the damage done to family financial planning by inexpert and erroneous advice. Lawyers, accountants and financial professionals often undertake to turn their clients' interests away from life insurance as an alternative to traditional investment vehicles without really comprehending either the benefits life insurance can offer or the terrible harm its lack of inclusion in a diversified portfolio can cause. I have long felt that the misrepresentations these so-called experts make about their own concepts and mine has bordered on malpractice. And now, we are beginning to see malpractice lawsuits brought against advisors who failed in their duty to fully examine and explain the merits of these concepts to their clients whose estates have suffered vast, unrecoverable depletions as a result of their negligence.

Of course, not ALL attorneys or accountants are culpable. But unfortunately, more of them are than aren't when it comes to the uses of life insurance for asset management and estate tax planning. I have never really understood their resistance to these concepts. Perhaps it is as simple as them fearing something they don't really understand or losing control of these situations. Could it really be that they are willing to let the interests of their clients suffer simply to try and maintain their egos?

175

I sometimes hear an attorney dismiss the value of insurance simply because it is a product that is being sold on which the agent makes his living. I have never understood this objection; of course I would expect to derive a livelihood from my profession and career. Don't they? When an attorney tells a prospect not to buy insurance but to draw up another complicated trust instead, isn't he or she simply selling their product, i.e. the crafting of the trust? But somehow it is bad that I am selling product while what they do is "lofty." I can not help but wonder how much better off our society would be if attorneys did not hold us in their sway quite so tightly.

I cringe when I hear that same attorney start to discourse on the perils and pitfalls of insurance. I am not allowed to practice law, though, in truth, when it comes to estate planning, I probably know much more about trusts and family partnerships and tax laws than any attorney knows about insurance. Yet many attorneys and accountants seem to think they are qualified and entitled to practice 'life insurance.' It would be laughable if people's lives were not being affected so direly. Many in my own industry fail to fully understand the utilization of the life insurance product as an Investment Alternative and they have unwittingly taken a backseat to the attorney's convoluted plans for saving taxes without optimizing assets for many years.

Hand in glove with the so-called financial professionals in misinforming the public about the power of life insurance is the media. Confronted with a topic about which most financial reporters know little or nothing, they respond with ridicule and scorn. And the public suffers for their arrogance. Frankly, it infuriates me. Of course, as probably the leading spokesperson for these plans, I personally come under a lot of individual attack. It is not pleasant, but it also is not what provokes my fury. Blithely and without any real concern for the terrible repercussions of their actions, these reporters dismiss a whole field of financial opportunity. With a reach far in excess of any single attorney's, they influence the decision-making of hundreds, if not thousands, if not tens of thousands of people whose families will suffer as a result.

THE MEDIA

Following are annotated reprints of articles which appeared in prestigious magazines and newspapers. You will see the authors' use of innuendo and tone to belittle my concepts. And you will see an example of one journalist apparently deliberately avoiding some of the facts which had been presented to him in order to further his unwarranted attack. I reprint these articles and their refutations not out of malice or self-defense, but to show you, specifically and directly, the harm you are suffering at the hands of these writers.

I will also relate to you some examples of the static attorneys and accountants create for their clients around the issue of using life insurance as an alternative to investing. The scenarios I present will be accurate depictions of the kind of misinformation or biased consulting which is preventing too many people from achieving their desired goals for me to remain silent anymore.

It is my hope that the reprinting of these articles and the exposing of these all-too-common occurrences of misdirection and misinformation will clear a path down which the public can more clearly see the truth of what is available to them through the use of life insurance as an alternative to some investments.

I could reprint many more articles in this section, but they are all the same. These should suffice if you understand how many more exist out there. Even worse are the articles that have not been written and the fact that this complete area of Investment Alternative solutions to estate planning has been overlooked.

Following is a reprint of an article which appeared in a prestigious regional magazine. Listen to the author's tone, observe the way he craftily uses language to convey his bias. Hopefully you are not so foolish as to be taken in by these rather obvious tricks. Unfortunately, most people, when confronted with an article of this type, feel that it must be accurate or it couldn't be printed. But when it comes to innuendo and inference, truth suffers from a clear lack of definition. And, as you will see, the author HAS included some outright misrepresentations which serve to damage both my credibility as a spokesman for these concepts and the integrity of the concepts themselves. I hope that as you read you will become as incensed as I am at the injustice being perpetrated upon you and the American people. Journalists, a once honored profession, under the guise of objectivity and fairness, are perpetuating their own misconceptions to the detriment of their readers. Perhaps it would not seem so heinous to me if the scope of the damage being done did not run so high.

I have no quarrel with the public being presented with a "second opinion" on the claims I make about the concepts I have developed. I simply demand that those second opinions be given in the interests of fairness, honesty and concern for the public's welfare, not in the self interest of some uninformed reporter or self-styled expert.

The first article is reprinted here verbatim. The notations in italics which you will see interspersed with the article are my comments intended to point out where the journalistic process breaks down into something dangerously less than accurate. It is my hope that you will read both sides, judge for yourself and perhaps learn something about the treachery and limited knowledge of some of the American financial press. Even when the intentions of the journalist are pure and his or her knowledge is extensive, the materials printed are often tainted by the information received from various legal and financial industry sources.

"You're going to be dead much longer than you've been alive."

This quotation belongs to Barry Kaye, the man who wants you to Die Rich, after having purchased a copy of his book by that name. Assuming you already are rich, the theme could perhaps be more accurately stated: How to Protect Your Millions From Estate Taxes, Thereby Allowing You to Pass More of Your Wealth to Your Heirs and Charity. But that's too long for a book title, not to mention a toll-free number (1–800-DIE RICH).

(Is there something wrong with the concept of Protecting Your Millions From Estate Taxes, Thereby Allowing You to Pass More of Your Wealth to Your Heirs and Charity? Is the idea deserving of such a scornful tone? Probably only if you are not already rich enough to benefit from the theme.)

*

Barry Kaye has written the book on how to voyage to that Undiscovered Country while not leaving those back there without a paddle. Tis a consummation devoutly to be wished for, no?

Kaye considers himself a sort of investment counselor. On close examination, however, you discover he's basically, um, a life insurance salesman. Kaye believes a healthy diversified portfolio has stocks, bonds, real estate and, of course, insurance.

(I emphatically state at the beginning of every seminar I present and on Page 15 of my book Die Rich and Tax Free *that I am a life insurance salesman. I sell life insurance and at no time do I intimate that I am an investment counselor. I am not ashamed of my profession as the author of this article seems to imply that I should be. Already, just by that subtle tone of derision, he is beginning his campaign to bias people against my concepts not because he has found anything inherently wrong with them, but simply because I accomplish my clients' financial goals using life insurance AND have the nerve to earn a living while doing so.)*

*

"If you're worth three million dollars or more, when you die, estate taxes will claim up to 55 percent of your net worth, leaving your heirs with less than half,' Kaye claims. He says you can protect most—if not all—of your money, provided you don't need it to live on. He figures if your pile of money is big enough, any dollars on the bottom are unnecessary, "junk money." After all, you don't need it to sustain your lifestyle. Junk money, he says, may not be worth anything to you in this life, but it can protect your heirs from estate taxes.

But before we continue, what was that about your heirs are going to lose more than half your wealth to estate taxes? Do the math. Since you're entitled to zero percent estate tax on the first $600,000, that leaves only $2.4 million of a $3 million estate which would be taxed at all—and that would be on a graduated basis, from 37 to 55 percent. Mr. Kaye's numbers don't add up here. It's pretty obvious you'd pay a heck of a lot less than 55 percent tax on a $3-million estate. But I digress.

(The author refers to my numbers not adding up and exhorts his readers to "do the math" and yet even he, in his attempt to undermine me, substantiates that estate taxes do run from 37–55 percent—an important point upon which many of my concepts are based. He then goes on to take completely out of context my examples regarding the costs of those taxes

to an estate worth $3 million. I clearly state in my seminars, one of which this author attended, and in all of my books, that the estate taxes are $1.1 million on the first $3 million <u>including</u> *utilizing your $600 thousand exemption and then 55% thereafter.)*

*

Kaye's philosophy of getting wealth out of your estate before you die is legitimate. The question is whether or not life insurance is the vehicle.

(Notice the lack of any suggestion of an alternative which can accomplish the same goals or any substantial disproof of life insurance's effects in this realm. Still the article relies solely on a sneering sort of dismissal that has no basis in any fact offered up as proof.)

*

TURN $1.1 MILLION INTO $11 MILLION

Kaye obviously understands numbers, and the numbers come at you like a Gatling gun, whether you're attending one of his seminars or watching his *Die Rich* video.

(Would the author prefer less numbers, less hard fact, less provable, calculable examples presented in a slower fashion? Would this make it more valid in his mind?)

*

Say you have an estate worth $20 million, and you're looking at paying $11 million in taxes at your death, leaving your heirs with $9 million. Kaye says if you and your spouse are average age 60, you can purchase a one-pay, "last-to-die" (that is, it pays only after both partners are dead) life insurance policy for $1.1 million.

Transferring the money to an Irrevocable Trust (simply put, a gift which cannot be revoked), the money is spent to purchase a policy worth $11 million. In other words, you'd replace the entire amount you would have lost in taxes, not to mention the fact that your $1.1 million insurance premium would, according to Kaye's math, be worth only $495,000 if you left it as junk money.

(This is not "according to my math." The 55% estate tax assessed on $1.1 million left in a $20 million estate is exactly $605 thousand thus leaving $495 thousand for the heirs. It is a simple, easily verifiable fact.)

*

OR TURN $20,000 INTO $3.1 MILLION

How about this: Kaye says, "You're allowed to give $10,000 each and every year to as many people as you want." So he gives his kid (son Alan) that amount, figuring it's out of his estate where it's worth only $5,000 a year. Alan buys a life insurance policy on Barry's life. At age 60, Kaye says, $10,000 buys about $500,000 in insurance. But wait: For the same $10,000, Mom can be insured for $1 million. Better yet, a last-to-die policy for Mom and Pop is worth $1,550,000. Since Mom can also give away $10,000 per year, Alan can buy another policy worth $1,550,000. Ergo, he gets $3.1 million when the second parent dies.

"Where are you putting $20,000 that will produce $3.1 million?" Where, indeed. Do you understand these numbers? If you don't, you can always dial 1–800-DIE RICH for your own "free, no-obligation proposal."

(Perhaps the author should have called me for a verification. If he had I would have pointed out to him that he had both misread and misquoted me. I very clearly state that it is a YEARLY $20 thousand which funds the insurance proceeds of $3.1 million and this happens to be the correct yearly premium for a last-to-die policy of this type at this age.)

*

DON'T PAY OFF THE LOAN

Then there's the Turning $200,000 Into $2 Million Trick.

(There is no "trick" involved. It is a mathematical fact. But by using words so heavily laden with innuendo, the author effectively discredits the plan before the reader even has a chance to review it. Personally, I'd call THAT a terrible trick being played upon the public.)

*

One of Kaye's clients had assets of $5 million. He made $200,000 income annually, and he had one loan for $400,000 against his real estate. It cost him $24,000 a year, which he could of course, easily afford, but he just wanted to eliminate the debt.

Kaye advised against paying off the loan.

"Pay off the $400,000," he says, "and you'll leave only $200,000 for your heirs."

A new plan emerged: Take $400,000 that the client would have used to pay off the debt and instead transfer it to an Irrevocable Trust and purchase a last-to-die policy for $2 million. One payment of $400,000 yields $2 million for the kids versus $200,000. The cost, of course, is the $24,000 debt service on the loan that didn't get paid off.

(This plan ignores an obvious third option: Invest the $400,000 in something other than life insurance.)

(First of all, the author has chosen to ignore the fact that I state in my book and seminars that my concepts are a part of a diversified portfolio. I do not discount the usefulness of investments nor do I ever recommend that an individual should use only life insurance to accomplish their financial planning goals. However, the fact of the matter is that in this instance life insurance is the best means of seeing to it that the $400 thousand, which will be reduced to $200 by estate taxes, will become worth $2 million immediately after having made the insurance purchase regardless of the time of death. This alone makes it an unequaled financial vehicle. Furthermore, the $400 thousand would have to grow to about $4 million if invested since its net value at the time of death will still be halved by estate taxes. This series of facts which the author chooses to overlook are why I believe that my client would be best served by using this small part of his assets to purchase the insurance.)

*

BORROW TO SAVE

You are worth $10 million. You're going to die someday. All of us can claim at least one of those facts. If you can claim both, says Kaye, you can make a fast $5 million. Merely by dying. Here's how.

(Again the author uses a tone in his writing which seems to imply that I invented the fact of death in order to exploit it. This ghoulish portrayal of me helps him to detract attention from the fact that his scorn has no basis in fact and helps him to bias people from concepts which could help them save millions of dollars for their families by biasing them against me personally. Remember, you are going to die whether you buy my insurance or not.)

*

At age 60, you can buy a $5 million insurance policy for $500,000 "based on current assumptions." You don't need your own principal or cash flow to make the insurance purchase. With an estate valued at $10 million, Kaye says, "you can easily borrow a half million at three percent." The loan would cost you $25,000 a year and buy you $5 million worth of insurance. That's a half percent interest.

(This is either a gross error on the author's part or an out and out lie. I have never stated such an interest rate. Throughout "Die Rich," I utilized a 5% interest rate which was accurate and current at the time the book came out. In fact, if you check the numbers above, you'll realize that a $25 thousand loan payment on a $500 thousand loan IS a 5% interest rate. Yet, even then I stated that interest rates were, of course, subject to change. In my current seminars, including the one the author attended, I base my examples on an 8% interest rate.)

*

Kaye has a million of these things.

(Well, not exactly a million. There are 50 unique concepts in "Die Rich," 20 money-saving, asset-optimizing ideas in the magazine the author took with him and approximately 12 more covered in my seminar. Some of them overlap from one source to the next.)

*

He's fond of bringing home the point of estate taxes by asking the question: "If you knew the stock market would crash 2,000 points guaranteed, what would you do?" Well, he says, you'd sell, of course, and sell short if you're aggressive to hedge the market. Well, he thinks he's created the ultimate hedge fund.

(This is the author's statement, not mine. I said that "if you bought insurance to offset the taxes that would have to be paid upon your death, you would be creating a hedge against that happening" and I made an analogy to the fact that the stock market will crash the day you die, since approximately 50% taxes will be due nine months after your death, thus decimating approximately half your stock market assets. Yet, for all his high-handedness, the author has still not been able to refute a single factual aspect of my concepts and has had to resort to misrepresentation in order to belittle their effectiveness.)

*

"The trick of course," he tells a recent seminar group at the Marriott's Desert Springs Resort and Spa, "is to know when the market will crash. But it's really not a trick at all. The market will crash the day you die, guaranteed. Estate taxes will decimate your portfolio as surely as a 2,000 point stock market plunge, cutting the value of your stocks in half." Your AT&T stock at $60 is worth only $27 at your death, but at age 70, you can buy $300 worth of insurance for $60. "Why would you keep $27 instead of $300?"

THE UGLY TRUTH ABOUT YOUR IRA

If you've amassed a million-dollar pension or IRA, "the sad truth is that it may be worth only $270,000," says Kaye. "If you don't need the income from your pension, and you have been thinking of it as a legacy for your heirs, you'd better think again. When you die, if you're worth more than $3 million, your $1 million IRA is subject to income taxes of approximately $400,000, leaving $600,000. Your heirs will pay about $330,000 is estate taxes, so they'll inherit $270,000." A better way, he says, is to turn the $270,000 into $5 million.

"Terminate the pension plan," he advises. "Take the $1 million," which by the way would have continued to grow tax-free if you had left it alone.

(Yes, the $1 million would continue to grow tax-free if you left it alone, but it would have to grow to $25 million so that after excise, income and estate taxes it would be worth the same $5 million to your heirs. It is only tax free as long as you don't touch it. As soon as it passes on to your heirs it is fully taxable. Does the author really believe that there is a possibility that the $1 million will grow to $25 million? And does he really believe that the chance of that happening is great enough to pass up the certainty of $5 million which the insurance proposal provides? Does he really understand what he's writing about?)

*

"You'll have to pay income taxes of $400,000, but your kids will get $5 million eventually, and it's better than paying $730,000 in income and estate taxes.

"Place the remaining $600,000 into an Irrevocable Trust, funding a last-to-die policy that, depending, on your age is worth about $5 million."

(Obviously a pretty good transfer: $5 million versus $270 thousand. Yet there is not a word of encouragement or acknowledgement from the author.)

*

WAIT, THERE'S MORE.

Chances are, you're still stuck thinking of paying your estate taxes with one lump sum. But why?

He says you've used financing vehicles all of your life to maximize your potential in business, to take out lines of credit and loans, to buy houses and to leave cars. Why not use financing to handle possibly the largest expenditure of your life, i.e., estate taxes?

Here's one you can adjust up or down for yourself, depending on how wealthy you are. Say you have a stock portfolio of $10 million. You borrow $2 million against this portfolio, at a cost of $100,000 a year (three percent interest).

(Not only does he once again incorrectly accuse me of slanting the truth in favor of my proposals by using an artificially low interest rate to support my claims, but he doesn't even bother to check that the very math he is quoting clearly demonstrates my use of a 5% interest: $100 thousand interest on $2 million equals a rate of 5%!)

*

Give $2 million to charity. They then use $1 million for funding operations. The second million is set aside by the charity and purchases a last-to-die insurance policy on you and your spouse. At age 60, Kaye says, the policy will produce an additional $10 million for the charity, "based on current assumptions." (The charity will undoubtedly be among the saddest to see you go.) Even if you're age 80, the policy will produce $3 million.

More for you to chew on: Your $2 million charitable contribution is fully tax-deductible, which means you'll realize a million dollars in tax savings in the first year. Using that saved million, you could buy an additional $3 million to $10 million for the kids. So, concludes Kaye, your annual premium of $100,000 buys 21 Big Ones ($11 million for charity, $10 for your heirs.)

(I'm relatively certain he did not mean to say $10 for your heirs. That he meant to be accurate and say $10 million. One would hope though that

someone so devoted to ferreting out nuance would be a little more careful. Meanwhile, he once again misquotes me by saying that I claimed the annual premium would be $100 thousand. It is the interest on the $2 million loan which would have been $100 thousand in 1994 and which I increased to $160 thousand—8%—to accurately reflect today's rate at the seminar which he attended. Even so, I think it is a pretty interesting program, creating $21 million for $160 thousand a year and I continue to wait to hear one solid refutation of it by this journalist.)

*

WANT TO PRODUCE $45,000 OUT OF THIN AIR?

OK, it was a dumb question. You're worth $15 million and you borrow $1.5 million. You pay no capital gains tax, and you don't touch your own cash flow. Using the $1.5 million you purchase an "immediate annuity" which will produce a guaranteed $119,000 annual income after taxes as long as you or your spouse is alive. From that, you pay $75,000 annual interest on the loan, and $71,000 on premiums of a $1.5 million last-to-die policy placed with an Irrevocable Trust to pay off the loan. This leaves $45,000 annually "out of thin air."

How does he feel about all the estate-tax avoidance? Does he toss and turn all night because Uncle Sam isn't getting his fair share?

(No taxes are avoided through the implementation of my plans. Families continue to pay the full 55% they are assessed. This is not legal tax avoidance as practiced by attorneys such as the one he uses for his second opinion. The only difference is that my client recoups the cost of those taxes through the insurance proceeds. Is this a bad thing? The only instances in which taxes are not paid occur when the bulk of the estate is given to charity and this is a perfectly legitimate, legal and approved method.)

*

"The recovery of estate tax costs through the purchase of life insurance leaves more principal to earn more income, which generates even more taxes and puts more money to work in investments, employing more people, creating more taxable income."

So . . . you can be rich, avoid taxes and still be a nice guy, apparently. And you can ask for second opinion and still be a nice guy, too.

As you can see, never once in that article did the author make any real case for his point of view. Though he tried repeatedly to tear down my concepts, he never succeeded in offering any viable alternative or valid proof against the workings of my programs. And yet, someone reading that article might come away with an impression that I was a charlatan and my concepts a fraud. The disservice done is horrendous. Not only is it insulting to the public that the author would so skew the truth in order to enforce upon them his own biased viewpoint, but the cost to families who were swayed by his writing could be in the millions of dollars of absolutely avoidable estate tax costs.

This is the sort of stuff which floods the media on the topic of life insurance as an estate planning tool. I do not understand where the bias stems from but I KNOW that it is there, needlessly poisoning people away from the one alternative which can answer better than any other their asset management and estate planning goals.

Running as a sidebar to that article, under the banner headline: "A Second Opinion," appeared the following discussion of the same materials. Given some of the crossover of the incorrect statements in both the article and this sidebar, one might almost have to wonder which came first, the facts or the opinions? I have deleted all names from this reprint; I do not intend my use of these articles as a personal attack against any single journalist, attorney or expert, simply as a means of educating you into the dangers that exist when the media can not be trusted to present the whole truth.

Just how important is life insurance in the estate tax planning field? We put the question to (attorney), a partner and estate tax expert with the law firm of (—). (—) is familiar with life insurance expert Barry Kaye's commercials on CNBC and his video *Die Rich.*

(—) thinks Kaye has part of the story right . . . but only part. He says Kaye's strategy of getting money out of your estate by giving it away and by establishing trusts for your heirs and for charity is valid. But he says, life insurance is not always the proper vehicle, and he questions some of the numbers that Kaye uses.

"He does, after all, have a lot of concepts correct," (—) says. "But insurance companies are not philanthropists. They're in it to make money. What Mr. Kaye is trying is to pump up the life insurance end of it."

(Is this attorney's law firm a philanthropic organization or is it "in it to make money?" Is it somehow supposed to detract from the credibility of the insurance industry that it is a profitable one? The attorney agrees only with those portions of my concepts which support his industry—the manufacture of gifts and trusts—while already dismissing the value of life insurance even when explained by a man who is stated in the article to be an "expert" on the subject. The fact of the matter is that no matter how much money a person gives away or shelters in trusts, there must always be some estate remaining for the well-being of its owners. And THAT means there is always a taxable event waiting to occur outside of the trusts and gifts.)

*

The most revolutionary thing—that he doesn't even talk about—is the 'family limited partnership,' and that doesn't involve life insurance at all. That's probably the biggest estate planning technique right now for large estates. People who do family limited partnerships may still have the need for insurance but it certainly cuts down the need.

(The attorney has artfully turned away from having to substantiate his disfavor with insurance concepts to push his own product: The family limited trust, which he says I don't even talk about. In fact, I refer to Family Limited Trusts in chapter 35, page 173 of my book "Die Rich." I credit these trusts with accomplishing some very desirable goals of estate planning, although I do point out that you may only achieve a limited discount using a Family Limited Trust in contrast to the very large asset you can create properly utilizing a life insurance policy.)

*

So what's a "family limited partnership" or FLIP? It's a limited partnership wherein the "limited partners" have both limited liability and limited control over the assets. The general partner is the person trying to reduce taxable assets. By slicing the asset into pieces for the limited partners, the overall value of the pie is reduced dramatically in many cases. If you're sitting atop a massive estate, it's probably a good idea for you to seek out an estate planner with a broad view of the options available.

(Is it beginning to seem like this is not a second opinion on life insurance but a commercial for a trust or document? Meanwhile, somehow, estate experts and legal experts and financial experts are supposed to be

deemed credible, yet insurance experts are not even when those other 'experts' are advising on a subject they are not expert in, namely life insurance.)

*

Another important tax-avoidance device, says (—), is the "qualified personal residence trust."

(Apparently, in the context of the attorney's comments, the suggestion of tax-avoidance is acceptable while, in the article on the insurance concepts I recommend the author asked, "how does he feel about all this estate-tax avoidance? Does he toss and turn all night because Uncle Sam isn't getting his fair share?" in a tone clearly intended to convey disapproval of me. How can any presumption of fairness or lack of bias be sustained in this environment? And, without fairness and a lack of bias, how can the media claim to be serving the interests of the public?)

*

A "QPRT" is a gift of your personal residence (which you own free and clear) to your heirs at some specified time in the future, while you retain the right to live in the home. The bad news: If you die before the specified time in the future, it's as if you haven't done anything—it doesn't work. The good news: If you outlive the selected term, the home is discounted to your heirs based on the length of the term. The longer the term, the lower the valuation, so it's possible to give away a million dollar home which would be valued at, say, a half a million when your kids get it. That half million would be tax-free if you haven't used your $600,000 one-time deduction.

(Still nothing of substance against life insurance. Nor any reference to my discussion of the QPRT on Chapter 29, page 146 and Chapter 36, page 177 of my book. Yes, Mr. (—) is right, using a QPRT in the above situation could, IF THE PARENTS LIVE LONG ENOUGH, effectively reduce the value of the home from $1 million to $500 thousand and that $500 thousand WOULD BE tax free if there was $500 of a one-time deduction remaining to one of the couple. But, what happens in the event the couple DOES NOT live long enough is completely glossed over as is the fact that the length of your life and the time of your death can not be guaranteed in a trust document. If the couple dies before the specified date, "it doesn't work," yet is this so much better than an insurance policy

which will pay its stated death benefit the very day it is purchased if need be? Furthermore, does anyone believe that a couple with a $1 million home doesn't have any other value in their estate? In all likelihood there are substantial other assets behind that $1 million house and THEY WILL BE SUBJECT TO ESTATE TAXES of up to 55%.)

Perhaps (—)'s biggest beef with Kaye is the interest rates Kaye quotes for money borrowed (for purchase of life insurance) against large estates. Prime rate is prime rate, says (—). You can't borrow money for three percent.

(Here is the exact same misquoted percentage rate as was used in the main article. I have never used a 3% interest rate. I used 5% in "Die Rich" which was appropriate at the time, and I use 7–8% now in my seminars and materials. Even in the examples quoted in the main article the interest rate was clearly 5% though the author miscalculated it and claimed it to be 3%. One might wonder whether this attorney is reviewing me and my materials—with which he is supposed to be familiar—or the article-author and his.)

*

"All these techniques involved gifts," he says. "Don't get me wrong. You have to do the gifts to get it out of your estate. But you're not creating money. You're not creating wealth."

(I'm not sure what the attorney would consider it, but every one of my clients who puts $100 thousand or $1 million in a policy and creates $1 million, $5 million or $10 million knows that his heirs have more money at any moment after the insurance is bought and the principals die than if no insurance had been bought.)

*

I think it is quite clear from reading these reprints that the authors of both the main article and the second opinion are enacting some personal agenda in their writings and are really unknowledgable about the usefulness of life insurance in estate tax planning. The attorney who gives the Second Opinion is clearly more interested in selling his own products than in fairly evaluating the benefits of life insurance and the journalist who wrote the main article pretty obviously had an inherent bias. It is sad for all the people who might have been affected by these writings not to proceed with the Investment Alternative methods available for estate planning and asset optimization that they are at the mercy of this sort of self-serving journalism.

But even when the writers are sincere in their attempts to report the truth of life insurance's many uses in estate and asset management, they are often given incorrect information from the sources they consult as they compile their data. The fact is that not many people really understand the nuances of how these insurance products work to create and preserve wealth. Attorneys, accountants and financial advisors rarely specialize in the fields of insurance, and most have never even taken classes or attended seminars to learn about it. Those who do all too often come into the learning situation from a position of having already made up their minds, based on some conventional wisdom which serves to bolster their own industry and position, and attend only to challenge the lessons. Even many insurance people do not fully comprehend these new uses for the products they sell.

For most of its history in the marketplace, insurance has been sold almost solely as a hedge against the tragic death of a family wage-earner. With the advent of the new types of policies and new concepts for how to utilize them in estate and financial planning, many insurance people find themselves trying to apply the old methods of structuring policies to the new plans. Unfortunately, the results are not always what they could be. Reeducation throughout any industry takes a long time and, as we are still in what could be called a transition period in which the new ideas are circulating but have not been entirely absorbed, it still happens that many insurance professionals are not yet as well versed about the best ways to implement these plans. As a simple example, the build up of cash values used to be a major consideration in the structuring of an insurance purchase. There were many good and valid reasons why a build up of cash value in the policy was a desirable thing. However, when we structure insurance purchases for estate planning we are not as concerned with cash values. Instead, we want the absolute lowest cost for the policy that will still offer the full needed coverage. So today it will sometimes happen that a client looking to use life insurance for estate planning purposes will be quoted a rate that is higher than necessary because the insurance salesperson is still locked into thinking about cash values when they don't actually apply in this situation as they once did.

What this means is that often, when a truly diligent and fair-minded journalist goes to write an article reviewing the new uses of life insurance as an alternative to and further diversification of traditional investing, he or she winds up inadvertently receiving professional counsel or advice from someone who is not wholly qualified to be speaking on the subject. What happens then is that, despite the best intentions of the writer, the public is once again given erroneous information which might serve to limit their understanding of the uniquely beneficial opportunity afforded by life insurance in a properly structured estate situation.

An article was published recently in a well-received Midwestern magazine that reviewed the concept of using insurance as an alternative means to achieving and preserving wealth. For the most part, the article was fair and correct. But look what happens when the writer, through no fault of her own, is given erroneous or incomplete counsel from an "expert" she consulted.

In one paragraph, the author credits her source, an insurance agent, consultant and attorney, with saying that:

Kaye assumes everyone wants to leave the majority or all of their estate to their kids. (Kaye says up front his concepts were designed to ensure that rich families stay rich families—after mom and dad die.) But according to (—), many people don't care about that concept. In fact, getting the kids through college may be enough of a commitment . Yet, an interesting balance is sometimes the answer. (—) cites this example: A Chicago family he worked with is worth $100 million and plans to leave the entire estate to a charitable foundation. The kids won't get the estate, but they will have lifetime jobs at the foundation, a $5 million interest portfolio, and there will be no estate taxes to pay.

(I have always said that giving all your money away to charity and establishing a foundation for your children to run for a salary is a viable and effective means of avoiding estate taxes. However, contrary to the author's source, in my 35 years experience in this field, fewer families with $100 million want to leave it all to charity than want to leave it for

the benefit of their heirs. More importantly, if this Chicago family is so devoted to their charity, why wouldn't they want to leave a significantly optimized gift then they will currently be able to do? Since they are waiting until death to give the charity the gift anyway, by making the charity their beneficiary, why wouldn't they put some of their $100 million into an insurance policy during their lifetimes to yield a 3, 5 or even 10 times return. If they are in their sixties, they could take $10 million and receive a 10 times return which would net AN ADDITIONAL $100 million for their charity. They can surely afford the $10 million. The bottom line is a greatly increased gift at virtually no additional cost to them. Of course, they could also choose to apportion some of this additional $100 million to their children without affecting the originally intended $100 million gift to the charity, but that's a personal choice.)

*

Kaye says you're going to lose more than half your fortune to estate taxes. But when you do the math, it doesn't add up. On the first $600,000, you're entitled to zero percent estate taxes, leaving $2.4 million on a $3 million estate. Your estate will probably end up with a graduated tax, from 37 to 55 percent, which is a lot less than the 55 percent tax that Kaye predicts.

(Once again a single point taken out of context is being offered as some sort of proof that my plans are built on an unstable foundation. I clearly state in my seminars, in my book and on the video the author of this article watched that the estate taxes are $1.1 million on the first $3 million <u>including</u> utilizing your $600 thousand exemption and then 55% thereafter.)

*

(—) adds, estate taxes are voluntary since any individual with wealth over $600,000, the threshold for imposing the tax, can arrange to dispose of his or her assets to avoid the tax. (—) comes up with this fast scenario. If Joe owns $5 million of stock in public companies, his estate tax will be $2 million, which only leaves $3 million for his kids. Instead, Joe can leave his kids $600,000 and $4.4 million to a charity. The result, points out (—), is that the IRS gets nothing.

(Has anyone else realized that this 'expert' has DONE NOTHING to benefit the kids. He talks about them ONLY getting $3 million if the

parents do nothing, yet, in his plan, he has reduced that $3 million to only $600 thousand. He didn't even try to establish the estate in such a way as to at least leave the children both parents' $600 thousand exemption for a total of $1.2 million. Which is still less than half what they'd get if you left the estate alone. Meanwhile, depending on their age and health, for a cost of $200 thousand, $400 thousand or $666 thousand, the parents could purchase a life insurance policy that would produce the $2 million needed for estate taxes allowing the children to inherit the entire $5 million without any loss due to estate tax costs. Did you really work that hard all your life to earn and grow and protect your $5 million, $10 million, $50 million, $100 million or more just to give it all away to charity to avoid estate taxes when there is a perfectly viable, legal and certain way to pass it on to your heirs intact?)

*

Later in this same article, the author quotes another expert source, a lawyer and estate planner, as saying that, "Employing life insurance as an investment tool can be very effective, but it's not the only tool to consider."

Anyone who has read my books or attended my seminars or seen my video knows that I only recommend insurance as a part of a diversified portfolio. Nonetheless, I wonder what other tools this expert would recommend that will come to the heirs income and estate tax free, will pay their return from the very first day they are purchased and will predetermine that yield based on current assumptions?

There is more, but you've heard it all already. Attorneys consulted for the article raising the question of my earning commissions through the sale of insurance but glossing over the fact that they earn their livings selling trusts and estate planning consulting. Self-appointed experts claiming that insurance isn't the be-all and end-all yet not being able to suggest a single alternative that achieves the same results. Insurance men questioning the costs of policies because they are still locked into old thinking and want to load up the cash values beyond what is necessary. The sad truth is, you can't rely on the financial media to accurately report the benefit of insurance in estate planning. Sometimes because the writers are biased, lazy or trying to elevate themselves by tearing down others. And sometimes because the 'experts' they rely on for background aren't really as expert as they like to think.

The real tragedy, is that these people go unchecked, spreading their misinformation while American families needlessly lose millions.

Recently, the New York Times ran a major, page one Sunday feature article on estate taxes and how the wealthy plan for them by David Cay Johnston and Christopher Drew. The article was extremely thorough and clearly every attempt had been made to examine the issue from all sides. The main focus of the article, however, was on the various means people use to avoid paying estate taxes and the repercussions these tax avoidance strategies have on them, their heirs, the nation, and the IRS.

Numerous experts were consulted for the article and quoted within it. Interestingly, though the article ran the day after the feature, written by the same journalists, which detailed the collapse of Jacqueline Kennedy Onassis' much-heralded estate tax plan, many of the exact same techniques which were utilized to such disaster for her were again quoted as being 'the way to go' by attorneys and accountants.

I am not going to reprint the whole article here; space forbids it and much of it is not germane to my purposes. But I would like to excerpt some of the contents to once again examine how and where the media goes wrong in its examination of this topic. This was a major article in a nationally renowned newspaper written as objectively as any I have seen, yet even it was skewed by the lack of understanding of some of its quoted sources and the general misconceptions about life insurance demonstrated by the public. In light of the revelations about Jackie's estate, I think it is desperately important to reiterate the way the press influences notions about estate taxes so that you can examine where some of your ideas may have come from and where they may be in error.

The article opens by telling a story of estate tax avoidance:

(—), who is 40 years old, knew that by the time he and his wife died and their house in (—), went to their three children, hundreds of thousands of dollars in taxes would be owed before the children could inherit it. But as a tax lawyer, he also knew a way around those taxes.

Using a popular strategy, the (—)s are giving the house to their children, the oldest of whom is 11, in exchange for permission to live there rent free for 25 free years.

It is all perfectly legal. In fact, Mr. (—) advises clients to take the sophisticated steps necessary to pull it off. And it is typical of a host of techniques that are being promoted aggressively so that affluent Americans can transfer much of their wealth to heirs while avoiding or deferring taxes.

(The 'popular strategy' this tax attorney is using and recommending is one of the 12 cookie cutter methods used by attorneys all across the country called a Qualified Personal Residence Trust or QPRT. While it does have some advantages, it disturbs me that the many disadvantages and better alternatives are not referred to at the same time. There is no mention of the emotional difficulties often faced when parents wind up renting their home back from their children after the rent-free term of the trust expires. In this case, the parents will only be 65 years old with, hopefully, years of life ahead of them yet they will have relinquished ownership of their home. More importantly, there is no mention at all of the fact that, if Mr. and Mrs. (—) are both in their 40's they could receive a 28–1 return on an insurance purchase. If their house is worth $500 thousand and their estate is worth enough that the taxes on it will be 55%—$275 thousand—a one-pay insurance policy to cover those taxes would only cost about $10 thousand. It might cost anyone who isn't their own attorney that much in legal fees alone to execute this complicated program and still they would be faced with all of its possible pitfalls. One of the advantages of making the transfer of the house now is that, by doing so, the asset is valued and taxed at only $83 thousand, a fraction of its value. But, if instead of transferring the home and risking the disadvantages inherent in this program the couple had transferred the same $83 thousand as a one-time payment, they could buy a $2.3 million last-to-die policy. This would more than cover the tax on the $500 thousand house even if it grew to $1.4 million and a larger tax had to be paid at their deaths. Why have $500 thousand out of your estate when you can have $2.3 million from the first day, which will more than cover the tax and leave an extra $1.6 million?)

*

The article goes on to examine some of the ways the rich avoid paying estate taxes and quotes the opinion of an economist at New York University who says that, "The wealthy already have huge advantages. (So) it is important to put teeth into the estate tax system now because otherwise this transfer of wealth will just exacerbate inequalities."

MYTHS, MISCONCEPTIONS AND MISINFORMATION   197

Conversely, duly reporting on both sides, the article also quotes government figures that place the revenue from estate and gift taxes at about $1% of total tax revenues and offers the opinion of the Heritage Foundation, a conservative Washington think tank, which says that estate taxes do reduce economic growth and are thus "hurting the jobs and incomes of the very people that wealth redistribution was intended to aid."

Meanwhile, what it _does not_ detail in its discussion of these issues is the fact that there is one estate tax planning method which accommodates the needs of both sides. By using life insurance proceeds to pay estate taxes, the wealthy families of America do not withhold from their country one dime that has been determined to be its due, continue to fund the supposed wealth redistribution which was the intended genesis of the estate tax and yet still retain enough of their fortunes intact for the kind of investment and development use which strengthens the economy as a whole. How can the article be complete without this additional information? How can the topic be separated into an either/or proposition—either tax avoidance is unfair because the rich are favored or the taxes themselves are an unfair penalty on industry and success—without any mention of the one technique which straddles the middle without loss to either side?

A New York estate lawyer and author is quoted as saying, "I think the estate tax is voluntary in two senses—how much you eventually need to pay within a family and when you pay it. I wouldn't say all of it, but you can eliminate much of it." The article then goes on the detail some of the ways the wealthy decrease or eliminate the need to pay estate taxes:

- Corporate executives have found ways to pass millions of dollars worth of stocks, and options to buy stocks, to their children without owing estate taxes.
- Investors are putting every sort of property, from vacation homes to stock portfolios, into partnerships for their children so that they are valued for tax purposes at 30 to 70 percent less than what they would be worth in the marketplace. Any rise in the property's value escapes the estate tax, and a separate gift tax is reduced.

- A Long Island widow has bought a $60 million share of her children's inheritance, shielding the proceeds from estate taxes and allowing the family to pay less to the Government. Tax counselors long insisted that nothing could be done after the death of a benefactor to reduce taxes. Now, perhaps, death is no obstacle.

(The technique being referred to in these examples is the use of a Limited Family Partnership, another of the cookie cutter legal methods for shielding assets from estate taxes. In many cases, A Limited Family Partnership is an effective tool as I discuss more in depth later in this book. However, it has several drawbacks as well. To begin with, since it exists pretty much solely to avoid estate taxes, it is always being closely examined by the IRS and Congress and I believe its existence may be greatly at risk. Moreover, the true benefit of these plans only comes into play if the asset placed into the trust grows significantly. Why would anyone pay all the money to an attorney to set up this trust, and run the risk of drawing the attention of the IRS in the process to protect an asset that might not even have the true potential or time to achieve the growth needed to make the trust worthwhile? An insurance policy would produce excellent results and does not antagonize the IRS. Yet no comparison or mention of this fact is included in the article. How are you to know your options if the professional community only supports proprietary techniques and the media doesn't tell people?)

*

When insurance is mentioned, it is brought up in the following manner:

Many heirs and benefactors have also provided for likely estate taxes by buying insurance that can help pay the bill, but that can involve hefty premiums over a period of unpredictable duration.

Avoiding taxes if you legally can is a favorite American pastime. Taxpayers would be foolish to pay more if they could find a legitimate way not to.

(Hefty premiums. Depending on the age of the people involved, insurance can net returns of 3, 5 10, 16, 28 or even 50 times! I'd say those are hefty

<u>returns</u> *and they are available the very day the purchase is made if need
dictates. The writer is correct when he says 'unpredictable duration' but
wrong in applying the term only to the possible length of insurance
premiums. In truth, what is of unpredictable duration is your LIFE and
when you enter that fact into the equation it makes the importance of life
insurance even more clear. Using 1/10 or 1/5 of the cost of the estate tax
you will eventually be faced with should leave more than enough funds to
establish trusts or make investments.*

*Furthermore, by following this minimal examination of insurance with
the statement that, "Avoiding taxes if you legally can . . ." suggests by
association that insurance is another means of attempted tax avoidance.
As we've already realized, it simply isn't. It is THE ONLY method which
discounts the estate tax costs without avoiding any taxes.)*

*

Yet, this is how the members of the public quoted in the article view
the inclusion of life insurance in their estate planning:

(—), a North Carolina farmer and business owner, recently wrote to
several members of Congress about how hard the estate tax can hit
families that do not take steps to avoid it. When Mr. (—)'s father died in
1964, his widow had to borrow $75,000 and sell a warehouse to pay a
$200,00 tax bill. "Ever since then, I've had a passion not to let this
happen again," he said.

Mr. (—), who estimated that his company was now worth $3 million,
argued that he could not put real estate in a trust for his two children or
give them big gifts of cash or stock. Such strategies, he maintained,
would prevent him from using the assets as collateral for loans his
company often needs.

So he has resort to an old standby, insurance. He pays $15,000 a year in
premiums for $1 million of life insurance to make sure that his heirs will
have cash to pay the taxes on his estate. He has also spent thousands of
dollars on expert advice to create a trust to hold the policies for his
heirs—protecting the insurance proceeds themselves from being hit by
estate taxes.

*(Maybe there is a reason why insurance is such an 'old standby.' Maybe
it's because as much as people try other ways to accomplish their goals,
they keep finding out the same thing. That nothing works like insurance to*

*accommodate all the needs and variables which must be taken into account when planning for the inevitability, unpredictability and expense of death. Yet even this man, who bemoans the inequity of the tax avoidance system to his representative overlooks the amazing benefits he is reaping. Only $15 thousand a year is protecting his entire estate from the decimation of estate tax. Is this a bad thing? The **really** tragic thing here is the money he was charged to establish his Irrevocable Trust to shelter the insurance proceeds from estate taxes. In fact, the establishment of such a trust should be a fairly simple, fairly straightforward and inexpensive thing as it is one of the most commonly used cookie cutter methods. Yet, while people begrudge the cost of the insurance premiums they accept the costs of legal services as being necessary and worthwhile.)*

*

Another concerned taxpayer tells that he is "pursuing a common technique of buying life insurance—in this instance a policy worth $50 million. They will pay the $1.2 million in annual premiums." There is no further positive statement that this is the total solution that benefits the taxpayer, the government and the American public. $50 million of insurance to cover taxes at a premium cost of only $1.2 million a year. An eventual net cost of less than $600 thousand yearly on a woman probably 70 years old. She could die tomorrow or live to 100. Her life expectancy is 15 years, age 85. Even at 15 years the net cost will be only $9 million with an additional net cost of gift taxes, which weren't mentioned in the article, of $5 million. A total of $14 million to pay the taxes of $50 million, more if she lives longer, less if she dies prematurely. Why is everyone complaining? Why are they looking for every convoluted plan of tax avoidance when nothing will compare with a life insurance policy? Why isn't everybody with a tax problem doing this? Why isn't anyone writing about this constructively, positively and in depth? When will the public catch on? When will the attorneys catch on? When will the public catch on to the attorneys? When will the attorneys prepare all the necessary documents, stop the more expensive tax avoidance plans and let the insurance pay the taxes?

Even this thorough, objective article does not delve enough beneath the surface of people's preconceptions to find the truth. It accepts, as so many do, the notions people have about life insurance and does not put them to the test in the same rigorous manner which it does the ideas about estate taxation, trusts, and the impact on America.

Perhaps, the time is right at last for The Investment Alternative. Perhaps, you understand now why I feel so strongly about this subject. Particularly when it is clear that almost every complex plan used by attorneys can be beaten every time at the bottom line by an insurance policy that, while it protects your family, does not take anything away from the government, does not require growth that may not occur, and is available the very first day it is needed. For the life of me, I do not understand what more people want.

THE EXPERTS

The fact of the matter is, you can get an "expert" to say almost anything if it is in his or her own best interest or supports his or her existing bias. We've seen it a hundred times. In televised trials where the defense and the prosecution each have established experts testifying on some crucial point of evidence yet the experts come up with radically different conclusions. In business meetings when different companies are bidding for the same job and each has 'hard evidence' to support why their approach is the better one.

The sad truth is that 'expertise' is up for grabs. And it doesn't always work in your favor. Consider these two tragic examples of expert advice gone very very wrong.

I tell a story in my book *Die Rich and Tax Free* that is germane enough to this topic that it bears repeating. Almost 20 years ago, Kenneth Langone offered Ross Perot a 70% stake in the new business he was starting—a chain of discount hardware stores called Home Depot. He offered the 70% share to Mr. Perot for a price of $2 million. On the basis of advice he received from one of his advisors, Mr. Perot turned down the offer. Today, 70% of Home Depot would be worth in excess of $12 billion. That's a more than 6,000 times increase and would have more than tripled Ross Perot's entire net value!

I make no suggestion that the advisor whose recommendation denied

Mr. Perot this opportunity did so for any clandestine or covert purpose. He was simply wrong. These things happen.

In his new book, _Rewrites_[1], Neil Simon tells a similar, tragic story.

". . . my new business manager came to me with a proposition. I don't remember if it was Paramount who offered it or my manager who dreamed up this deal. I had recently formed my own corporation called Ellen Enterprises. Its only holdings were two properties, _The Odd Couple_ and _Barefoot in the Park_. The offer was for Paramount to buy Ellen Enterprises from me for a $125,000 capital-gains deal. It was a great deal of money but I didn't understand the benefit of the deal . . .

"Why would I want to do that?" I asked my manager.

"I'll tell you why. You still keep the stage rights to _The Odd Couple_. You still get your money for the _Barefoot_ movie. And on top of that, you get a hundred and twenty-five thousand dollars. Look, you've had two small hits and two gigantic hits. Do you know what the possibilities of your writing more hits are? Even _one_ more. A thousand to one. No, _ten_ thousand to one. There are maybe three or four writers in the history of the American theater, playwrights I'm talking about, that have done that. You could have two, three, five more flops before you wrote another hit. It could take you seven, eight years, _if_ you even wrote another hit. I think you're nuts if you pass this up."

My lawyer shrugged and I got the feeling he was agreeing with my manager. The final decision, obviously, was left to me. No one was telling me what the downside was. Maybe there _was_ no downside; I had no way to know what the right thing to do was aside from the prodding of my manager. I accepted the deal.

In total, this is what I got: $125,000. Although it didn't become clear to me for some time, this is what I lost. Paramount made a TV series of _The Odd Couple_ starring Tony Randall and Jack Klugman. Those were one of the ancillary rights Paramount got in buying Ellen Enterprises. I never received one cent from the series. I had my name on every episode but I never saw a dime, a nickel, or a penny. It ran for years and will run in syndication for years and years to come. Not just in America but all over the world. The value of what I had given up for _The Odd Couple_ series was in the millions. Probably a great deal of millions. It gets worse. I also gave up _all_ the stage rights to _Barefoot in the Park_. It's one of the most

---

[1] _Neil Simon Rewrites, A Memoir._ Copyright © 1996 by Neil Simon. Simon & Schuster.

performed plays of all the plays I've written. They're still doing it today in Japan and Russia and Germany and India. From the day I signed that agreement, I never received a penny in royalties. And I never will. Add another million or two to my losses on *The Odd Couple.* My children will never see that money nor will my grandchildren."

The moral of this tragic story is clear. Advisors can be terribly, terribly wrong. Yet, Mr. Simon makes a honest and courageous statement when he says, "The final decision, obviously, was left to me."

The final decision about how to handle your estate planning is YOURS. It is YOUR children who will be affected; your lawyer, accountant, tax expert or financial advisor will not suffer from the depletion of your estate. Their fees will have already been paid. It is YOUR life's work, YOUR treasured collectibles, YOUR business and acquisitions that are at stake. And so the responsibility for deciding what to do is YOURS.

And yes, this applies to me as well. You must use your own judgment even over mine on this subject.

So how do you know what to do? It is simple. Look at the bottom line. Get advise, and lots of it, but then use the skills and wisdom which earned and preserved your wealth to begin with to evaluate what you are being told. Don't believe everything you read in a newspaper or magazine. Think for yourself what makes sense and what doesn't, what fits with what you want to accomplish and what doesn't.

As I've said before, estate planning and capital optimization is a financial event. A matter of arithmetic and bottom lines. Compare the outcomes of all the different plans being put before you and then embrace that one which will support your desires most closely. And remember: Yes, I have a financial interest in selling life insurance. But that does not disqualify my expertise or the value of my concepts any more than the fact that a lawyer charges to draw up a trust, or a tax planner charges to evaluate your estate, or an accountant charges to prepare your taxes. These things are all given and equal among the various advisors you might consult. If they are a consideration for the validity of one, they are a consideration for the validity of all. Therefore, you need to include that concern across the board to the extent that it is a factor for you and then evaluate the proposed plans from the basis of a clean and even slate.

Because this point is SO important, let's look at a few more examples of how the press and financial community, as well as attorneys and accountants, misunderstand and/or misrepresent the concept of insurance as an alternative to traditional investing.

The first story is an especially sad account of what can happen when a person abrogates the responsibility for their estate planning decisions to experts who are too wrapped up in their own worlds to honestly and thoroughly consider alternatives that are unfamiliar to them.

Over the past ten years on two occasions I had met with a prospective client I will call Mr. B. On the first occasion he had me analyze his assets and needs to determine how much insurance would be appropriate for his situation. He understood the need and the tremendous problem his daughter would have at his death due to the estate taxes which would be due on his assets. He was particularly concerned with the possibility of a forced liquidation and the havoc it would wreak on his estate since it was heavily concentrated in real estate.

Mr. B felt that he wanted to proceed with some of the concepts I have espoused but said he would have to confer with his accountant upon whom he had relied for many of his financial decisions over the past two decades. While he understood the need and the urgency as well as the common sense of the purchase of insurance, he wanted his accountant's assurance.

Unfortunately the accountant was busy as it was tax season at that time. This caused a tremendous delay in securing the accountant's attention and concentration. There was no understanding of the client's changing health and age and the manner in which they would impact the pricing of the insurance policy. While insurance is paid for with money, it is bought with good health. Any change in health before the purchase was consummated could increase the premium or negate the purchase all together thus eliminating the most efficient method of paying the estate tax.

The accountant's reason for delay and hesitation in recommending the insurance soon became apparent. He simply did not understand the insurance, how it worked or its effectiveness in discounting the cost of paying estate taxes. Instead of admitting his ignorance on the subject and his preconceived bias against insurance, he just told his client he did not think it was right for him.

In spite of the fact that Mr. B agreed with my assessment of his situation, he turned the whole program down rather than offend his long standing relationship with his accountant.

I have seen other situations like this where the children who suffered the consequences of this bad advise from the father's accountant are now suing the professional for malpractice in telling the father that the insurance program was not for him.

In any event, the same Mr. B contacted me 6 years later, just 4 years ago. Once again he asked me to design a program that would avoid the decimation of his assets at his death. His health had deteriorated and I suggested using a surrogate to be insured in his place to accomplish his goals. Everything proceeded in excellent fashion and it looked like we would initiate a plan that would finally benefit his children. This is when his new attorney was brought in for a final review. Once again I was confronted by an attorney with a strong bias against insurance and a total lack of understanding of insurance concepts. The prospect's inability to make a decision on his own coupled with his advisors' ignorance once again resulted in a turndown.

I heard nothing further on this situation until shortly before this book went to press. It was at the Friars Club in Los Angeles where I was holding one of my regular seminars for the public. I did not know Mr. B's daughter was in the audience. In the middle of one of my statements she posed a question and then tearfully related the above story and told us that Mr. B had died last year. She went on to explain that she had just finished paying the IRS an awesome amount of money and she was seriously considering taking legal recourse against the professionals who had given her father such bad advise. Incidentally, the attorney and accountant are not suffering one dime's worth of consequence today for their actions.

There is no need for these horror stories. If only the uninformed professionals would either learn or admit their ignorance and not offer up an opinion and the public would follow the bottom line to realize the value of these concepts and not rely on someone else to do their thinking for them, millions of dollars of needless loss could be saved for families all across America.

Yet even when the experts are open minded and creative in their thinking they can often overlook solutions simply because they are not aware of them. Though I have been promoting these wealth creation and preservation programs for more than 35 years, the fact remains that only a very small segment of the financial community is really aware of them and an even smaller percentage of those people comprehend in-depth the manner in which they work. So, though they do not mean to overlook an important opportunity, they simply do not know to include life insurance in their planning. Those that do, limit their insurance purchase to the minimum to cover the actual tax with no regard for the Investment Alternative potential. Following is a dramatic example of what can happen when estate planning is executed creatively—but not creatively enough.

JACQUELINE KENNEDY ONASSIS, AN UNFORTUNATE EXAMPLE

There was and continues to be a lot of news discussion about the estate planning used by Jacqueline Kennedy Onassis to protect her estate for the benefit of her heirs. The subsequent auction of many of her personal affects re-raised questions of the estate's solvency in the face of estate taxes.

Using one of the more effective and popular 'cookie cutter' legal approaches to estate planning, a Charitable Lead Generation Skipping Trust, Mrs. Onassis did successfully manage to save the bulk of her estimated $100 million estate from total decimation and pass on $98 million out of $100 million of it instead of the $20 million which is all her heirs would have been left with from the $100 million had she not enacted the plan. However, if Mrs. Onassis had utilized the Investment Alternative concepts detailed here, she could have increased her estate to $469 million for her heirs instead of the optimized $98 million they received.

The attorneys assisting Mrs. Onassis drew up a very special plan which has since received great press and accolades from estate plan-ning attorneys all over America. The chairman of the trusts and estates department at a major Boston law firm said that he planned to use the Onassis will as a case study for partners and associates. "It is an interesting will," he said. "It is a rare look at how a good estate plan is done." However without the utilization of life insurance it is less than one fourth as effective as it might have been. This once again proves how these antiquated conventional cookie cutter plans are incapable of optimizing assets beyond the vision of those who created them so many years ago. And they are costing the rich and society in general a fortune. These plans are methods of the wealthy to keep their estates intact, often avoiding huge taxes by donating portions of their wealth to charities and placing their assets in various trusts. However, while this may avoid taxes, it does nothing to increase and optimize their assets at the same time. It is a shame when something works so well that it limits the thinking to go way beyond.

Many professionals are unaware of the methods and techniques that are available utilizing the Investment Alternative system. But most of all they close the door to even taking advantage of these ideas because of their biases toward insurance.

But it isn't the rhetoric from either side which should convince you one way or the other. Let me show you my recommendation for the handling of Mrs. Onassis' estate. Then let the bottom line determine your opinion of the best method. I am fairly certain that you will come to agree that the utilization of life insurance produces superior results than those which were achieved through the convoluted plan that was used.

In situations like Jackie's, conventional wisdom dictates using charitable lead trusts and generation skipping trusts to protect the estate. As an example, when these trusts were combined, Jackie could transfer $100 million to them as a means of sheltering her estate. The trust then transferred $6 million income yearly to charity for 24 years and because of the way the trust is structured, at the end of the period her grandchildren can receive approximately $98 million. This serves charity and the social good of our country with approximately $150 million over a 24 year period going to charity while keeping the estate practically intact for the eventual benefit of the grandchildren. But that's where these plans stop when there is really so much more that can be accomplished.

Had Jackie been my client I would not have waited until her age 65 to make these hurried plans when the options were limited. I would have recommended at age 60 that she utilize up to 30% of her presumed assets of $100 million—$30 million—towards achieving her estate planning goals. With that $30 million I would have shown her how to create $469 million which her designated heirs would receive income and estate tax free. While my plan may have ultimately required her to outlay $30 million it does produce an extra $371 million for her heirs. A fair exchange, I think.

I would have recommended that she purchase $50 million worth of insurance on herself. This insurance would be bought in a generation skipping trust at a one payment cost of $8 million, based on current assumptions. There also would have been an additional gift tax of $4.4 million and another $4.4 million of generation skipping taxes, for a total of $8.8 million. Coupled with the insurance premium, this would have cost $16.8 million and produced $50 million completely tax free at her death. The $50 million remaining in a generation skipping trust after her death based on 6% net after taxes, would have grown in 24 years to approximately $200 million for the benefit of her grandchildren. They would then have had $200 million rather than $98 million for each $100 million transferred.

In addition, I would have recommended that she transfer $2 million to the generation skipping trust to insure her children for the benefit of her grandchildren. A $2 million one payment premium on a last-to-die policy would produce approximately $100 million at the deaths of the two people covered, based on current assumptions. There would be a gift tax of $1.1 million and an additional generation skipping tax of $1.1 million, plus the original premium of $2 million for a total of $4.2 million for each child. Doing this with both children for the benefit of her grandchildren would require a total outlay of $8.4 million.

Following my procedure, her grandchildren would receive $200 million on the deaths of the four named parties. At any time prematurely, or at some time, based on life expectancy, in the next 45 years, there would be a regeneration of assets available in a generation skipping trust of approximately $200 million, increasing the total to $400 million totally tax free, instead of $98 million.

In all probability, the only reason anyone would create the original plan that transferred $6 million to charity each year for 24 years from a charitable lead trust would be to produce the tax free elements that fall into place once such a trust is set and the charities get the income. However, assuming that Jackie had a genuine interest in producing $150 million for charity, I would have recommended that she transfer the remaining balance from the $30 million (she had already spent $16.8 for insurance and taxes on her life, and $8.4 for insurance and taxes on her children's lives for a total of $25.2 million) to her favorite charity. The remainder from her $30 million would be $4.8 million. This will allow her to give approximately $8 million to charity for a net after tax cost of $4.8 million. Meanwhile, since the $8 million to charity is tax deductible, it really only costs her estate $4 million.

My next recommendation would be to suggest that she take $6 million of the $8 million that went to charity and buy approximately $36 million worth of insurance payable to the charity on her death. This is much more than the original $6 million she was going to leave for at least the first 6 years, and it can be compounded at interest to bring it in excess of $50 million.

Using the same idea as above, the remaining $2 million contribution to charity could purchase an additional $100 million of insurance on her children that will be released upon the joint deaths of the children, their spouses, et al, as described above. In this manner charity would eventually receive approximately the same $150 million which was produced in the plan she did utilize.

The heirs' money has now been optimized from $98 million to $400 million and charity has still received $150 million. The total cost to do this was $30 million. If she didn't do this, the net result after all taxes on the $30 million to the grandchildren would be less than $7 million.

It is indeed doubtful that she could equal these figures using the conventional wisdom plan which only nets $98 million to her family. The only possible way to equal the benefits from the insurance would be to take the total $100 million and somehow increase it to approximately $2 BILLION. After estate taxes of $1.1 billion, there would be $900 million left and after generation skipping taxes of $500 million, her grandchildren would ultimately receive the same $400 million created so efficiently by insurance. WHY WAIT FOR $100 MILLION TO GO TO $2 BILLION TO PRODUCE THE SAME $400 MILLION WHICH CAN BE CREATED INSTANTANEOUSLY WITH LIFE INSURANCE?

I created this entire $400 million using only $30 million (30%) of Jackie's assets and while 30% may seem like a hefty share, remember there is still $70 million of the original $100 million left. The lawyer's way, if her estate totaled $100 million, she had to transfer ALL of it. (It had never been published as to the exact amount of her estate valuation. Estimates ran from $100 million to $200 million.) THEREFORE I WOULD NOW TAKE THE REMAINING $70 MILLION AND FOLLOW THE ATTORNEY'S ORIGINAL CHARITABLE LEAD PROGRAM AND CREATE AN ADDITIONAL $69 MILLION THUS PRODUCING A TOTAL OF $469 MILLION INSTEAD OF HER CONVENTIONAL APPROACH WHICH NETTED $98 MILLION.

There was nothing wrong with the plan her advisors intended for Jackie. It accomplished a significant benefit for her estate. But so much more could have been achieved. The use of life insurance as an alternative to investing and as an alternative to legal machinations is not commonly recognized or understood well enough for the majority of people who call themselves estate planning professionals to comprehend how best to integrate it into an overall plan of asset optimization. In most cases there is no malice involved in the advisors' failure to include life insurance; it is simply a lack of knowledge. Unfortunately, the damage done to your estate and the losses suffered by your heirs are the same whether they were engineered through malice or neglect.

At the time and since then, the plan for Jackie's estate was touted as one of the finest examples of estate planning this country had ever seen, accomplishing tremendous goals for her heirs and charity while avoiding the bulk of debilitating estate taxes. It was said that she, "left behind as much or more to the rest of us in the form of a model of smart estate planning," and that, "though not all of us may have her estimated $200 million in wealth, we can still learn from the expertise that guided her." One Florida CPA and estate planner was quoted as saying, "The will made a real impression. She wasn't just saying, 'Here are my assets.' She said why she gave them. She made plain her intent for social good in describing the charities. She passed power on to her children as trustees. You could see the thought beyond the legal verbiage, and that's what a last will and testament should ultimately reflect." But recently, new information has come to light which reveals the truth about the dangers of estate tax planning as undertaken by the traditionalists in law and accounting today. Suddenly this architectural wonderment of estate planning which had all the 'experts' so impressed is shown to be built on a foundation of expensive, flimsy paper and documents which have served no purpose.

Following is an article by David Cay Johnston which appeared in The New York Times on Saturday, December 21, 1996, detailing the sad truth about the needless difficulties this great lady's estate is suffering:

NEW YORK—Jacqueline Kennedy Onassis' estate was worth far less than was widely estimated at the time of her death, and her two children will get most of her assets, leaving very little for charity, according to the state attorney general's office.

The former first lady's executors valued her estate at $43.7 million, court documents show, though the fantastic prices some of her property brought at auction have prompted an IRS audit to determine whether its true value was closer to $73 million.

(There has been speculation and it is my belief that the auction was needed to help raise funds to pay the estate taxes. Now, as I feared and predicted would happen, the estate is being audited, something no one wants to have happen as it is expensive and ties up the estate for a long time. The use of life insurance to raise the funds to pay the taxes might well have avoided the audit while, at the same time, left her heirs with more than the IRS will.)

*

In any case, the amount falls well short of the estimates of $100 million or more in many news reports after her death in 1994. So far, less than $500,000 of the estate has gone to a nonprofit organization, the John F. Kennedy Library near Boston.

($500 thousand instead of the $150 million which was previously believed to have been going to charity.)

*

Mrs. Onassis' will left her two children valuable properties, ranging from a Martha's Vineyard retreat to stocks. But is also gave them the option of letting some or all of these properties pass to a charitable trust, which would have made annual donations to charities for 24 years and then dissolved, passing the money on to Mrs. Onassis' grandchildren.

The devise of the charitable trust was essentially a way for Mrs. Onassis' children, Caroline Kennedy Schlossberg and John F. Kennedy Jr., to allow some of her assets to pass to her grandchildren without paying estate taxes. But there was no requirement in the will that any money go to the trust, and the children have apparently determined that it makes more financial sense for them to pay the estate taxes and invest the balance.

(So they have determined that it makes more financial sense to pay the estate taxes than to shelter the money in the charitable trust. This is tragic when you consider that the device of life insurance has been available all along, without the need of lawyers or advisors, to pay the estate tax for them. This expensive, involved trust has been conceived and, ultimately, its value has been discarded. So now Caroline and John Jr. will pay the taxes out of the estate assets and then reinvest the depleted balance in the hopes of building it back up for the sake of their children, the grandchildren the trust method sought to benefit. If the estate is $43.7 million, estate taxes could take up to $24 million, leaving $19.7 million which Caroline and John Jr. must somehow build back into $43.7 AND then protect from estate taxes as it passes to their heirs. Meanwhile, a single outlay of $4 million for insurance could have produced the entire needed $24 million, based on age 60 and current assumptions. If the estate is worth the $73 million the IRS suspects, the estate taxes which they have determined it makes more sense to pay, could be as much as about $40 million, leaving $33 million. In that case, it would have taken an outlay of only $6.6 million plus gift tax to protect the entire estate.)

*

The trust would have been called the C&J Foundation, after the first initials of the children.

Mrs. Onassis' executors have told the state that after distributing the property that the children decided to keep, making specific bequests and paying administrative expenses, the estate has $18 million, but owes $23 million in estate taxes.

"Given the administrative expenses and the taxes and the consequences of the choices of the children, there will not be a residuary to create the C&J Foundation," said Jennifer Farina, a spokesman for Attorney General Dennis Vacco.

The $5 million shortfall—which the children are liable for—almost certainly means that "there will not be a C&J Foundation," said Sean Delaney, chief of the attorney general's charities bureau.

(—), one of the executors, confirmed that Mrs. Onassis' charitable lead annuity trust does not exist, though he would not rule out the possibility that it might still be created.

(The trust which was held up as THE measure of successful estate planning does not exist and the children are faced with a $5 million shortfall between their assets and the estate taxes owed so far. This is the tragic and completely avoidable result of conventional estate planning in America today. How amazing. What a tragedy. This is so unnecessary.)

*

Many publications and outside analysts had assumed that Mrs. Onassis' real estate and personal property would go to her children and that the remainder of her estate would go to the charitable trust. Based on estimates that the estate would be worth $100 million or more, there was widespread speculation that charities would receive as much as $192 million and the grandchildren would inherit perhaps $98 million in 2018, when the trust was to have dissolved.

Many publications cited the charitable trust feature in Mrs. Onassis' will as a shrewd way to reduce estate taxes while passing money on to the grandchildren. Fortune magazine called her will "a model of smart estate planning."

(These are the same articles and publications which you may have been relying upon to help direct the course of your estate planning. Certainly there was no intention to misinform you, but, nonetheless, I can not help but wonder how many people, based on the support of those articles, chose to undertake involved legal directions in their estate planning and are now faced with similar failures of those methods.)

*

Many of the properties that the Kennedy children decided to keep were auctioned last April by Sotheby's for $34.5 million. Earlier, those items were valued at less than $6 million, according to an informal accounting document made available to (a prestigious newspaper).

(One of the executors) said that he was unwilling to discuss specific amounts involving the estate, but did observe that "if you have an estate where the residuary bequest exceeds the amount in the estate, then you would not have a residuary with which to create the foundation."

The charitable donations already made consisted of property that the Kennedy children renounced, which under the terms of the will meant the property was then donated to the Kennedy library. The 11-page list of items, including a copy of the Warren report on the assassination of their father, was valued at $449,000, according to the informal accounting report.

So there you have it. It is not my doing and I certainly take no joy in having my predictions verified at the expense of this great lady and her family. But perhaps this needless financial tragedy can become Jackie's last gift to America. If the drama of this story will help others to avoid the same mistakes then good can come of it still.

Ultimately, of course, as we discussed above in regards to the Neil Simon story, the responsibility for making decisions regarding your estate planning is *yours*. Obviously, if you are never given the information about all the alternatives, you can't make a fully informed choice and it is then, I believe, mostly a failure of your advisors who have not offered up all the options fairly and comprehensively.

But many times a client comes to me and goes through the whole proposal and exam process, admits a great need for the insurance, becomes excited by the outcomes we show them they can achieve and acknowledges the value insurance has as an estate planning tool. Then, they go home, present the plan to their lawyer or accountant, someone who can not be considered to be an expert in the field of insurance, and allows that attorney or accountant to dissuade them from doing what they have said they believed was the right thing to do. In those instances the ultimate blame for the tragedy of estate devastation which will almost assuredly occur must be shared by both the not-so-expert-experts AND the clients who allow their own better judgment to be compromised. While I felt very badly for Mr. B's daughter from the example above, I found myself getting at angry at Mr. B for having so needlessly put her through such turmoil and anguish.

The bottom line is the bottom line. Yet time after time I talk to people who have decided against utilizing an insurance policy to protect their estates despite the fact that they tell me they understand and agree with what I am telling them. When I press them for some explanation into why they are then choosing not to implement the program, they can't even really tell me other than to say that it is on the advice of their attorney or accountant or tax advisor. What a sad thing that is. People whose opportunity to take advantage of these programs diminishes every month and every year wind up subverting their own belief in what is best for them and their families because some less-knowledgeable advisor told them to.

Jackie, the most admired, the best planned, the one person with the most access, working with one of the best law firms, utilizing one of the most sophisticated plans, acclaimed as the epitome of estate plan-ning—a dismal failure! What a difference one insurance policy would have made.

PART THREE

Incomparable Comparisons

INSURANCE VS BANKS

As part of the myth against life insurance, people tell me that my concepts are only of value if they die. And though they know they will die, they have an aversion to undertaking a financial course which is best the sooner they pass away. Maybe it's superstition. Maybe they think if they avoid making plans for the inevitable outcome of mortality, they will somehow escape its notice. Unfortunately it doesn't work that way. Death finds us all sooner or later and about the only say we have in the manner is whether we are caught prepared or not. You are going to die whether you buy life insurance or not.

This is the primary need for life insurance as a crucial and central part of a diversified financial portfolio. Its unique properties, properly structured, make it superbly suited to the task of preparing for the inevitability of death. No investment can accomplish what life insurance does for financial optimization and estate preservation in the face of an uncertain future.

But even many of those people who concede the point that nothing functions as insurance does to create and protect wealth still have the misconception that its value is only excellent if you die early. Insurance's value to your heirs if you were to die tomorrow is incontrovertible. NOTHING will produce the returns insurance will the very day after it is purchased. And since any of us could die tomorrow it seems clear to me that insurance is a MUST. But there is a more important fact being overlooked here.

The fact is, insurance is not only a good buy if you die soon. In the concept entitled "The Most Incredible Policy Of Them All," I showed you how cash values built up in a policy through over-funding can reap

217

an unbelievable return of up to $1 billion in fact. **This is the first time that 'life insurance' and '$1 billion' have been seriously mentioned in the same breath within my industry.** In that example, the longer the policy holder lived the greater the cash values that the policy built up and the higher the death benefit those cash values would fund.

Although that example was exceptionally dramatic because of the extreme over funding that occurred in order to fully guarantee the policy, all properly structured insurance policies build up cash values. You never want to utilize a policy that is so thin, so cut to the margin in terms of premium and return, that it could collapse. Those cash values, though not an investment or a savings plan, function in much the same way; they can be borrowed against or even withdrawn from the policy. Which means that the value of the policy is NOT only vested in the short term 'hope' for an early death to best take advantage of the death benefit. The fact of the matter is, insurance compares extremely favorably throughout the course of your life against practically any bank or savings institution which holds people's money and returns them a profit in the form of earned interest. In fact, an insurance policy completely surpasses the bank return in value because it not only builds up this cash value which is closely equivalent with the performance of savings in a bank, but it also always has available the highly optimized death benefit against the eventual inevitability of your family's need of it.

Look at the five pages of charts on pages 220–224. They detail the course money takes when placed into a savings account versus being used to purchase insurance. The results of the comparison are very important.

As you can see, in the beginning the savings account is worth more than the insurance policy. $1.05 million in the bank equates to a little over $800 thousand in the policy. While you're alive. However, please don't neglect to fully consider the meaning of the far right column. While the bank is about $250 thousand ahead of the insurance policy with you alive, should tragedy strike, the policy would immediately optimize and become worth $5.8 million more than the savings account. You CAN NOT discount this advantage as the possibility of tragedy is unfortunately all too real. Where else could you put $250 thousand and have it become worth $5.8 million if need be?

Look how closely the insurance policy keeps pace with the savings account through the twelfth year. The gap between cash value and compounded savings gets narrower and narrower. Yet the ONLY growth the savings offer is the interest while the insurance continues to have in reserve in the background a $6.85 million death benefit. Would you really prefer and consider more valuable an additional $14 thousand—$176 thousand over a $6.85 million death benefit?

Now look at year thirteen. The insurance policy cash values have SURPASSED the compounded savings. Suddenly this financial vehicle which has been held to be only of value if the insured dies early on has surpassed the performance of a conventional savings account investment. The policy has developed higher cash values than the savings account has earned interest. AND the policy STILL has that $6.8 million death benefit waiting in reserve for the day it is needed.

By year twenty the policy has over $200 thousand more in cash values than the savings account has earned. And the $6.85 million remains in reserve.

The policy continues to surpass the savings account through the thirty-second year by which time the owner is 92 years old. Do you think consideration of that death benefit might be in order now? The savings account contains about $4.76 million while the policy only has $4.75 million. But the policy still has the $6.85 million death benefit which, at age 92, has to be something the owner is thinking about.

Only if the owner lives to be 100 does the savings account surpass the insurance death benefit and then only by about $150 thousand. Is that extra $150 thousand worth running the risk that you don't make it to 100? At virtually any lesser age the death benefit of the insurance policy is greater than the amount in savings.

And now here's something that I hope will really make you understand the phenomenal nature of the Investment Alternative methods. To be truly accurate, you must go back to the chart and the model and cut all the savings account numbers in half.

As long as the funds held in the savings account remain within the estate of the owner, they will be subject to estate taxes as they pass on to his or her heirs. Those estate taxes will reduce them by as much of 55%. So the $7 million accrued in the savings account by year 40 will be reduced by about half to $3.5 million while the death benefit proceeds from the insurance, if they have been properly structured within an Irrevocable Trust or are owned by the children, will come to the heirs

BANK VS. INSURANCE POLICY

The Power of Compound Interest and The Investment Alternative

Age 60	**Bank**	**Insurance**			
		Plan 1		Plan 2	
Year	**Life or Death at 5% Tax Free**	**In Life Cash Value**	**At Death Policy Pays**	**In Life Cash Value**	**At Death Policy Pa**
1	1,050,000	801,322	6,850,000	735,288	8,748,21
2	1,102,500	882,554	6,850,000	820,213	8,748,21
3	1,157,625	959,930	6,850,000	898,906	8,748,21
4	1,215,506	1,039,126	6,850,000	978,443	8,748,21
5	1,276,281	1,120,336	6,850,000	1,058,949	8,748,21
6	1,340,095	1,209,246	6,850,000	1,147,469	8,748,21
7	1,407,100	1,289,812	6,850,000	1,223,353	8,748,21
8	1,477,455	1,380,916	6,850,000	1,310,751	8,748,21
9	1,551,328	1,470,459	6,850,000	1,394,178	8,748,21
10	1,628,894	1,572,504	6,850,000	1,491,457	8,748,21
11	1,710,339	1,678,048	6,850,000	1,590,692	8,748,21
12	1,795,856	1,781,194	6,850,000	1,684,212	8,748,21
13	1,885,649	1,895,409	6,850,000	1,788,932	8,748,21
14	1,979,931	2,014,234	6,850,000	1,896,362	8,748,21
15	2,078,928	2,138,682	6,850,000	2,007,607	8,748,21
16	2,182,874	2,268,654	6,850,000	2,122,188	8,748,21
17	2,292,018	2,403,264	6,850,000	2,238,416	8,748,21
18	2,406,619	2,549,930	6,850,000	2,365,379	8,748,21
19	2,526,950	2,694,646	6,850,000	2,484,579	8,748,21
20	2,653,297	2,881,304	6,850,000	2,613,144	8,748,21

Bank money usually in estate and cut in half at death by estate taxes.
Investment Alternative usually out of estate and tax free.

*All figures are based on current assumptions.

BANK VS. INSURANCE POLICY

The Power of Compound Interest and The Investment Alternative

ge 60	**Bank**	**Insurance**			
		Plan 1		**Plan 2**	
Year	**Life or Death at 5% Tax Free**	**In Life Cash Value**	**At Death Policy Pays**	**In Life Cash Value**	**At Death Policy Pays**
21	2,785,962	2,990,835	6,850,000	2,712,755	8,748,212
22	2,925,260	3,133,599	6,850,000	2,808,358	8,748,212
23	3,071,523	3,279,170	6,850,000	2,898,055	8,748,212
24	3,225,099	3,428,864	6,850,000	2,982,514	8,748,212
25	3,386,354	3,582,103	6,850,000	3,059,060	8,748,212
26	3,555,672	3,738,796	6,850,000	3,125,381	8,748,212
27	3,733,456	3,898,716	6,850,000	3,178,395	8,748,212
28	3,920,129	4,062,389	6,850,000	3,215,679	8,748,212
29	4,116,135	4,228,497	6,850,000	3,230,368	8,748,212
30	4,321,942	4,397,874	6,850,000	3,218,402	8,748,212
31	4,538,039	4,571,741	6,850,000	3,175,111	8,748,212
32	4,764,941	4,751,514	6,850,000	3,094,433	8,748,212
33	5,003,188	4,939,593	6,850,000	2,970,299	8,748,212
34	5,253,347	5,139,148	6,850,000	2,795,969	8,748,212
35	5,516,015	5,353,664	6,850,000	2,562,022	8,748,212
36	5,791,816	5,587,795	6,850,000	2,258,057	8,748,212
37	6,081,406	5,847,024	6,850,000	1,870,452	8,748,212
38	6,385,477	6,137,912	6,850,000	1,380,981	8,748,212
39	6,704,751	6,468,894	6,850,000	768,039	8,748,212
40	7,039,988	6,850,386	6,850,000	2,973	8,748,212

Bank money usually in estate and cut in half at death by estate taxes.
Investment Alternative usually out of estate and tax free.

*All figures are based on current assumptions.

BANK VS. INSURANCE POLICY

The Power of Compound Interest and The Investment Alternative

Age 70	Bank	Insurance			
		Plan 1		Plan 2	
Year	Life or Death at 5% Tax Free	In Life Cash Value	At Death Policy Pays	In Life Cash Value	At Death Policy
1	1,050,000	816,609	3,970,000	745,758	5,247,
2	1,102,500	890,494	3,970,000	820,883	5,247,
3	1,157,625	958,198	3,970,000	885,522	5,247,
4	1,215,506	1,026,735	3,970,000	948,540	5,247,
5	1,276,281	1,099,371	3,970,000	1,014,980	5,247,
6	1,340,095	1,172,435	3,970,000	1,079,844	5,247,
7	1,407,100	1,251,545	3,970,000	1,150,403	5,247,
8	1,477,455	1,331,552	3,970,000	1,219,686	5,247,
9	1,551,328	1,420,747	3,970,000	1,298,472	5,247.
10	1,628,894	1,511,568	3,970,000	1,376,576	5,247
11	1,710,339	1,607,745	3,970,000	1,457,491	5,247
12	1,795,856	1,701,769	3,970,000	1,530,806	5,247
13	1,885,649	1,798,086	3,970,000	1,601,839	5,247
14	1,979,931	1,901,126	3,970,000	1,675,796	5,247.
15	2,078,928	2,002,654	3,970,000	1,740,700	5,247.
16	2,182,874	2,106,198	3,970,000	1,797,886	5,247
17	2,292,018	2,211,199	3,970,000	1,846,381	5,247
18	2,406,619	2,321,964	3,970,000	1,889,978	5,247
19	2,526,950	2,435,053	3,970,000	1,921,896	5,247
20	2,653,297	2,555,177	3,970,000	1,945,714	5,247

Bank money usually in estate and cut in half at death by estate taxes.
Investment Alternative usually out of estate and tax free.

*All figures are based on current assumptions.

©1997 The Investment Alternative - Barry Kaye Associates

BANK VS. INSURANCE POLICY

The Power of Compound Interest and The Investment Alternative

	Bank			**Insurance**	
ge 70			Plan 1		Plan 2
Year	Life or Death at 5% Tax Free	In Life Cash Value	At Death Policy Pays	In Life Cash Value	At Death Policy Pays
21	2,785,962	2,657,511	3,970,000	1,923,496	5,247,211
22	2,925,260	2,762,872	3,970,000	1,877,989	5,247,211
23	3,071,523	2,872,706	3,970,000	1,805,473	5,247,211
24	3,225,099	2,988,922	3,970,000	1,701,798	5,247,211
25	3,386,354	3,113,659	3,970,000	1,561,254	5,247,211
26	3,555,672	3,249,728	3,970,000	1,377,480	5,247,211
27	3,733,456	3,400,441	3,970,000	1,142,118	5,247,211
28	3,920,129	3,569,757	3,970,000	844,012	5,247,211
29	4,116,135	3,762,744	3,970,000	469,887	5,247,211
30	4,321,942	3,985,644	3,985,644	2,039	5,247,211

Bank money usually in estate and cut in half at death by estate taxes.
Investment Alternative usually out of estate and tax free.

*All figures are based on current assumptions.

BANK VS. INSURANCE POLICY

The Power of Compound Interest and The Investment Alternative

Age 80	**Bank**	**Insurance**			
		Plan 1		Plan 2	
Year	**Life or Death at 5% Tax Free**	**In Life Cash Value**	**At Death Policy Pays**	**In Life Cash Value**	**At Death Policy Pay**
1	1,050,000	894,963	2,420,000	829,158	3,571,408
2	1,102,500	947,139	2,420,000	864,929	3,571,408
3	1,157,625	1,000,180	2,420,000	897,458	3,571,408
4	1,215,506	1,059,366	2,420,000	935,124	3,571,408
5	1,276,281	1,117,756	2,420,000	967,350	3,571,40
6	1,340,095	1,178,119	2,420,000	997,852	3,571,40
7	1,407,100	1,242,804	2,420,000	1,029,702	3,571,40
8	1,477,455	1,310,003	2,420,000	1,059,796	3,571,40
9	1,551,328	1,381,860	2,420,000	1,090,247	3,571,40
10	1,628,894	1,457,781	2,420,000	1,118,460	3,571,40
11	1,710,339	1,534,425	2,420,000	1,133,984	3,571,40
12	1,795,856	1,612,437	2,420,000	1,134,945	3,571,40
13	1,885,649	1,692,242	2,420,000	1,117,847	3,571,40
14	1,979,931	1,774,536	2,420,000	1,078,439	3,571,40
15	2,078,928	1,861,133	2,420,000	1,014,615	3,571,40
16	2,182,874	1,950,085	2,420,000	904,634	3,571,40
17	2,292,018	2,049,255	2,420,000	758,590	3,571,40
18	2,406,619	2,156,666	2,420,000	562,152	3,571,40
19	2,526,950	2,290,272	2,420,000	327,764	3,571,40
20	2,653,297	2,425,172	2,425,173	1,209	3,571,40

Bank money usually in estate and cut in half at death by estate taxes.
Investment Alternative usually out of estate and tax free.

*All figures are based on current assumptions.

©1997 The Investment Alternative - Barry Kaye Associates

income and estate tax free. Pick any year and do the math. The results are unarguable. In every way and every sense, the life insurance out performs the safe, conservative, solid financial vehicle of a bank savings account. Insurance is NOT something which only has value if you die right away; its value extends throughout your life in cash values that accrue and in the highly optimized, tax free death benefits it keeps available until your coin is tossed and falls tails up.

INSURANCE VS THE 12 "COOKIE CUTTER" LEGAL PROGRAMS

The Final Test—The Bottom Line

Following are 12 'cookie cutter' trusts and applications universally used by attorneys to accommodate their clients' estate tax problems. In most instances, these are legally approved methods of tax avoidance. However, they are expensive and often do not accomplish the desired goal. While they may be applicable at the time of inception, changes in clients' portfolios may negate the whole original purpose, as we saw in the tragic Jacqueline Kennedy Onassis example described earlier.

While these plans are "cookie cutter" in nature, each following a proscribed legal formula for their consummation, a good attorney can apply various twists and combinations to accomplish the most advantageous way of reducing taxes for your estate.

However, in almost every instance, these plans can do nothing more than reduce your estate thereby *reducing* your estate taxes. In many cases they are obviously legal avoidance approaches that have nothing to do with the economics of your situation or your real intentions, but only serve the purpose of doing anything necessary to reduce your estate taxes. **AT NO TIME DO THESE PLANS ALSO OPTIMIZE YOUR ASSETS**. Only life insurance can both reduce your estate tax costs and optimize your assets at the same time without any complex, convoluted program of charitable giving, which is being implemented only for the purposes of saving taxes and not to accomplish your real end purpose of reducing taxes and optimizing assets.

More and more clients have utilized Charitable Remainder and Charitable Lead Trusts or have even established Charitable Foundations, in order to avoid estate taxes. They have done this **ONLY** and **SIMPLY** in order to save estate taxes even though they really had only minimal or no charitable intentions. More importantly, most ultimately discovered that their plan didn't increase or replace the assets used to pay any remaining estate taxes.

I have stated earlier and re-state now, that any rhetoric from an attorney, an insurance man or a financial planner should be overlooked in favor of your going to the actual bottom line of each concept to see which program is best for you, produces the most for your heirs and reduces the estate taxes the most efficiently.

In this chapter, you will see each "cookie cutter" plan illustrated versus the Investment Alternative approach. I believe that after you see this, no more 'rhetoric' will be necessary. The numbers will be obvious and you can go to the bottom line and do what is best for your specific family situation.

I also believe that all people with large businesses and substantial estates achieved their success with common sense, logic and gut feelings as well as a steady eye to the bottom line. Why, when you reach your 60's, 70's or 80's, after following this intelligent approach all your life relative to building your assets, would you change your techniques, listen to things you don't really understand and completely overlook what the bottom line says when it comes to preserving and optimizing those hard-earned assets?

Don't do anything until you have implemented the programs that are best for your heirs in accordance with the bottom line. You will have found, by the end of this chapter, that in almost every instance, the smartest, least expensive, and most effective method of paying your estate taxes will be by utilizing the discount method of the Investment Alternative, funded with ordinary universal life insurance policies. The ordinary really becomes quite extraordinary after you understand this material. Only after the point where you achieve that understanding will it become imperative that you consult with your attorney, since there will be no additional methods necessary beyond creating the maximum exemption applicable in your situation, based on all of the above mentioned variables. Then and only then should you be visiting your attorney for all of the legal documents necessary to implement any of these plans. Only an attorney specializing in this subject should be utilized to draw up the Irrevocable Trust, your wills, special trusts and other necessary tax saving devices. But those devices will only be necessary after you have completely maximized your exemptions or 'bought' the additional exemptions your estate planning requires.

Remember, each additional exemption, after you have used your original $600 thousand (or yours and your spouse's combined $1.2 million) only costs approximately $300 thousand. So, to buy a $10 million exemption, to cover a $10 million estate, after you have utilized both exemptions you would simply pay $500 thousand in gift taxes on a $1 million premium, depending upon your ages, to an insurance company to create $5 million of life insurance death benefit so that the insurance company can effectively pay the $5 million taxes on your $10 million estate.

In this manner, instead of the children paying $5 million in estate taxes, you will have paid only $250 thousand net in gift taxes since the $500 thousand cost to buy the exemption comes from within your estate and in almost every case is effectively tax deductible thereby reducing it by half to $250 thousand.

Read on and be amazed as estate planning as we have always known it takes an incredible change for the benefit of all taxpayers in America. This new technique will provide a method of eliminating "cookie cutter" legal tax avoidance strategies and simply allow the life insurance company to pay the estate taxes for you without any tax avoidance to the detriment of other American taxpayers.

1. USE YOUR $600 THOUSAND—$1.2 MILLION IF MARRIED—EXEMPTIONS now or at death.

Many people hold them until death as if they were something sacred. They do not realize the advantage of using them during their lifetime in order to get any increasing asset out of their estate. By waiting until death the asset continues to appreciate inside the estate and, in all probability, will be substantially larger at death and therefore exceed the $600 thousand exemption at that time.

Your attorney will usually recommend that you use one of the upcoming 11 plans at least to the extent of your exemptions, if you can afford the cash flow impairment, in order to stop the appreciation inside your estate, thus helping to reduce the eventual estate taxes.

While each plan will speak for itself, the main purpose of the above action is to get the most and largest appreciating asset out of your estate for the maximum leverage. Depending on your age(s), it probably will be a 10–1, 5–1 or 3–1 life insurance policy. This means that any other asset transferred will only be worth $600 thousand or $1.2 million, or slightly more, while the life insurance policy can be worth $1.8 million to $12 million from the first day of the transfer. How long do you think it will take your $600 thousand exemptions to increase to $12 million? Obviously the bottom line should prove to you that the largest appreciating asset that should come out of your estate will be any insurance policy you buy.

One more point. If you like the above leverage, you can buy as many additional exemptions as you want by simply paying approximately $300 thousand gift tax for each. In this manner you can buy as much life insurance to the maximum allowable until you have increased your exemption beyond your assets. There will be no estate taxes to be paid beyond your exemptions since the insurance company will have effectively paid the taxes for you. The bottom line will prove you only paid an effective tax deductible gift tax on the insurance purchased. Furthermore you only effectively paid 1/3 to 1/10 of the original estate tax.

2. REVOCABLE LIVING TRUSTS AND WILLS are recommended in many cases. This excellent trust will provide an avoidance of any probate fees, and help protect your heirs and estate from any publicity about your personal matters. This will also act as a will relative to the disposition of your assets and determine how you wish to be treated in case of extreme death threatening health problems. It is also an excellent method of handling any $600 thousand exemptions that have been retained.

*Be careful. The above is approximately **all** your living trust will do. It* _**does not** shelter your assets from estate taxes beyond your $600 thousand exemptions as many think. Since it is revocable, your assets are not considered to be out of your estate until your death(s), at which time they will be subject to the full decimation of estate taxes._

3. IRREVOCABLE TRUSTS are the best way to transfer assets out of your estate. These are used to hold the assets you gift to your heirs in accordance with your instructions, called indentures, at the origination of your trust. This trust can be used to hold any life insurance policies outside your estate and will assure that your death benefit proceeds will be completely estate tax free.

The same estate tax free protection is afforded your children if your assets or gifts to buy insurance are given directly to them. There is absolutely no advantage if they are held in an Irrevocable Trust other than the control offered at the inception of the trust. The tax results are the same. You should use whichever serves your purpose better. Remember, the bottom line will prove that 5 unfunded Irrevocable Trusts will only provide good reading at death compared to the money provided from one in-force life insurance policy.

Too often the Irrevocable Trust is emphasized as being the most important first step in estate planning, prior to the policy purchase. The bottom line will prove that a finalized trust with no insurance due to long delays, procrastination, and the emphasis in the wrong place will never compare with a completed life insurance policy ready to pay off in case of premature death or any change in your health prior to completion of your policy. Why pay expensive legal fees to set up a trust before you know if you are insurable?

4. CHARITABLE REMAINDER TRUSTS are excellent ways to effectively receive a stepped up basis in your lifetime, avoid all capital gains tax, receive a 50% increase in your income and avoid all estate tax while giving a part of your assets to charity. Since this usually is excellent for the charity and your personal income tax and estate tax situation, it is currently a very popular technique for estate planning. The drawback however, is absolutely devastating to your heirs since, once you've given your money away to charity, they do not receive even the after tax proceeds they would have had you just left your estate alone and let it be diminished by estate taxes. While a portion of this loss is often made up by using the tax savings on the charitable donation and/or some other funds from the donor to purchase a life insurance policy, doing so only recovers the loss. It does not maximize the estate for the benefit of the heirs. The charity receives whatever remains in the trust at the death(s) of the donor.

While this is an excellent plan, I have rarely found that this is a charitable move by the donor. It is almost exclusively done for the tax advantages involved with little or no real intention of being charitable. While it serves its purpose, it is an excellent example of using an expensive, convoluted plan to legally avoid estate taxes that is not as efficient as a much simpler plan to pay the estate taxes and maximize the heir's inheritance. If someone is really interested in giving to charity, increasing their income and avoiding estate taxes while still taking care of their heirs, there can be better arrangements as the bottom line will prove.

This plan depends on the age of the donors. I usually find them to be in their late 70s or 80s. At those ages, they could very effectively use an Investment Alternative approach where they sell their property, pay the capital gains tax and purchase an Immediate Annuity. In spite of the tax that has been paid, they will possibly still receive more net income than the CRT will provide depending upon their age(s). This net excess income can be used to purchase a life insurance policy in excess of what the CRT produced for their heirs and they could use the remaining income to increase their own, boost what they leave their heirs or even give it to charity to purchase a life insurance policy on them to be paid at their deaths, the same as the CRT, if they were really inclined. This plan will only work in certain situations and the bottom line will prove when. Remember, any reduction in the capital gains tax—something Congress constantly promises—will be devastating to the donor who wasn't really charitably inclined in the first place.

5. CHARITABLE LEAD TRUSTS are a variation on the charitable remainder trust described above. In this arrangement the income goes to charity for a prescribed number of years and the remainder goes to your heirs with a great discount in the taxes that must be paid. If the income is not needed, this is an excellent devise for reducing taxes even if the donor is not charitable.

But be careful. Any change in your estate composition can cause a disaster. This is particularly true if this plan is offered as a specific solution to reducing estate taxes in lieu of any other. A false sense of security can develop. No further planning is arranged and other steps utilizing an Alternative Investment approach are precluded that might have avoided this horror story.

This may be best illustrated in the case of Jacqueline Kennedy Onassis. As stated earlier, when the estate was settled it was found that there wasn't enough left after taxes to fund the carefully, cleverly drawn, estate plan which had received such accolades. The heirs felt that they would be better off if they paid the estate taxes. Isn't this exactly what the taxpayer Jackie was trying to legally avoid? Can you see the difference in the final execution of her wishes if one simple life insurance policy was in place to pay the taxes? If the plan had only been executed on a timely basis, in anticipation of her eventual death, instead of as a last minute necessity, the difference of the bottom line would have been monumental.

Why wasn't there life insurance in place to cover the contingency of a premature death? They occur all the time. No mortality table of how long she should have lived is of financial solace to her family. Would an auction have been necessary if one insurance policy had been in place? Would that life insurance policy have precluded the costly audit that has now ensued? What would the discount have been on the taxes paid using this Investment Alternative technique for the family? Couldn't she easily have afforded the reallocation of assets necessary to secure this policy? Was there no advisor available for a person of her standing and asset level to explain the value of insurance? When will the insanity stop? The bottom line for what happened is devastating. If they could only go back, what a difference it might be!

6. GENERATION SKIPPING TRUSTS are an excellent method for wealthy people to pass their wealth on to their family legally in the most tax advantaged way possible. Once transferred to such a trust, the assets can escape further estate taxes for possibly 100 years. This is a method of taking great sums out of your estate for the benefit of your grandchildren before they appreciate substantially. The government allows each taxpayer to transfer up to $1 million to a generation skipping trust without the onerous, flat 55% generation skipping tax that must be paid on such a transfer. In this manner a married couple could take advantage of both of their exemptions resulting in a $2 million generation skipping tax free transfer.

This is often combined with other techniques described above for maximum tax advantage. Such was the case of Jacqueline Kennedy Onassis who attempted to use a Generation Skipping Charitable Lead Trust.

If this is such a tremendous technique for tax advantaged transfers, which it is, why would you settle for only a $1 million or $2 million exemption? The same Investment Alternative approach that was used to increase your $600 thousand exemptions can be applied here. Why settle for $1 or $2 million out of your estate when you can take $50 million to $100 million out using my formula? This is described earlier in detail; basically you would buy a last to die policy on you and your spouse and, depending on your ages, effectively increase your exemptions up to 10 fold or $20 million.

For maximum leverage, you would purchase the same type policy on your children for the benefit of your grandchildren. If your children are between the ages of 30 and 40 you will be able to increase the value of your exemptions up to 50 times. This means two exemptions could total $100 million, from the first day of execution! Even at age 50, two exemptions can be increased to $40 million. Is there any question at the bottom line?

7. GRITS, GRATS, AND GRUTS are not cereals or sounds in the night. They are excellent estate planning tools when used by knowledgable attorneys. A GRAT is a Grantor-Retained Annuity Trust. The grantor transfers assets into the trust. He retains the right to annual payments of a fixed amount of principal and interest for a prescribed number of years. At the end of the period the assets go to your beneficiary in accordance with your original intentions.

A GRUT is a Grantor-Retained Unitrust. It is similar to the GRAT described above. The only real difference is that the grantor receives a fixed percentage of the trust's assets each year rather than a predetermined annuity. Both GRATS and GRUTS allow you to transfer assets at a significant gift tax discount. As long as you survive the term of the trust, the potentially-increasing value of the assets transferred are out of your estate and therefore avoid estate taxes.

Similar instruments are used in Charitable Remainder Trusts called CRATS and CRUTS. Using just one example of a GRAT, a client receives a recommendation to transfer $1 million to a GRAT in order to remove principal and future appreciation from his estate. The government assesses the value of the $1 million asset at less than $600 thousand. This provides a 40% discount on the gift and therefore saves an approximate 50% tax on the $400 thousand. This amounts to a savings of $200 thousand in gift tax. If the property appreciated 10% a year, it would be worth $2 million in 7 years and $4 million in 14 years at age 84, it the client started the program at age 70. This is only one example but it does give you an idea of how this and similar cookie cutter concepts work.

This may be better than an outright gift of the asset but we are not looking for what is better. We are looking for what is best. That is the true meaning of the bottom line. You must also consider the costs associated with this technique. They include set-up and administration expenses, attorney fees, property title costs, accounting fees, appraisal fees, and trustee's fees. Furthermore you lose potential opportunity and control of the asset and there is always a possibility of your death prior to the end of the term thus causing your asset to go back into your estate and be exposed to estate taxes once again. Sometimes insurance is suggested just to offset that possibility.

If you used the Investment Alternative concept in lieu of the GRAT or GRUT the results would be as follows. You could have transferred only $600 thousand out of your estate leaving $400 thousand to be exposed to an eventual estate tax or gift tax of approximately $200 thousand.

This could be covered with a one payment life insurance policy at a cost of $40 thousand with an ultimate net cost of $20 thousand. In other words, for a net cost of only $20 thousand you could cover the tax on the extra tax free asset value you removed from your estate. If you used the entire $1 million, at a net gift tax cost of only $20 thousand, you could purchase a last to die policy with a death benefit of approximately $5 million, or at combined age 60, $10 million. This would be effective immediately instead of starting at $1 million and waiting for it to eventually, if you're lucky enough for 'eventually' to come, be worth $4 million.

The above approach would eliminate the income you would have received. This proves once again that ONE SIZE DOESN'T FIT ALL. You must determine which bottom line is best for you depending on whether your objective is to save gift taxes, save estate taxes, produce income for you for a limited number of years, optimize greatly what you give your heirs or avoid appreciation on an ever increasing asset. It seems to me that the usual purpose of this plan is to get the most out of your estate, at the least tax cost, and obviously $5 to $10 million out of your estate is better than $1 million, even at an extra cost of $20 thousand.

8. QPRT IS A QUALIFIED PERSONAL RESIDENCE TRUST VERY SIMILAR TO A GRIT, A GRANTOR RETAINED INCOME TRUST. This is a plan which is described earlier in the book. It has been heralded as an excellent and outstanding method of reducing smaller estates where your home is a major asset. The house is given to your children in a QPR Trust. They agree that you can live there for a negotiated period of years after which the house belongs to them. Since they will not receive the actual gift for many years it is appraised at a great discount for the present value of the future gift. This allows a low evaluation for gift taxes and removes what may be an appreciating asset out of your estate.

While this can be an excellent plan in the right situation, it is too often written about incorrectly in the media, quoting attorneys with their own biases or lack of knowledge about superior alternatives to this cookie cutter approach. One actual comparison appears earlier. The disadvantages of this plan include the set-up and administration costs including attorney fees, appraisal fees, property titling costs, possibly real estate transfer tax and trustee fees. If you die before the term of the trust is over the home will be back in your estate and your heirs will face full-value estate taxes on it.. Furthermore, by setting up the QPRT, you also may have lost the opportunity to use a better alternative plan.

You also will lose control over your home and your spouse may not be pleased to live in a house now owned by your child's spouse. This can happen in second marriage situations with either you or your children. THIS MAY EVEN BECOME WORSE WHEN YOUR SPOUSE UNDERSTANDS THAT SHE COULD ONE DAY WIND UP RENTING HER HOME FROM HER STEP-SON'S WIFE. You also lose the stepped up basis normally available at your death.

Once again, review your objectives as they pertain to your tax situation and your emotional comfort, so you accomplish what you want, not the conventional wisdom. Once ascertained THE BOTTOM LINE WILL LEAP OUT AT YOU as illustrated. My experience has shown, in most situations, the Investment Alternative technique produces a far superior result due to the leverage of a life insurance policy, the stepped up basis and the capital gains tax, which is usually not referred to, while avoiding the worst of family discomfort and combat.

9. FAMILY LIMITED PARTNERSHIPS ARE THE LATEST VOGUE IN TAX AVOIDANCE SCHEMES. The IRS is not happy about this shelter and is threatening to reevaluate its use, but so far, they are working, though overly aggressive evaluations and discounts are being audited. The main purpose of this approach, once again with slight variation, is to transfer out of your estate $900 thousand to $1 million at a discounted evaluation of $600 thousand thus avoiding any gift tax on the additional $400 thousand transferred. The other important purpose is to remove an appreciating asset from your estate at its current discounted value and assure your heirs that any future gains in value will escape estate taxation. This is accomplished by transferring assets to a family limited partnership in return for a minority interest in the partnership. This still gives you control, but the asset is out of your estate.

In addition to the tax advantages outlined above, there is a presumption of less exposure for the assets to creditors. It is imperative that you use an attorney who is totally conversant with every aspect of this approach.

I have great concern with this technique. It really has no purpose other than tax avoidance and these are the challenges that the IRS enjoys the most. In any event, I usually find that the bottom line favors my Investment Alternative concept. The discount sounds good, but once again, the tax savings are only based on approximately $300 thousand to $400 thousand. The actual gift taxes will be between $120 thousand and $200 thousand. The net cost to offset this 'extra tax' using a life insurance policy is only approximately $12 thousand to $40 thousand depending upon your ages. This may be less than the legal fees and other administration expenses, as well as any additional legal fees, if your Partnership is challenged for any reason.

Then, there is always the appreciation of the transferred asset to consider. This really was the main purpose of the FLP. Why would you want to accomplish this convoluted plan with your assets in order to avoid paying estate taxes on your current $1 million even if it grows? Realistically, do you really expect it to double, triple or quadruple to $4 million and how soon will that occur? The Investment Alternative plan would, using the same transferred $1 million and a last to die life insurance policy, instantly produce $3 million to $10 million income and estate tax free, if necessary. Which do you want to use your exemption for immediately, removing $1 million from your estate or $10 million? Go to the bottom line. IT NEVER LIES!

10. INTERNAL REVENUE CODE SECTION 6166 is the government's method of relief for those who are not liquid and can't afford to pay the estate tax within the prescribed nine months. If you qualify, you can take advantage of it. It allows you to pay off your taxes over a 14 year period. Due to the 14 year schedule of principal and interest, it effectively doubles the tax. Based on a $10 million estate, with a $5 million tax, you would pay a total of $10 million over the 14 year period. This is sometimes offered by an accountant to his client as an excellent method of paying off the estate tax instead of purchasing a life insurance policy.

How uneducated and unknowledgable must a professional advisor be to offer this as a tax solution. If there is no other solution, under the absolute worst scenario, this may make sense. But only if it is at your option, and then appropriate. No client, advised by a professional, should be allowed to find themselves in this position. Proper planning, under the worst circumstances, should have used The Investment Alternative loan program. At age 60, a one payment last to die policy, would have cost $500 thousand based on current assumptions.

THIS MONEY COULD HAVE BEEN BORROWED. $5 million would have been available at death to pay the taxes. Is there any question that the heirs would have an easier time paying back the tax deductible $500 thousand personal loan than the $5 million non deductible government loan? Is there any question whatsoever about the bottom line? Yet, this insanity really happens.

11. PRIVATE ANNUITY is a less frequently discussed technique, but it is still being used. It is an arrangement between two parties without an insurance company. It is a method of selling a business usually to a child, grandchild or favored employee. This will remove the asset from the estate and due to the sale approach, avoid gift tax or even generation skipping transfer tax. There are other applications that must be reviewed with a skilled attorney in this area and it does lend itself to highly customized situations.

The obligation of the transferee is unsecured. You must use life insurance to guarantee the transferor in case of the transferee's premature death. There may be no alternate approach. Even in this case a look at the bottom line will prove the best method of proceeding.

12. FOUNDATIONS are usually arranged not to avoid estate taxes as much as to create an institution to handle the philanthropic

wishes of the creator of the foundation. This can facilitate the charitable intentions of the party. It can be created during his lifetime or at his death, for small estates and large. It is primarily used by the more wealthy and affluent who have no heirs or only want to leave limited amounts to named beneficiaries and the rest to charity through their own foundation. Often their children will be appointed paid trustees. Competent attorneys must be consulted in order to assure the proper implementation of these programs.

Remember, if you want to maximize contributions to these Foundations, life insurance policies can produce exceptionally large amounts at no additional cost to you. The leverage of using a life insurance policy can greatly increase the grantor's wishes in maximizing his gifts with soft dollars. It can be tax deductible during his life if the Foundation or charity is the owner of the policy from the inception. Or the grantor can maintain the ownership during his lifetime if he wishes to control the cash value equity until his death at which time it can be donated to the Foundation and avoid all estate taxes. The bottom line will always be enhanced when the leverage of life insurance is included.

Many of the above charitable approaches have been created and are used strictly for estate tax avoidance and tax savings. The above is not written to avoid charitable approaches. But I do not believe they should be used when charity is not your main objective and there are better techniques available to accomplish your real purpose of estate tax cost discounting and asset maximization using the Investment Alternative techniques.

There are many methods available for people who really wish to give to charity that will still provide them with tax advantages. Only then should these plans be implemented. In all cases always consider giving away the smaller soft dollars which can create larger dollars by using leveraged life insurance policies. In this manner you can more than satisfy your family, heirs and your philanthropic dreams, desires and wishes.

Always use an attorney who specializes in taxation when necessary to draw up the proper documentation and implementation of customized plans that are appropriate as described above. Use the best insurance expert to implement The Investment Alternative ideas. Call the accountant for consultation on your specific numbers and questions within his discipline and a trust officer for the administration of trusts. Never use an insurance man for the legal questions and decisions that only your attorney can provide. Finally, never use an attorney for the questions, comparisons and decisions relative to insurance that only a professional life insurance man can answer. Always stay within each professionals discipline for the best and most knowledgeable results.

The Moment of Truth or "How to Stay On the Forbes 400"

In my last book, _Die Rich and Tax Free_, I quoted a Forbes magazine article which stated "in short, the odds against a family staying rich are many times greater than the odds of getting rich."

Estate taxes are a financial disaster. The tragedy of cutting the fruits of a lifetime's success in half is devastating. BUT THERE IS HOPE. While the government is looking for a redistribution of your wealth, a simple reallocation of your assets can SAVE IT ALL!

In this chapter I cover 10 specific cases of people with different situations listed in the Forbes 400 issue. I will show you what recommendations I would make if they were my clients at this time. Of course, my information is limited to what has been published and is public knowledge. I know nothing of a personal nature about any one of them and am only basing what I write on already known information. You can make an analogy to your own situation by taking a % of the figures, or removing or adding a zero or two. What a waste, if nothing is done.

OPRAH WINFREY

Oprah Winfrey (42 worth $415 million) is a unique situation, and therefore interesting for my first example since she has no children or apparent blood heirs. However that doesn't preclude the possibility of her having children and grandchildren one day. Even now there may be close relatives that she has a great concern for and whom she would rather receive her hard-earned and rather incredible fortune than her Uncle Sam. Certainly there are causes she has a deep concern for and she would undoubtedly like to optimize what they receive at her death, without the government determining who gets what, and when, if anything.

If Oprah were my client I would first ascertain whether there is family, which specific individuals she wants to leave her fortune to, and how much she wants to leave each one. Any additional assets that she wishes to leave to her favorite causes, charities and her own foundation will escape, in most cases, all estate taxes. Later I will show how she can capture her wildest financial dreams for whatever purpose she desires using my Investment Alternative ideas.

For the first $100 million not going to charity but to named heirs, the estate tax will be $55 million. I would recommend she raise her $600 thousand exemption to an effective $100 million so that it completely covers the $100 million asset and therefore effectively eliminates any estate tax. This can be accomplished by her buying a $55 million policy, owned by an Irrevocable Trust for a one time premium of approximately $3 million, based on current assumptions. Assuming she had not used her $600 thousand exemption as yet, this would cost her a gift tax of approximately $1.1 million to make the entire $55 million tax free. She could pay for this on an annual basis, if she wished, for approximately $210 thousand a year plus gift tax.

Her Investment Alternative approach with an insurance policy would have used $3 million to produce $55 million and the insurance company would have effectively paid the estate tax.

In this manner she has reduced her estate tax on $100 million from $55 million to the only tax she will effectively pay which is only a net gift tax of approximately $495 thousand. While it is highly unlikely that anything would happen at her young age, I would want her completely prepared for any unforeseen accident or change of health. I believe that anything less would be unprofessional and constitute malpractice.

If she has a cause or charity that is so meaningful to her, she could maximize any gift she wants to leave to them with 'soft' tax deductible dollars. A single payment of about $593 thousand will buy $10 million based on current assumptions. This can be given immediately to her charity or own foundation and so be completely tax deductible. Or she can retain the control and cash value equity of the policy and give it at her death thus avoiding any estate taxes. Most importantly, she would have created $10 million at a net cost of only $267 thousand for each cause she was interested in. It also could have been financed at a cost of $50 thousand a year, which is fully tax deductible as a charitable donation and so is really a net cost of only $25 thousand a year, for the entire $10 million. What a turn on; what satisfaction, what a lifetime accomplishment for Investment Alternative pennies on the dollar!

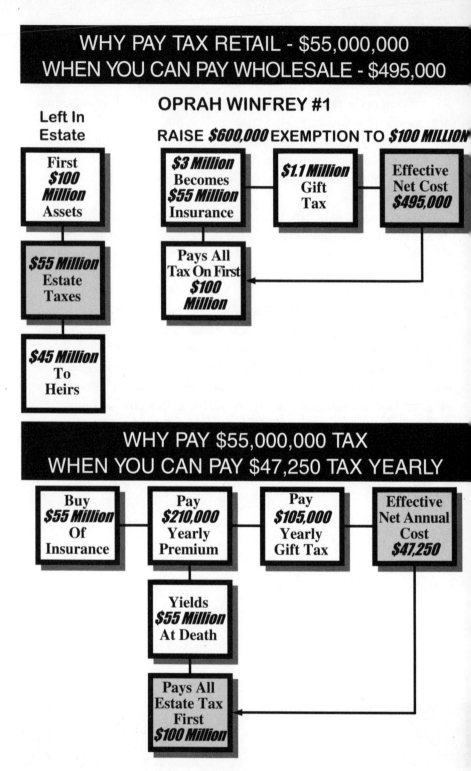

WHY PAY TAX RETAIL - $55,000,000
WHEN YOU CAN PAY WHOLESALE - $495,000

OPRAH WINFREY #1

RAISE *$600,000* EXEMPTION TO *$100 MILLION*

Left In Estate

First *$100 Million* Assets

$55 Million Estate Taxes

$45 Million To Heirs

$3 Million Becomes *$55 Million* Insurance

$1.1 Million Gift Tax

Effective Net Cost *$495,000*

Pays All Tax On First *$100 Million*

WHY PAY $55,000,000 TAX
WHEN YOU CAN PAY $47,250 TAX YEARLY

Buy *$55 Million* Of Insurance

Pay *$210,000* Yearly Premium

Pay *$105,000* Yearly Gift Tax

Effective Net Annual Cost *$47,250*

Yields *$55 Million* At Death

Pays All Estate Tax First *$100 Million*

All figures are based on current assumptions. Charts are for illustrative purposes only.
This illustration used an insurance policy for a female age 42.
©1997 THE INVESTMENT ALTERNATIVE - Barry Kaye Associates

OPRAH WINFREY #2

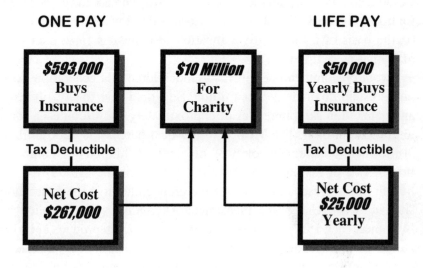

ONE PAY

LIFE PAY

| *$593,000* Buys Insurance | *$10 Million* For Charity | *$50,000* Yearly Buys Insurance |

Tax Deductible

Tax Deductible

| Net Cost *$267,000* | | Net Cost *$25,000* Yearly |

All figures are based on current assumptions. Charts are for illustrative purposes only.
This illustration used an insurance policy for a female age 42.
©1997 THE INVESTMENT ALTERNATIVE - Barry Kaye Associates

ROSS PEROT

My next client by choice would be Ross Perot (66 worth $3.3 billion). I have chosen him since you would think, with his billions, there is nothing more to be accomplished with my techniques. However, I would recommend a plan that could eventually increase his gross assets for his family by 33% and his net assets by 50%. I would show it to him on the basis of a further diversification of his assets for a man who really has everything.

I would recommend he gift his grandchildren in a generation skipping trust approximately $5.4 million. He would have to pay gift taxes and generation skipping taxes of approximately $3 million each for a total of $6 million. The Trustee would then purchase a $200 million last-to-die life insurance policy on his married children or a combination of two of his daughters (assuming approximate age 35) for the benefit of his present and prospective grandchildren in the generation skipping trust. Using this Investment Alternative system funded by insurance, each $5.4 million spent in this manner will produce upon his children's ultimate deaths $200 million. The total cash flow outlay will be $11.4 million, thus reducing his estate by that amount, resulting in a $6.3 estate tax saving. Therefore the net cost to create $200 million for his grandchildren will be $5.1 million.

If he purchased 5 units of $200 million each on a combination of his children and their spouses he would produce $1 billion at a net cost of $25.5 million. This is optimum diversification, and it will prepare his grandchildren to pay the eventual estate taxes which will be due upon his children's deaths, when the cost for the tremendous estate tax costs discounts are at their lowest and his children are their healthiest. If there are no estate taxes at that future date, then the grandchildren will have an extra $1 billion in their portfolio, thanks to their grandparents. This is probably easier than selling a business for a billion dollars after all capital gain and estate taxes. Best of all, my recommendation never really impacted Ross Perot's lifestyle or estate.

There is another aspect of this plan which I think would be of interest to Mr. Perot. Given his love of his country and his fierce determination to help improve it, as evidenced by the formation of his political party and self-funded, two-time run for the Presidency, I am sure Mr. Perot would have some reservations about implementing any estate planning strategies which have, as their basis, a philosophy of tax avoidance. Not wanting to cheat the country he loves out of a single dollar that is due it, Mr. Perot will probably be relieved to know that he can efficiently and cost-effectively discount his estate tax costs to his heirs while still paying every dime of taxes assessed on his estate.

INCREASE NET ASSETS 66%
FROM $1.5 BILLION TO $2.5 BILLION

ROSS PEROT

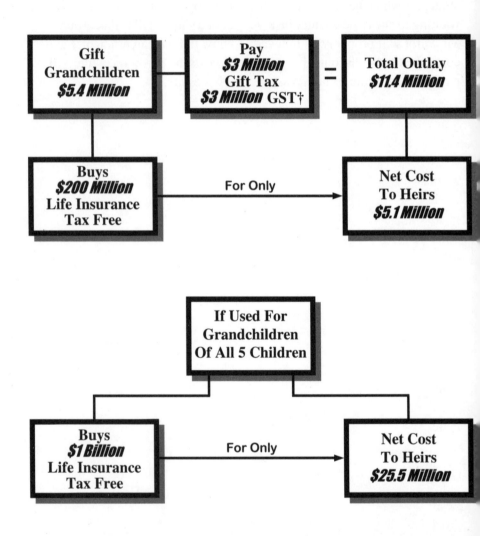

| Gift Grandchildren *$5.4 Million* | Pay *$3 Million* Gift Tax *$3 Million* GST† | = | Total Outlay *$11.4 Million* |

Buys *$200 Million* Life Insurance Tax Free — For Only → Net Cost To Heirs *$5.1 Million*

If Used For Grandchildren Of All 5 Children

Buys *$1 Billion* Life Insurance Tax Free — For Only → Net Cost To Heirs *$25.5 Million*

†Generation Skipping Tax

$1 BILLION COSTS $25.5 MILLION

All figures are based on current assumptions. Charts are for illustrative purposes only.
This illustration used a last-to-die insurance policy for a male and female both age 35.
©1997 THE INVESTMENT ALTERNATIVE - Barry Kaye Associates

JEFF KATZENBERG

My next choice would be Jeff Katzenberg (45 worth $400 million). He recently left Disney and became a part of the Hollywood 'dream team.' Since his assets are estimated at approximately $400 million, I can practically eliminate his estate taxes completely. As Mr. Katzenberg has unfortunately been exposed to deaths at an early age of associates and other show business personalties, he should now have first hand knowledge of how important planning for the possibility of this sort of tragic occurrence can be.

I would recommend that he increase his exemptions to their maximum which would be $363 million. He would buy a last-to-die policy on his wife and himself for $200 million. In this manner, at their deaths, the insurance company would effectively pay the taxes and therefore you could say that instead of his children paying no taxes on the first $1.2 million, they paid no taxes on the first $363 million. The one pay outlay for this Investment Alternative approach would be $9.4 million. The gift tax to increase his exemption to the maximum $363 million would be $5.1 million. His total cash outlay would be $14.5 million. This sum would now reduce his estate thus reducing for his family the eventual estate taxes by approximately $8 million. The net cost to cover the first $200 million of his family's estate taxes would be $6.5 million, probably less than some options that went astray or were found. No complex legal plan of tax avoidance can do better than my recommendation for Jeff Katzenberg.

INCREASE EXEMPTION TO $363 MILLION

JEFF KATZENBERG

$1.2 Million Exemption	**Effectively Increases To**	**$363 Million** Exemption

$200 Million Estate Tax	**Decreases To**	**$5.1 Million** Gift Tax

Estate Tax Effectively Paid By Insurance Company For $9.4 Million Premium

Net Gift Tax Cost $2.3 Million

PAY ONLY $5.1 MILLION GIFT TAX VERSUS $200 MILLION ESTATE TAX

All figures are based on current assumptions. Charts are for illustrative purposes only.
This illustration used a last-to-die insurance policy for a male and female both age 45.
©1997 THE INVESTMENT ALTERNATIVE - Barry Kaye Associates

MARVIN DAVIS

Marvin Davis (71 worth $2.2 billion), a perennial part of the Forbes 400, would receive my next recommendation. I would suggest he use my leverage-designed Investment Alternative to benefit his grandchildren. This will be a program that will create $200 million for his family but there will be ABSOLUTELY NO OUTLAY DURING HIS LIFETIME. He can purchase a policy for his grandchildren on his children's lives, borrow the premium, accrue the interest to the principal, pay nothing until his and his wife's deaths, at which time it will be completely tax deductible in a 55% estate tax bracket.

The premium for a $200 million last-to-die policy on a combination of his children's or their spouses' lives, based on age 40 and current assumptions, will be approximately one payment of $7 million. If he borrowed the $7 million at current LIBOR rates of 7% interest and accrued the interest, the loan would double in 10 years to $14 million and when Mr. Davis was in his 90's the loan would grow to $28 million. Assuming he died at that time, his estate would be reduced by the loan liability thus reducing his tax and saving his family $15.4 million. This means Uncle Sam effectively paid off more than half the loan and the net cost was only $12.6 million to create $200 million and NOT ONE CENT WAS PAID DURING MARVIN DAVIS' LIFETIME. In other words there was no cash flow impairment to accomplish this for his family.

Mr. Davis would incur an estate and generation skipping tax of $7.7 million which could be paid immediately or added to the loan, to also be paid off at his death. Other options include retaining the policy in his estate, giving him control of the cash values, but the transfer would then be more at his death, due to the growth of the cash values. The loans could also be taken yearly, based on an annual premium of approximately $460 thousand.

If Marvin Davis did this with all 5 of his children, he could create $1 billion with no outlay during his lifetime! Are there really many investments that are comparable to this Alternative, particularly when you realize you do not need any more during your lifetime and everything you do now is for your heirs at your death?

MARVIN DAVIS

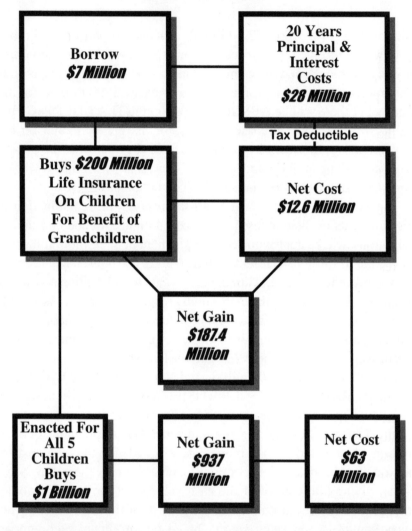

All figures are based on current assumptions. Charts are for illustrative purposes only.
This illustration used a last-to-die insurance policy for a male and female both age 40.
©1997 THE INVESTMENT ALTERNATIVE - Barry Kaye Associates

JACK KENT COOKE

Jack Kent Cooke (84 worth $825 million) would be the next choice that I would like to make a recommendation to. The possibilities with older people are really very exciting—much more so than most people realize—and among the best uses of the Investment Alternative methods.

I would suggest Mr. Cooke use my Municipal Bond Alternative program. The older you are, and in some cases the sicker you are, the better this plan works. I would want him to buy an Immediate Annuity in lieu of any CDs, T-bills, and Munis he might be holding. At best, triple A municipal bonds are paying at this time only 5% to 6%. An immediate annuity is currently paying at his age 84, 22%. Since this represents a return of your own capital, the government gives you an exclusion for your life expectancy and therefore there is income tax usually on less than 20% of the annual income. He would probably net 20% yearly until he had recovered his principal in approximately 7 years. Thereafter, the entire 22% would be taxed.

This means he would receive $2 million yearly for each $10 million annuity he bought, rather than $500 thousand yearly from his municipal bonds. By using this Investment Alternative technique, he will create an extra $1.5 million yearly. He would then gift approximately $1 million to an Irrevocable Trust and the trust would purchase $10 million of insurance. The remaining $1 million would cover the necessary $500 thousand of gift taxes and replace his original $500 thousand of Muni or T-bill income.

This is a simple reallocation of Mr. Cooke's assets, but at his death, his three children would receive the $10 million life insurance proceeds completely income and estate tax free. If he did not use this technique, his children would receive only $4.5 million after paying $5.5 million in estate taxes on his original $10 million.

This reallocation method could be used with $100 million once Mr. Cooke was comfortable with the technique. This would enable him to transfer $100 million to his children after all taxes, $55 million more than they would have received, and Uncle Sam still received his yearly gift taxes.

If Mr. Cooke wanted maximum return, he could employ my GST program for the benefit of his grandchildren. Assuming he did not need the income of $500 thousand he had been earning from his Munis, going back to the original $10 million, he would transfer to his grandchildren's trust approximately $1 million over a 5 year period. The remaining $1 million would be used to pay the necessary gift and generation skipping taxes. The trustee would buy a 5-pay, last-to-die policy on his son and daughter-in-law for the benefit of his grandchildren. Based on age 55 and 50, it would buy approximately $57 million. In this manner, he has turned $10 million which would have been worth $2.5 million after all taxes into $57 million totally tax free on the death of his children.

Naturally, I would customize the plan to his specific objectives, possibly including a combination of all of the above. This is what I particularly enjoy, putting together my own creations with my client's objectives and making sure they are executed properly and then nurtured through the on-going changing economic and political climate.

REALLOCATION OF ASSETS
TURNS $4.5 MILLION INTO $10 MILLION

JACK KENT COOKE

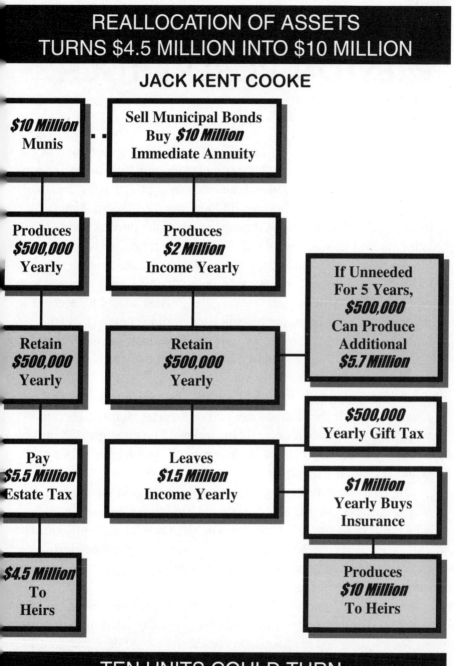

$10 Million Munis

Sell Municipal Bonds Buy *$10 Million* Immediate Annuity

Produces *$500,000* Yearly

Produces *$2 Million* Income Yearly

If Unneeded For 5 Years, *$500,000* Can Produce Additional *$5.7 Million*

Retain *$500,000* Yearly

Retain *$500,000* Yearly

$500,000 Yearly Gift Tax

Pay *$5.5 Million* Estate Tax

Leaves *$1.5 Million* Income Yearly

$1 Million Yearly Buys Insurance

$4.5 Million To Heirs

Produces *$10 Million* To Heirs

TEN UNITS COULD TURN
$45 MILLION INTO $157 MILLION
AT NO COST TO YOU

All figures are based on current assumptions and life expectancies. Charts are for illustrative purposes only. This illustration used an immediate annuity for a male age 85, and a last-to-die insurance policy for a male and female both age 55. ©1997 THE INVESTMENT ALTERNATIVE - Barry Kaye Associates

PRESTON ROBERT TISCH

Preston Robert Tisch (70 worth $2 billion) would receive one of my newest recommendations. This particular Investment Alternative concept combines the leverage of an insurance policy with charitable giving and a no-interest, to-be-paid loan, since it is accrued during his lifetime providing him with the advantage of the interest and the loan being tax deductible at his death. While there is obviously no need for Mr. Tisch to borrow this money, it does avoid any cash flow impairment in his lifetime thereby making this more attractive and comparable to any leveraged business transaction. The interest would be accrued to the loan and nothing would be paid back until his death at which time both the principal and interest would be tax deductible in a 55% estate tax bracket. His estate would pay off one half of the loan and effectively Uncle Sam pays off the other half.

Mr. Tisch would borrow $10 million. He would transfer the borrowed money to his foundation or his favorite charity. The charity would use $2 million for current operations. The remaining $8 million would be used for a future endowment by purchasing a last-to-die policy on Mr. Tisch and his wife for $40 million.

Mr. Tisch would write off the $10 million donation to charity. This would create tax savings of $5 million. Using the savings, he would gift $3.2 million to his children and pay gift taxes of $1.8 million. His children would take the $3.2 million and buy a one payment, last-to-die policy on Mr. and Mrs. Tisch for approximately $16 million, based on current assumptions.

Assuming Mr. and Mrs. Tisch lived 18 years, the net cost of the loan, based on current interest, would be covered by the $16 million received by the children and his foundation or charity would have received $42 million for each $10 million loan employed in this manner.

PRESTON ROBERT TISCH

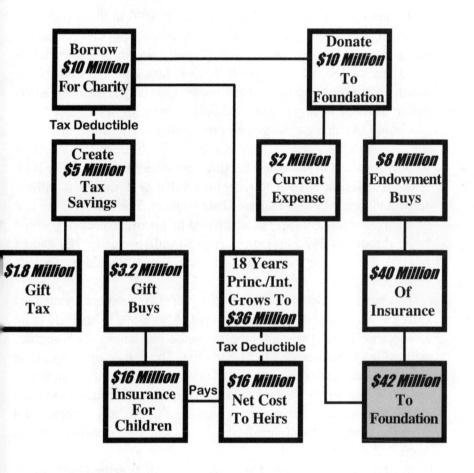

All figures are based on current assumptions. Charts are for illustrative purposes only.
This illustration used a last-to-die insurance policy for a male and female both age 70.
©1997 THE INVESTMENT ALTERNATIVE - Barry Kaye Associates

257

ZACHARY FISHER

I am interested in Zachary Fisher (85 worth $500 million) because I believe I could more than double his net estate without any complicated, convoluted, expensive estate planning which is usually advocated in situations of this type. If it is too late, I will still be able to adjust and improve antiquated techniques using my Investment Alternative methods of augmenting and optimizing his assets.

I would like this to cost him nothing during his lifetime thus avoiding any cash flow impairment. Since he and his family have been heavily involved in real estate for three generations, I am sure he is no stranger to leverage. I would recommend that he borrow $30 million. He would then purchase an Immediate Annuity. The return for the rest of his life would be 22%. The tax, based on his life expectancy would bring the net to 20%, thus producing $6 million yearly. His annual interest paid on the loan, based on current rates, would be approximately $2 million.

This would still leave him $4 million yearly to spend as a result of his loan. He would transfer $2.6 million out of his estate to his child or an Irrevocable Trust. The child or trust would purchase a life insurance policy for $40 million on Mr. Fisher's life. The remaining $1.4 million would be paid yearly in gift taxes to make the $40 million completely estate tax free on Mr. Fisher's death. So far, Mr. Fisher hasn't used any of his own money. The interest, premium and gift tax has been paid from the income on the Immediate Annuity that Mr. Fisher bought with borrowed money.

You buy. You die. It pays. The moment of truth. Whether death occurs in the first year or in 10 years, the beneficiary receives $40 million tax free. The $30 million debt must be paid off. Mr. Fisher's beneficiaries pays off $13.5 million and Uncle Sam pays off the remaining $16.5 million. This is simply accomplished because the debt is a liability thus reducing your gross estate thus reducing your estate taxes. This effectively makes his loan (or any loan) at his death, principal and interest, completely tax deductible in a 55% estate tax bracket.

258

Mr. Fisher has produced approximately $26.5 million at no cash flow impairment during his lifetime, *and no cost to him or his heirs* at his death. Furthermore, this means that the free $26.5 million that I created will pay the estate taxes on the first $48 million of his estate. If I and Mr. Fisher could arrange the capacity, he could take a total of 4 comparable loans for a total of $120 million, producing income of $24 million, to pay the interest, premiums and gift taxes, to purchase $160 million of life insurance, to pay off the net loan, to cover the estate taxes on the first $192 million of his assets and all of this AT NO COST WHATSOEVER.

I have two more Investment Alternative concepts that I would discuss with Mr. Fisher that would be helpful in covering and offsetting the rest of his estate tax and assure that his heirs eventually receive the total estate of $500 million instead of $225 million or some convoluted series of trusts and foundations.

CREATE $26.5 MILLION AT NO COST

ZACHARY FISHER

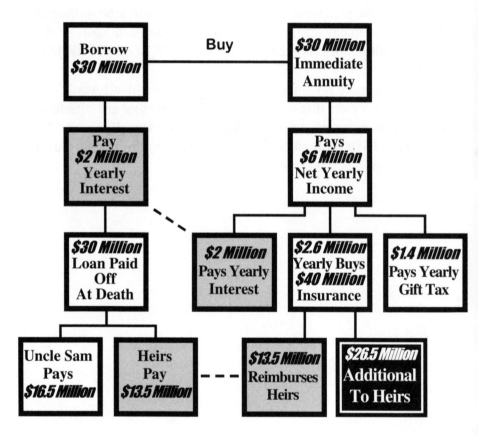

THE MORE YOU BORROW
THE MORE YOU CREATE

All figures are based on current assumptions and life expectancies. Charts are for illustrative purposes only.
This illustration used an immediate annuity and insurance policy for a male age 85.

JON MEADE HUNTSMAN

Jon Meade Huntsman (59 worth $2.5 billion) is a family man. He has 9 children and 26 grandchildren and therefore presents a wonderful and exciting challenge to me. I have many recommendations for Mr. Huntsman and I would hope I could increase his assets at least 4 times ultimately for his heirs. Yes, up to $10 billion!

He has the money and can afford the right moves of reallocation if they make sense. He is very charitable and therefore will be able to see the on-going method of continuing optimization for his charities after he has taken care of his family. Mr. Huntsman recently gave $100 million to cancer research and has made his fortune through acquisitions and great leverage. Using the same techniques that he has employed in his business will enable this quadrupling to happen.

I would recommend that he allocates $90 million to this project. This is less than 4% of his assets. He would then transfer $10 million to each child's family Irrevocable Trust. Each Trustee would purchase on the parents and siblings, Mr. Huntsman's children, approximately $50 million of life insurance depending upon their age and health. There would be a total of 9 policies for an initial total of $450 million. The premium is over-funding the policies and thereby guaranteeing the $50 million. The over-funding is so substantial that the death benefits will grow almost immediately. While each policy will start with a $55 million death benefit, it will grow by age 40 to $60 million; age 50 to $78 million; age 60 to $105 million; age 70 to $147 million; age 80 to $218 million; age 90 to $348 million; and by age 100 to $552 million based on current assumptions. This should produce ultimately for Mr. Huntsman's heirs based on the time of deaths and current assumptions a minimum of a guaranteed $450 million to a potential $5 billion. He may want these funds to eventually be used for his charitable endeavors, optimization of family assets or to offset estate taxes paid or to be paid or a combination of the above. He can further avoid any estate taxes or generation skipping taxes by paying them up front on the $90 million instead of on the potential up to $5 billion to be received. These figures could be doubled or halved in accordance with the budget and return he desires. Half the figures with premiums and taxes would amount to approximately $90 million and still produce a guaranteed $225 million to a potential $2.2 billion.

If he wanted to remove the guarantee and the awesome potential, he could still buy $450 million ($50 million on each child and spouse or sibling) for only $11.7 based on current assumptions. The $450 million would be tax free if he paid the gift and generation skipping taxes of $6.5 million for a total expenditure of $18.2 million.

I would also recommend that Mr. Huntsman purchase a $200 million last-to-die policy on himself and his wife, the maximum he can buy at this time since he will never be younger or healthier and the premiums will never be cheaper. I have a new Investment Alternative approach that may be perfect for his situation. In the meantime he will have all his charitable, tax discounting, and asset optimizing options open at a one-payment outlay of $20 million for the entire $200 million.

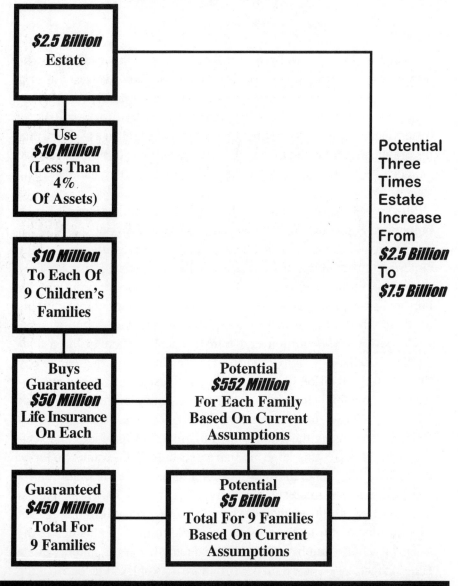

LIFE INSURANCE INCREASES
$2.5 BILLION TO POTENTIAL $7.5 BILLION

JON MEADE HUNTSMAN

$2.5 Billion
Estate

Use
$10 Million
(Less Than
4%
Of Assets)

$10 Million
To Each Of
9 Children's
Families

Buys
Guaranteed
$50 Million
Life Insurance
On Each

Potential
$552 Million
For Each Family
Based On Current
Assumptions

Guaranteed
$450 Million
Total For
9 Families

Potential
$5 Billion
Total For 9 Families
Based On Current
Assumptions

Potential
Three
Times
Estate
Increase
From
$2.5 Billion
To
$7.5 Billion

USE 4% OF ASSETS TO TRIPLE ESTATE
FOR FAMILY OR CHARITY

All figures are based on current assumptions. Charts are for illustrative purposes only.
This illustration used a last-to-die insurance policy on a male and female both age 30.
©1997 THE INVESTMENT ALTERNATIVE - Barry Kaye Associates

SAMUEL J. LEFRAK

Samuel J. LeFrak (78 worth $1.3 billion) is one of the leading philan-
thropists in America today. He has benefited many causes. He is a
family man and very concerned for his grandchildren. My recommendation would be an excellent Investment Alternative for Mr. LeFrak,
better than almost any investment he could make and an assurance that
his grandchildren would eventually receive as a result of his ingenuity
as much as he left his children regardless of how they handled their
estates.

Mr. LeFrak is very aware of his cash flow. He has done enough
building to appreciate the advantage of leverage. My goal is to leave to
his grandchildren the same $580 million that he leaves after taxes to his
children, thus doubling his net estate without impairing his cash flow
during his lifetime. In other words, I want him to spend nothing by
borrowing the money and accruing the interest to the principal until his
death, at which time, it will be completely deductible.

He borrows $50 million and transfers $24 million to his grandchildren's generation skipping trust. He uses the rest of the loan to pay
the gift and generation skipping taxes. The Trustee purchases a guaranteed one payment $100 million last-to-die policy on his children (or
child and spouse) for $24 million. The policy is substantially over-
funded thus causing the death benefit to grow. This provides an excellent method of creating large tax free assets outside his estate. So far he
has paid nothing out of his own pocket for the potential $100 million tax
free proceeds. The interest is accrued each year to the loan principal. At
age 88 (based on current interest) he would owe $100 million; at age 93,
$150 million and if he lived to age 98, $200 million. At his death, the
loan is paid off from his estate, thus reducing his assets and his estate
taxes. Effectively Uncle Sam paid off more than half of the loan making
the entire loan tax deductible. The total net cost of the loan would be $45
million to $90 million depending upon the time of his death.

Meanwhile, the life insurance policy has started to grow from the
original $100 million to $134 million by age 55; by age 65 to $182

million; by age 75 to $260 million; by age 85 to $400 million; by age 95 to $652 million and if they live to age 100, $809 million. Using borrowed funds a guaranteed $100 million to a potential $809 million has been created at a net cost of $45 million to $90 million. Mr. LeFrak's gross estate has been eventually doubled and the grand-children have received more than the children's net $580 million, based on current assumptions.

Mr. LeFrak has the option of paying only $4.9 million for the same $100 million policy, based on current assumptions. This would also reduce the taxes and the loan to $7.6 million but there would be no potential growth to $809 million. The extra $42 million loan which doesn't have to paid off until death, at which time it will be tax deductible, provides the potential of up to an extra $700 MILLION TAX FREE!

SAMUEL J. LEFRAK

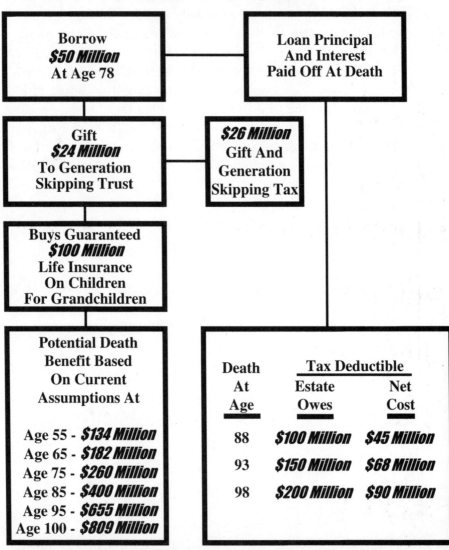

Borrow
$50 Million
At Age 78

**Loan Principal
And Interest
Paid Off At Death**

Gift
$24 Million
**To Generation
Skipping Trust**

$26 Million
**Gift And
Generation
Skipping Tax**

Buys Guaranteed
$100 Million
**Life Insurance
On Children
For Grandchildren**

**Potential Death
Benefit Based
On Current
Assumptions At**

Age 55 - *$134 Million*
Age 65 - *$182 Million*
Age 75 - *$260 Million*
Age 85 - *$400 Million*
Age 95 - *$655 Million*
Age 100 - *$809 Million*

Death At Age	Tax Deductible Estate Owes	Net Cost
88	*$100 Million*	*$45 Million*
93	*$150 Million*	*$68 Million*
98	*$200 Million*	*$90 Million*

BUY INSURANCE AT NO COST
DURING YOUR LIFETIME

All figures are based on current assumptions. Charts are for illustrative purposes only.
This illustration used a last-to-die insurance policy for a male and female both age 45.
©1997 THE INVESTMENT ALTERNATIVE - Barry Kaye Associates

266

BILL GATES

Bill Gates, (40 worth $18.5 billion) the richest man in America, would produce the most interesting results of all, because of the leverage of his young age. He is very philanthropic and recently gave $100 million to his foundation. He could give up to another $1.5 billion to them at no cost to him whatsoever!

MY RECOMMENDATION WOULD SHOW MR. GATES HOW TO GIVE HIS FOUNDATION UP TO $1.5 BILLION AND ALSO UP TO AN ADDITIONAL $1.5 BILLION TO HIS FAMILY FOR A TOTAL OUTLAY OF $52 MILLION. IN 22 YEARS THE ENTIRE $52 MILLION OUTLAY OR MORE WOULD BE RETURNED TO HIM. THE MINIMUM THE CHARITY AND HIS FAMILY WOULD RECEIVE IS $200 MILLION *GUARANTEED* TO A MAXIMUM OF $3 BILLION *AT EFFECTIVELY NO COST.*

Using the most dynamic Investment Alternative technique of all, providing excellent diversification, Mr. Gates purchases two $100 million policies on his life for a total return of $200 million. His total one pay premium is $52 million, based on current assumptions. He retains both policies thereby controlling the cash value equity which exceeds the original outlay within 4 years.

In 22 years he gives one $100 million policy to his foundation, retaining the other for his family. The approximate cash value of each policy at that time is $104 million. The amount of the cash value equity transferred at that time to the foundation is tax deductible. This creates income tax savings of approximately $52 million completely replacing his original outlay. He did give up the return on his $52 million during the 22 year period. However, if he had died, his heirs would have received $200 million, more than making up the original outlay.

The foundation and his heirs now have individual policies for $100 million each and the policies are constructed to grow substantially beyond their original face value based on current assumptions. The longer he lives the more the policy pays. At his age 70, the face value of each policy would be $210 million; at age 80, $387 million; at age 90,

$768 million; and at age 100 each policy would be worth $1.5 billion for a total of $3 billion! ALL WITH THE ORIGINAL PREMIUM HAVING BEEN PAID BACK RESULTING IN NO COST. Quoting my 11 year old grandson Peter, *"it doesn't get much better than this."*

One final concept worth $55 million to $550 million in estate tax savings for Mr. Gates. If he would like to make the guaranteed $100 million to potential $1 billion death proceeds to the family completely tax free, he could pay at the inception of the policy gift taxes of $14 million on one policy's premium and this would remove that policy from his estate. This would make the entire potential $1.5 BILLION TO HIS FAMILY TAX FREE.

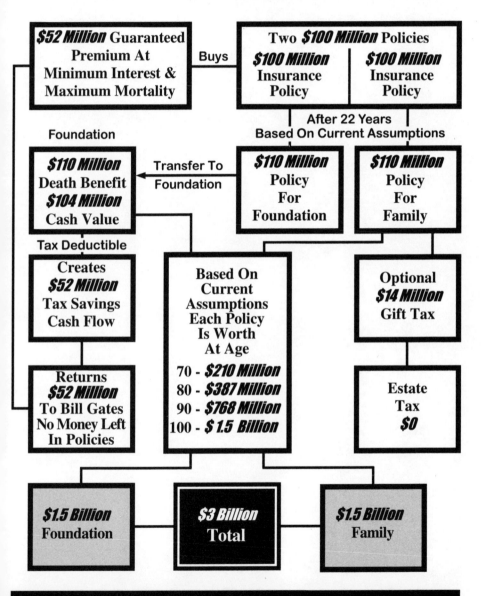

UP TO $3 BILLION
AT NO COST - ALL PREMIUMS RETURNED

BILL GATES

$52 Million Guaranteed Premium At Minimum Interest & Maximum Mortality

Buys

Two **$100 Million** Policies

| **$100 Million** Insurance Policy | **$100 Million** Insurance Policy |

After 22 Years
Based On Current Assumptions

Foundation

$110 Million Death Benefit **$104 Million** Cash Value

Transfer To Foundation

$110 Million Policy For Foundation

$110 Million Policy For Family

Tax Deductible

Creates **$52 Million** Tax Savings Cash Flow

Based On Current Assumptions Each Policy Is Worth At Age

70 - **$210 Million**
80 - **$387 Million**
90 - **$768 Million**
100 - **$1.5 Billion**

Optional **$14 Million** Gift Tax

Returns **$52 Million** To Bill Gates No Money Left In Policies

Estate Tax **$0**

$1.5 Billion Foundation

$3 Billion Total

$1.5 Billion Family

ALMOST AS GOOD AS MICROSOFT ITSELF

All figures are based on current assumptions. Charts are for illustrative purposes only.
This illustration used a last-to-die insurance policy for a male and female both age 40.
©1997 THE INVESTMENT ALTERNATIVE - Barry Kaye Associates

PART FIVE

Too Good To Be True

Having seen how the concepts work and how life insurance can be used as an alternative to investments to create and preserve great wealth, you're probably sitting there wondering what's the catch. Even though I've shown you where the media and other financial professionals go wrong in their understanding of these plans, you may still be skeptical. It is generally at this point in my seminars that skeptical people begin to reach for some means by which to discredit my approaches. Lacking anything more substantial or specific, they often fall back on a sort of generic, all-encompassing "It's just too good to be true."

I wonder at this. I wonder at people's reluctance to believe that something really wonderful and something equal to its own claims could truly exist. And it seems to me that people's reluctance is more broadly applied to the products of life insurance. Whether this really is just a product of the bad information they get from the media or a reflection of the ignorance of many legal and financial professionals or a reaction to some of the historical associations that accompany thoughts of insurance, in general, life insurance, in particular, and life insurance salespeople, I do not know. What I DO know is that the "Too Good To Be True" mentality is harming people. It is preventing them from taking advantage of a financial opportunity that, as an alternative to investing and part of a fully diversified portfolio, fulfills many of their estate goals far better than any of their investments.

Part of the problem is that, as previously presented, the purchase of life insurance has been a complicated process. The structure of policies and means of calculating costs and returns was intimidating. But, in truth, as an alternative to stocks, bonds, real estate and other investments, the nuts and bolts of how life insurance performs its miracles of financial wizardry is really quite simple: You buy a policy . . . You die . . . It pays. In truth, there really isn't much more to it than that. Yes, there are details and yes those details are just as involved as the complications of stocks, bonds, real estate, etc. But the bottom line, the most important aspect of the product and the one which will allow you to accomplish your desired financial goals in a way no other vehicle can, never changes.

YOU BUY. YOU DIE. IT PAYS.

No stock can claim that. Neither can any bond or real estate investment. With them you could very well buy, die and lose. Even if the investment has gone up, due to capital gains taxes and income taxes and estate taxes, there is no firm part of their equation that says "It pays." And that is where life insurance triumphs over any investment vehicle. You buy. You die. It pays.

Simple. And perhaps within that simplicity lies the notion that it must therefore be "Too good to be true."

In this chapter we are going to try and put that notion to rest for ever. I'm going to take you through the various 'nuances' of the life insurance purchase and explain how each aspect works to provide the returns which you have seen at work in the many examples of wealth creation and preservation presented to you in the earlier chapters. With this information you will be able to make an informed, knowledgeable assessment of life insurance's value to your financial planning. You will be able to answer for yourself and for those detractors who might seek to warn you off life insurance by dismissing it in that offhand, denigrating way of sneering that its claims are simply "Too good to be true." You will see from this material that it **IS** true. That life insurance **DOES** perform as claimed.

On the following pages we will take a frank and detailed look at exactly what "based on current assumptions" means to you and how it can affect the return your policy will yield. We will examine different types of policies and different means of payment and how the choices you make might affect your overall outcome. We will address what cash values are and what their place is in making a life insurance purchase. I will show you how to buy insurance even if you are uninsurable.

These are the nitty gritty aspects of policies which most attorneys, accountants and financial advisors don't understand, which the media doesn't understand and which, in all likelihood, you don't understand. These are the exploited aspects, the areas which the detractors point to in their attempts to dismiss life insurance. Armed with an understanding of these things, you will be able to make an intelligent decision that could benefit your family in huge ways. In ways that might very well seem to be "Too good to be true."

Throughout human history there have always been those concepts and their supporters which the general population has dismissed as being "too good to be true." When air travel was first seriously envisioned as a means of moving people vast distances in short periods of time, of making the world smaller and more efficient, of transporting goods and services, people undoubtedly scoffed and said it was an idea that was too good to be true. Until the Wright brothers proved otherwise.

When the concept of a means of communication that would link people over great distances instantly and make keeping in touch or reaching out for help as easy as lifting a handset off a cradle was first introduced to the masses, I am certain most people shrugged the idea off as one of those pipe dreams that can't be achieved because they are too good to ever be true. And then Alexander Graham Bell showed the world that sometimes the truth can exceed our hopes and dreams.

What do you suppose people said when news of a means of generating light without flame or fire began to filter through society? Or when they first heard about a means to safely remove the health threat from cheese, milk and other dairy products? I have no doubt that many, if not most, people, upon first hearing of these things that they greatly desired, passed them off as being too good to be true. Perhaps they didn't want to get their hopes up only to have them dashed. Perhaps they wore skepticism as a protection from being taken in. In any event, Thomas Edison and Louis Pasteur reached out and proved that sometimes things which are too good to be true are, nevertheless, true.

Now the news is spreading of a way to discount your estate taxes, to turn any tax into an asset, to effectively exempt your entire estate from estate taxes, to significantly optimize gifts to charity, to double the proceeds from the sale of any asset, to optimize IRAs and pensions many times over, to create and preserve great wealth for your family. Is it as groundbreaking as electricity or telephones or flying? Maybe not. But on a personal and individual level it can make almost as huge difference in your family's well-being. And it's true.

BASED ON CURRENT ASSUMPTIONS

Throughout this book, I have told you of the predetermined nature of life insurance benefits in contrast to the risk involved of investment. This aspect of how policies work is part of what makes life insurance so incredibly valuable as an alternative to investments.

A large part of life insurance's value has to do with the unalterable guarantee of death. You WILL die. It is a certainty. The only thing not guaranteed is WHEN you will die. And it is for this reason that life insurance as an alternative to traditional investments is so crucial. Since you know you will die but don't know when, you can't safely make any financial plans that depend on some foreseen passage of time to come to fruition. Stocks, bonds, the real estate market, the collectibles industry . . . all require time to achieve their return. Rarely does it happen that you buy a stock one day and it increases in value to any significant level the next. But that is EXACTLY what happens with life insurance. You buy it and even it you die the very next day, it pays the full amount of the stated return.

Your other advisors might try to gloss over this hard truth by quoting mortality statistics and, in fact, it is these same statistics that are used by the insurance companies to determine what your return will be when you make the insurance purchase. But the cold, hard truth is that those statistics are meaningless on an individual basis. They work out in large groups of people to provide an average or a mean which is what allows the insurance industry to function. But they have absolutely no real bearing on YOU. I use the following alliteration in my seminars to explain the importance of this point: If you were to flip a coin a thousand times, the law of averages would apply to the expected results you would achieve over those times. But if each of those flips were a person, there is no telling whose toss comes up heads and whose comes up tails. Every day of your life is like that coin toss and difficult as it may be to consider, the law of averages could care less which of the thousand you are. This is one of the aspects in which life insurance is so superior to every other financial vehicle out there. It doesn't require you to fit the average or to come up heads in order to provide an optimized return. In the event you are a 'tails', it will be there, paying in full for the good of your family. Given this reality, how could any responsible advisor not insist that you include life insurance in a diversified portfolio of asset management?

So you can see how impactful the guarantee of death is on your financial decisions. Given that you COULD die at any time, you MUST be financially prepared for death to occur at any time. At least some portion of your portfolio must be designed to accommodate this possibility or it can not be considered thorough, prudent, balanced and responsible. And only life insurance, utilized as an alternative or in addition to your other investments, can accomplish that goal.

Because death is guaranteed to happen at any time to anyone, life insurance is guaranteed to provide a financial benefit no other financial vehicle can.

But I speak of life insurance's benefits as extending beyond the protection it affords against just the fact of death. I have talked about the returns a life insurance policy will yield at different ages and in different situations and then noted that those returns are *based on current assumptions*. It is this caveat that many lawyers try to use to pick apart my claims. It is this caveat that some accountants try to use to disprove the financial feasibility of these plans.

What exactly does *Based On Current Assumptions* mean? How does it impact a policy's cost and return? These are very fair, very important questions which I will try to answer as fully as possible without becoming obscure.

The return on a life insurance policy is calculated by the insurance company based on two primary factors: your expected mortality (how long you can be statistically assumed to live given your age and current health) and the interest rates they can expect to earn on the money you pay them and how those earnings go to their bottom line of expenses to dictate their profit. Those interest and mortality rates, factoring in the insurance company's expenses, are what determine the insurance company's profitability and fiscal soundness.

When you apply for a policy, you are quoted a price which will yield a quoted return *based on the current assumptions.* Which means that as long as the mortality assumptions made about the group you fall into and the interest rates the insurance company is earning on your money hold to current levels, you will receive the death benefit that was presented to you. Even given the limits implied by the caveat, this is still far more of a certainty than you could expect from virtually any investment. But even so, the lawyers and financial advisors try to pick it apart and paint these dire, dreadful images of policy costs ballooning into the stratosphere as the assumptions upon which they were made, change.

But let's be realistic. Let's look at the factors upon which "based on current assumptions" rests. First, mortality. The longer you live, the longer the insurance company has your money to invest and earn returns on. Therefore, the less your policy costs. When you purchase your policy, you are examined by a doctor. On the basis of this examination you are assigned a 'level' which is a designation of the state of your health. This level, i.e. preferred, standard, etc., is used to determine your expected mortality. Once assigned, that level will not be altered by changes in the status of your health. It is not changes is YOUR mortality expectations which can effect the cost of an insurance policy. It is changes in the mortality assumptions of the whole pool of potential insureds, basically the population of America, in most cases. The mortality assumptions for the United States have improved for many years. Medical advances, lifestyle improvements, preventative measures have all served to increase the average life expectancy. And so the insurance companies' expectations of how long they will have your money to invest grows and they are able to charge you less for the same amounts of coverage. Is there ANY reason to think that this trend will change in any significant way for the worse through the rest of your lifetime? I don't believe there is.

There is however, based on the recent historical performance of the mortality expectations EVERY reason to believe that it is possible they will continue to grow. When the assumptions are recalculated, if there is an increase of life expectancy within the health level you were assigned, your expectation will go up and so, the amount of money needed to fund your stated policy return could go down. Your policy will build up greater cash values and produce a higher return than you had expected for the same amount of cash outlay on your part.

Clearly, the portion of the life insurance policy guarantee which is based upon assumptions of mortality can be fairly judged to be, at worst, static and, at best, in your favor. But there is a maximum guarantee in your policy that the insurance company can charge you to cover this contingency.

What then about the assumptions based on interest earnings? Remember, the more interest the insurance company can be expected to earn with your money, the less the cost for your desired return. If interest rates go up, allowing the insurance company to realize higher yields on their investments, the cost of the return you want goes down. If interest rates go down, causing the insurance company to earn less with the same money, the cost to produce the originally determined amount of death benefit, goes up.

It is this point which detractors from life insurance blow out of proportion in a lame attempt to belittle its value and usefulness.

Yes, changes in interest assumptions can impact your policy. This is why I so carefully caveat the statements of return I make whenever I discuss these products. But THINK ABOUT THE REALITY of the situation. Right now we are living in a world of approximately 6%–7% interest. What do you think is the likelihood that interest will drop much beyond that? Could it go down a point to 5%–6%.? Look at what happens to the cost of a policy at age 60 on page 352 if it does. Clearly, the increased cost is minimal and, when measured against the return, its tax free nature and the fact of its immediate availability, almost negligible in relationship to the resulting death benefit.

See the charts at the back of this book for what happens if interest rates go up just a single point to 7%–8%. The cost for the same return drops so you can either pay less or build up substantial cash values to have in the policy in the event rates drop again. Or it can wind up funding additional death benefits at no additional cost.

Once again, use your best judgment. Do you think it is likely that interest rates will drop more than a point below their current low levels at this time?

In fact, aren't all your investments, with the exception of some very conservative, safe but low-yielding bonds, interest sensitive? Our whole economy is. There is nothing so different or so fearful about life insurance. Your stocks offer you NO GUARANTEE at all. Your real estate offers you NO GUARANTEE at all. Your CD's and savings account are completely dependent upon the current interest rates exactly as a life insurance policy is. Yet, again, NONE OF THEM can perform as a life insurance policy, structured within an Irrevocable Trust, can for the ultimate good of your family whether their need of it comes tomorrow, a year from now or twenty years from now. Even with the caveat of current assumptions, interest is guaranteed never to be lower than 4% depending on the individual company.

There have been times in our history when *"based on current assumptions"* for a life insurance policy was not favorable for a potential insured. When interest rates are artificially high and likely to come down a significant amount, an individual can find that the cost of the return they need is at its lowest but most valuable. I believe that it is carried-over thinking from these times that fuels the ongoing misunderstandings about the truth of insurance returns being *based on **current** assumptions*. Given the interest and mortality assumptions being utilized to determine policy returns today, it is my opinion that there is no better time for consumers to benefit from the many financial opportunities afforded by a properly structured life insurance policy used as part of a diversified financial portfolio. Remember, you can always add money to a policy if necessary, borrow against it or cut the death benefit to more than salvage the policy. In most cases if an investment goes bad, you could lose everything.

One last note on the subject. As I showed you in Concept #21, there is a fully guaranteed policy available for those who remain uncertain about relying on current assumptions. Of course, this fully guaranteed policy costs considerably more but, for many, the absolute guarantee of the return is well worth the increased price. Furthermore, as I demonstrated in that example, should the rate the insured is paying to secure the guarantee turn out to be significantly more than what the current assumptions would have demanded, the "extra" payments build up substantial cash values which can ultimately wind up funding death benefits beyond the guaranteed death benefits. For people who can afford it, these fully guaranteed policies can represent a remarkable growth vehicle over the long run. On the downside however, this is one type of policy that does not take full advantage of the timing element of life insurance policies. Should it happen that the insured were to lose the coin flip and die early on in the policy's life, they would have paid far more than they had to for the return they received. The longer they live, however, the greater the potential for significant returns. It is a trade-off. The security of a full guarantee and the potential for incredible growth against the added expense and decreased return percentage in the early years of the policy. Which type of policy best addresses your specific needs and concerns only you can decide. But having either one, or even a combination of both, will surely do more for your estate planning than not having either. This is incredible for very wealthy people who wish to transfer huge estate tax free maximum amounts out of their estate at minimum gift taxes.

TYPES OF POLICIES

WHO TO INSURE

The outcome of your usage of a life insurance policy as an alternative to investing is also dependent upon the type of policy that you select. Throughout most of the examples I've used in this book, I have shown the results based upon using a Last-to-Die policy. I do this for two reasons. One because Last-to-Die policies offer the best return. And two, because Last-to-Die policies are most appropriate for the type of tax cost discounting and wealth creation and optimization which we have been discussing.

But there are other types of available policies and each has their usefulness in different situations. As in any field of financial planning, an informed decision is the best decision. Let's take a brief look at the three basic choices for the insured—Male, Female and Last-to-Die—to examine how to select which might be best for your specific situation.

A policy based on the life of a man only is perhaps the most traditional and familiar of policy types. In the history of the insurance industry, policies were sold to serve as protection in the event of the unforeseen and tragic death of the household breadwinner, for the most part in those days, the man of the house. Insurance proceeds were intended to provide the widow with the means to continue providing for herself and her family.

Ironically, of the three choices for who to insure, the male only policy receives the lowest return. There are two basic reasons for this. To begin with, statistically men do not live as long as women. As we just learned, this lower mortality assumption makes the cost of the policy go up. Secondly, in most marriages the man is older than the woman so, at the time that they begin to consider the purchase of a life insurance policy to diversify their investment portfolio for the good of their heirs, he can be presumed to have already lived a higher percentage of his full expectancy.

Of course, if the purchase of life insurance is being undertaken for the reasons it was traditionally sold, to protect a widow left without resources, a policy on the life of the man is the only way to go. But unfortunately, all too often that same approach is inappropriately carried over onto the use of life insurance as an alternative to investing for estate management and planning and couples wind up paying far more than they should to achieve their goals.

Insuring the woman alone makes a little more sense than insuring the man alone since, as was just stated above, she has a greater life expectancy and is probably younger. Therefore, it is fair to presume that she will receive a better return then he will. Keep in mind, an estate may pass from one partner to the other in a marriage without any death taxes being levied. Estate taxes only come into play when the estate passes out of the marital situation. Since it is assumed that the woman will live longer, it can make sense for estate planning purposes to insure her life. But, as I have reiterated many times throughout this book, there are no guarantees when it comes to death except that it will happen sooner or later to us all. Should the woman be insured and die first, the heirs will come into the insurance benefits but not the estate, which would most likely remain in the possession of her widower. The proceeds can be structured to remain in a trust in order to ensure they are still around to pay the taxes at the time of his death, but then what was the point of having the coverage be on her only?

Of course, there are some situations and conditions which will necessitate making a choice that is not solely based on age and life expectancies and rates. Instances where the decision about whether to insure the man or the woman will be determined by the circumstances of the couple's lives. Perhaps it is a second marriage for one or both of them and there are children from the previous marriage to be considered in the estate planning. If the woman's children are to be provided for separate from the man's, it stands to reason separate policies would be needed.

Or, perhaps one of the two is uninsurable. In that event, there would be no choice but to insure only the other.

However, in most instances of estate planning, I recommend what is commonly called a Last-to-Die, Survivorship or Second-to-Die policy.

A Last-to-Die policy basically combines the ages of the man and woman and arrives at an "average age" for the life expectancy of the two of them. Since the expected combined survivorship of the two people is greater than that for either one of them, the insurance company will have longer to collect premiums and earn interest. That means the premium for the policy can be less for the same amount of benefit than a comparable Male Only or Female Only policy. As we are not concerned with earning returns for a surviving spouse in these situations but instead have as a focus the protection of the estate as it passes to the heirs, the Last-to-Die type policies offer by far the most optimized returns. The second death that creates the need to pay the taxes also creates the proceeds with which to pay the taxes.

To see illustrations of how the cost and return are impacted by your choice of policy type, study the charts included at the back of this book. They will provide a comprehensive comparison and allow you to best assess your own needs.

HOW TO PAY

The other major factor which will affect the cost and performance of your policy is the manner in which you elect to pay for it. Policies can be paid for in full or financed and paid for over time, they can even be structured to be paid over your entire lifetime, but, as with any financed purchase, there is an increased cost involved. In the examples I use in this book, I have usually utilized a one-pay method in order to best demonstrate the incredible benefit of life insurance as an alternative to investing. But I have also shown several concepts where we use financing in order to demonstrate the fact that, even with financing costs included, life insurance still offers a uniquely beneficial opportunity for wealth creation and preservation. I have also shown you how to have your policy absorb the cost of the financing, how Uncle Sam actually pays half of it, and how to recoup the cost of financing for your family. Now, let's make a slightly closer examination of how these different policies are structured and how those differences impact your decision.

There are three basic types of payment options: One-Pay, Limited-Pay and Life-Pay.

A One-Pay policy is the most cost effective in the long run. Because it receives the full cost of your desired coverage up-front, the insurance company has the funds on hand longer and will therefore earn a longer period of time's worth of interest. Because they make more, they are able to charge you less. Of course, the cost of a One-Pay policy is still based upon the current assumptions which determined your rate to begin with and so even this type of policy can see some changes in its cost that might require subsequent, additional payments. Although it is just as possible, especially in light of today's assumptions, that changes in those assumptions could work in your favor to build up higher cash values or to increase the ultimate death benefit. Meanwhile, the cost of the single payment plus any additions that might be needed because of changes in the original assumptions would still almost assuredly be considerably less than paying for the policy on a Limited-Pay or Life-Pay basis. Remember, the One-Pay rate is significantly less to begin with AND any increases that might impact the a Limited-Pay or Life-Pay will also affect a One-Pay policy.

There is only one major drawback to consider in an One-Pay policy. Because you have paid for the entire policy from the beginning, should the coin toss of life go against you and death were to occur sooner rather than later, you would have paid more than was necessary. With a Limited-Pay or Life-Pay policy, you have only paid for coverage through a certain period. In a manner of speaking, each new payment continues the coverage, extending it through the next portion of your life. If you die before you have paid the whole amount, it is the insurance company's loss, not yours. They will pay the whole stated return without having collected the full premium cost.

This is where it is up to you to make the decision. If you go for the Limited or Life Pay to avoid overpaying in the beginning and wind up living through the terms of the policy, you will have paid, in total, more than if you had made One Payment. But if you opt for the One-Pay plan and die too soon after having purchased it, you will have significantly overpaid for the return you receive.

The Limited and Life payment options are versions of the same thing. You extend the payments of your policy premium over time. With a Limited-Pay plan, there are a fixed number of payments to be made and those are usually made yearly for the defined period of time;

generally Limited-Pay policies are structured to be paid within five, seven or ten years although almost any plan you prefer can be accommodated.

With a Life-Pay you very simply pay a premium every year for the rest of your life. It is the same as a Limited-Pay except that it is structured so that the premium continues forever rather than reaching an end at some point.

Of course, all premium quotations are still based on the current assumptions at the time of the purchase. Yet, no matter which option you choose, the product still produces its incredible return.

As discussed above, the Limited-Pay and Life-Pay options both have advantages and disadvantages. By spreading your payments out over time, you incur what is basically, for the sake of this model, a finance charge and so the total cost of your coverage is higher than that for a One-Pay plan yielding the same result. And the longer the time over which you spread your payments, the higher the total for the policy will be. However, by paying over a larger period instead of in one lump sum, you can positively impact your cash flow possibly allowing you to afford much greater coverage than if you had to pay for the whole thing at once. Furthermore, remember that, if you elect a Limited-Pay or Life-Pay option and die early on in the policy's life the insurance company will still provide the full return you had purchased even though you had only paid a small portion of the total stated cost of the policy. However, please do keep in mind that changes in the assumptions which were current at the time that you purchased your policy will impact its performance no matter whether you elected a One-Pay, Limited-Pay or Life-Pay plan. I prefer a Life-Pay to a Limited-Pay because you can buy more for the same yearly outlay. I call it 'option' insurance. You can always cut back but usually people want more insurance when they get older and they are pleased that they bought more at the lower price when they were younger and possibly healthier.

There is another objection you might hear raised about insurance and the structuring of policies. Sometimes it happens, either through ignorance or, in truth, greed, that a policy is structured in such a way that the coverage only extends through years 80, 85 or 90 of a person's life. This usually happens when an insurance salesperson is trying to get the premium down to a level that satisfies or entices the client. By structuring the policy in such a way that the coverage ends at age 80, 85 or 90 the cost can be reduced because there is an added element of chance in the insurance company's favor. Should the insured live past 80, 85 or 90 years, the insurance company would not have to pay any death benefit even though they had collected the premiums for all those years. This can leave a person at 80, 85 or 90 years old exposed to the reality of death without any coverage or a huge premium to keep the policy in force.

We only use and recommend policies which cover through age 100 or even beyond. Yet, even so, some detractors from life insurance in general will use the fact of its age-based limitation to suggest it is not a valuable, viable form of economic protection. We all hope to live forever, but, of course, none of us will. Will you really live to be 100? I certainly hope so. Be truthful, how likely is it? Only a handful of people out of the BILLIONS who inhabit earth have ever done so. In fact, just to put things in perspective, look at the following list of personalities and the ages at which they died over the past 25 years. It's not statistically accurate, but I think it's pretty telling.

George Burns	100
Russell Colley	99
Harold Tinker	99
P.L. Travers	96
Lyle Talbot	94
Sir Arthur Whittle	93
Claudette Cobert	92
Greer Garson	92
Max Factor	92
Rene LaCoste	92
William Powell	91
Diana Trilling	91
Marlene Dietrich	90
Martha Entemann	90
Lawrence Welk	89
Sir Frank Whittle	89
Lincoln Kirstein	89

Sidney Korshack	89
Fred Astaire	88
Charlie Chaplin	88
Mae West	88
Myrna Loy	88
Roger Tory Peterson	88
Joseph Mitchell	88
Albert "Cubby" Broccoli	87
Morey Amsterdam	87
Jimmy Durante	86
Groucho Marx	86
James Cagney	86
Whit Bissell	86
Austin Hansen	86
Helen Wallenda	86
Marshall Korshack	86
Jessica Tandy	85
Burl Ives	85
Bill Monroe	85
Gloria Swanson	84
Greta Garbo	84
Rudy Vallee	84
Ginger Rogers	83
Gene Kelley	83
Fred MacMurray	83
Minnie Pearl	83
Walter Kerr	83
Mel Allen	83
Minnesota Fats	83
Barbara Stanwyck	82
Cary Grant	82
Laurence Olivier	82
Rex Harrison	82
Vincent Price	82
Morton Gould	82
Rene Clement	82
William Vickrey	82

Bette Davis	81
Jerry Siegel	81
Dorothy Lamour	81
E. Digby Blatzell	81
Herbert Huncke	81
Jack Benny	80
Alfred Hitchcock	80
Burt Lancaster	80
Walter Brennan	80
Barry Gray	80
Brownie McGhee	80
Edward G. Robinson	79
Charles Boyer	78
Martha Raye	78
Dean Martin	78
Ella Fitzgerald	78
Stirling Silliphant	78
David Opatoshu	78
Irving Lewis	78
Charles O. Finley	78
Spiro Agney	78
Henry Fonda	77
Kate Smith	77
Mary Martin	77
Danny Thomas	77
Jimmy "The Greek" Snyder	77
Raymond Burr	76
Dinah Shore	76
Mercer Ellington	76
Martin Balsalm	76
William E. Colby	76
Ethel Merman	75
Timothy Leary	75
Ben Johnson	75
Saul Bass	75
Eva Gabor	74
Phil Silvers	74

Lana Turner	74
Danny Kaye	74
Joanne Dru	74
Thomas S. Kuhn	74
David Niven	73
Bing Crosby	73
Jo Van Fleet	73
John Wayne	72
Lorne Greene	72
Ed Sullivan	72
Tennessee Ernie Ford	72
Marcello Mastroianni	72
Louis Armstrong	71
Jackie Gleason	71
Jack Weston	71
Orson Welles	70
Telly Savalas	70
Joan Crawford	69
Desi Arnaz	69
Audrey Meadows	69
Erma Bombeck	69
G. David Schine	69
Merle Oberon	68
Rita Hayworth	68
Jerry Mulligan	68
John Chancellor	68
Ingrid Bergman	67
Ava Gardner	67
Agnes Moorhead	67
Vince Edwards	67
Tomas Gutierrez Alea	67
Sarah Vaughn	66
McLean Stevenson	66
Tiny Tim	66
George Peppard	65
Rosalind Russell	65
Yul Brynner	65

George Starbuck	65
Donna Reed	64
Sammy Davis, Jr.	64
Audrey Hepburn	63
William Holden	63
Anne Baxter	62
Elizabeth Montgomery	62
Greg Morris	62
Carl Sagan	62
Peter Lawford	61
Ted Bessell	61
Johnny "Guitar" Watson	61
Van Heflin	60
Barbara Jordan	60
Loret Miller Ruppe	60
Bill Bixby	59
Conway Twitty	59
Juliet Prowse	59
David Viscott	58
Betty Grable	59
Lee Remick	55
Susan Hayward	55
Haing S. Ngor	55
Jerry Siegal	55
Ron Brown	55
Michael Landon	54
Peter Sellers	54
Jill Ireland	54
Raul Julia	54
Krzysztof Kieslowski	54
Mario Savio	54
Veronica Lake	53
Steve Tesich	53
Roy Orbison	52
Don Simpson	52
Helen Kushnick	51
Steve McQueen	50

Franklin Israel	50
Gilda Radner	48
David Janssen	48
Don Grolnick	48
Howard Rollins	46
Norman Rene	45
Marvin Gaye	44
Dan Blocker	43
John Candy	43
Margaux Hemingway	41
Bobby Darin	37
Andy Kaufman	35
Jonathan Melvoin	34
Bruce Lee	32
Karen Carpenter	32
Dana Hill Goetz	32
Bradley Nowell	28
Jim Morrison	27
Tupac Shakur	25
River Phoenix	23
Freddie Prinze	23
Jessica Dubroff	8

Average Age at Death   70

Maybe you will beat the odds and be the George Burns of the group. Or maybe you will achieve the average. Then again, there is always the possibility that you will be the Michael Landon of your group. It's hard to contemplate but avoidance won't change fate. Insurance, however, can greatly improve your economic fate.

Is the likelihood that you will live past 100 greater than the likelihood that you won't? More importantly, is the likelihood that you will live past 100 great enough to void the incredible benefits available through these Investment Alternative programs? Particularly since you can arrange it to go to 110 and beyond.

It may well be that all these choices and options are what concern people about using life insurance as an alternative to investments to protect and optimize their estates. It CAN all seem so very complicated and uncertain. There is something to be said for the simplicity of selecting a stock, buying it and waiting for it to achieve your hoped-for result. No caveats. No payment options. Yet you must keep in mind that along with the loss of caveats and options you are losing some other extremely important benefits as well. Those caveats are protecting a predetermined return which no stock can ever offer you. Those options help to make it possible for the return you need the policy to return to be available the very first day after you buy it. NO STOCK can EVER make that claim under ANY circumstances.

Life insurance operates differently than any investment because it IS different. And it is those differences which make it so uniquely valuable to you. There is simply not another financial vehicle which can perform as life insurance does, nothing else which can predetermine its return under any terms or caveats, nothing else which can make its full return available from the first day, nothing else which can come to your family both income and estate tax free for its full promised amount. Having seen the true impact of the caveats and the real considerations of the payment options, you should by now have realized that the horrible dangers which your advisors may have warned you about are simply not true. A properly bought and structured insurance policy is not an open-ended document which an insurance company can change over night to massively inflate its costs and deflate its returns. It is a tightly devised and well-regulated financial vehicle which very clearly and very specifically states it possibilities and potentials for your review. There are some risks involved in terms of changes to the current assumptions, but then again I know of absolutely NO risk-free investments and absolutely no other vehicles whose risks are balanced by such a wealth of benefits and potentials. Now, having the facts to replace the fearful insinuations you may have been exposed to, you can decide for yourself.

HOW TO BUY

I stated above that it was understandable that the purchase of life insurance, with its payment options and terms, could seem so much more complicated than a purchase of a stock which you simply select and buy and own and then sell when it, hopefully, achieves its potential. But, in fact, don't you occasionally buy your stocks on margin?

In several of the sample concepts which appeared earlier, I showed you how to borrow the cost of your insurance policy using the margin available from your existing stock portfolio or the loan power of your asset base. In this way, you can still purchase your policy on a One-Pay basis, thereby getting the absolute best rate, without having to be out of pocket for the full purchase price.

You may be wondering now why it would be advantageous to borrow the money from another source rather than simply use a Limited-Pay or Life-Pay plan. The answer is rather simple. When you finance the money for the insurance premium by selecting a Limited-Pay or Life-Pay option from the insurance company, the cost of that financing is built into the payments that you make. But when you borrow the money for the premium from an outside source, many options become available for its ultimate repayment. Though we examined those options in the concepts presented earlier, let's review them again.

To begin with, you can pay cash for your policy, reallocating funds from existing stocks, CD's, T-Bills, Municipal bonds or your IRA or pension fund. Remember, we looked before at how much more advantageous a life insurance policy can be for your family's welfare than your IRA or pension fund due to the tax-free nature of the insurance proceeds, if you did not need it to support your lifestyle. So, while there might initially be some taxes or penalties to be paid in liquidating those accounts, the benefits will still greatly out-weigh them. I can not more strongly recommend that you consider this reallocation of your available funds to diversify your assets and include life insurance, not for what it is, but for what it does in your overall financial plan. Its unique benefits add an element of valuable security to your plans that no other financial vehicle can match in terms of rate of return, tax advantages, and certainty. It is my belief that NO effective, efficient estate planning can occur UNTIL AND BEFORE life insurance has been looked into.

However, even if you do not want to reallocate existing funds or are not in position to be able to do so, you can still take advantage of the marvelous opportunities presented by life insurance at almost no cost to you whatsoever while still receiving the best rate from the insurance company. You do this by using the leverage of your existing portfolio to borrow the funds for a One-Pay policy. By buying a One-Pay policy, you get the best rate available for your coverage, thereby protecting your family's future for the least cost available and earning the best return. More importantly, *you can do so at a mere fraction of the cost of the policy or at virtually no cash flow impairment to you whatsoever*!

Consider this. Your broker call rates or LIBOR rates are probably about 7.5% right now. So you could borrow the cost of your One-Pay insurance premium for a 7.5% annual interest cost. Assuming you have a substantial enough portfolio to even require estate planning at this level, your brokerage firm would surely be more than accommodating of any loan you wished to make and would almost as certainly not be concerned with repayment of the principal loan amount. Clearly, with your portfolio as collateral, they know they are covered. This means that if you have purchased an insurance policy for $500 thousand premium in order for your heirs to receive a $5 million death benefit, you are really paying only $37.5 thousand of interest a year for it. Is there any investment of which you are aware that can perform like that? That will net $5 million tax free at your death for a cost of only $37.5 thousand a year and will do so even if you have only paid one year's worth of the interest cost? If cash and CD's and T-Bills and Munis are considered liquid assets to be used during your lifetime, or by your heirs at death, how can you not have the most liquid asset at your death of them all, with the built-in optimizer, maximizer ready to go to work at a moment's notice which may well be all you get just before dying? You could also borrow the annual premium on a Life-Pay basis if you thought it was only necessary for a few years before you have the money to pay the payments.

This is the point where some people bring up the question of the principal loan amount. They question my numbers, saying that I am 'gilding the lily' by failing to take into account that expense. But consider this. You NEED NEVER PAY THE PRINCIPAL LOAN AMOUNT BACK during your lifetime. If cash flow is a concern in your financial planning, you can simply allow that principal loan amount to remain in place until such time as your estate passes on to your heirs. At the time of your death, the loan can be repaid by your heirs as they inherit your estate.

Let's assume that you needed the $5 million of coverage because your $10 million estate was going to be faced with $5 million in estate taxes. The One-Pay cost for a $5 million policy, assuming you and your spouse average age 60, would be about $500 thousand which you are borrowing at the rate of $37.5 thousand a year. Those yearly $37.5 thousand payments are funding a return, based on current assumptions, of $5 million. Without the insurance, your heirs will inherit only $5 million of your $10 million estate. With the insurance, they will inherit the full $10 million minus the $500 thousand which will go towards repaying the principal loan amount. $9.5 million for $37.5 thousand a year, or $5 million—the choice is yours but it seems clear to me.

Furthermore, consider this: Had you not paid the $37.5 thousand per year in interest costs, it would have remained in your estate and been subject to estate taxes. And since every dollar which remains in your estate at the time of your death is subject to the up to 55% estate tax, each is worth only half to your heirs. That means that the $37.5 thousand yearly payments really only cost $18 thousand and the $500 thousand principal loan repayment only costs your heirs half. In effect, Uncle Sam has repaid the other half of your loan. Now, effectively, $18 thousand net annually is funding a net return of $5 million. It is all in the math and it is indisputable. You have created $5 million at a net cost of $250 thousand plus net interest. Can you get the same return anywhere else? If you think you can, I'd like to know where and I want to be first in line to buy.

As a further point to consider, you need not even make the loan payments in the financing model described above. Rather than pay the $37.5 thousand annual payments, you could simply let them accrue. Your brokerage firm, holding as security your millions of dollars worth of stocks and bonds, will allow you to borrow up to the margin regulations maximum. They would simply add the unpaid yearly interest fees to the original principal loan amount of $500 thousand and, at the time that your estate passed onto your heirs, would be repaid the entire amount. Suppose you live twenty years beyond the date on which you took out the loan. For the couple featured in this example, that would put them into their 80's. Accruing for twenty years, the unpaid, compounding $37.5 thousand annual interest payments and principal would total about $2 million. The net cost to your heirs would be $1 million to fund a $5 million—over 4 times net—return to your family, based on current assumptions. Will any of your stocks increase more than 4 times over their current value in the next 20 years? More importantly, will they increase the more than 8 times over their current value they would have to before estate taxes cut them in half in order for them to net the same 4 times return? Your heirs could receive $5 million from your $10 million estate if you do nothing but follow the course you are already on or they could receive $9.5 million even after repaying the principal loan amount and the accrued interest. Your current portfolio would have to increase from its present value of $10 million to more than $19 million to net the same $9.5 million for your heirs. ***In this model, $1 million buys $5 million effectively without it ever costing you a single dollar during your lifetime.***

The options available for you to utilize in designing a purchase plan that best fits your situation and desires are virtually endless. Policies can be structured to accommodate any estate, marital and financial situation. The only thing that does not change from situation to situation is the fact that NOTHING works as an alternative to investing like life insurance does. NOTHING can match the tax-free yields and the immediate availability of the full promised return. No diversified portfolio intended to provide a secure legacy for your family can possibly be said to be effectively or efficiently designed if it does not include life insurance to optimize and maximize your assets and recoup the losses of estate taxes.

When this is fully realized and completely accepted, the Investment Alternative will become a part of every portfolio and not being recommended by advisors will be tantamount to malpractice.

UNIVERSAL LIFE VS. WHOLE LIFE

There is much misinformation on this subject. If you speak to an agent who is associated with a company that sells whole life, they will tell you their policy is best. If you listen to an agent who sells Universal policies they will tell you that it is best. The bottom line will show you the truth. It's simple; just look at the prices. You don't want to pay more than you have to. All insurance companies pay when you die, so why overpay when you can save the money or buy more for the same price.

The real facts are that the Universal Life premiums were substantially lower than Whole Life when they were first released in the late 70's. This caused an immediate barrage of false and misleading propaganda about Universal Life in order to protect the turf and status quo of the long existing Whole Life and, more importantly, to protect the commissions, since the new Universal Life paid much lower commissions to the agents in most cases, based on much lower premiums for the buyer.

This propaganda has remained with many attorneys who first heard this years ago. I can't tell you how many times an attorney has insisted on Whole Life to the detriment of the client because of this predetermined mindset. I recommend to my client whichever policy is best, usually based on price, if both policies are really equal. This is where the misinformation works to the disadvantage of the client. The client is told the policy is guaranteed. It usually is not. Only the premium is guaranteed. The dividends are based on current assumptions as is Universal Life, and can and do change. This will change the end result of the Whole Life policy in the same manner as Universal Life.

The Universal Life premium is flexible, allowing the premium to be higher, lower or skipped in accordance with the contract. Whole Life policies were almost always more expensive than Universal Life so it wasn't long before they simply could not compete on a price basis. Many mutual Whole Life companies started subsidiary companies in order to sell Universal Life policies on a more competitive basis. Most Whole Life dividend companies created new term riders that brought the premium and the commissions down so they could compete with

Universal life. The term element removed whatever guarantee was left completely from the Whole Life policy.

Agents were now selling various combinations of 50% Whole Life-50% Term. This has proliferated to 40%/60%, 30%/70% and even 10%/90% combinations thus completely diluting the Whole Life Policy and its guarantees. However most advisers are not really familiar with this and many agents overlook stating anything beyond the original guarantee. If term is not introduced to the Whole Life policy it just won't be competitive.

Universal Life is easier to understand, less complicated, more flexible and almost always less expensive. It is interesting to observe that you can always make a Universal Life Policy into a Whole Life policy by over-funding the premium and paying too much but you can never make a Whole Life policy into a Universal Life policy. My clients are usually sophisticated and want to bring the premiums down to the lowest possible price and this is accomplished by funding for a minimal cash value at age 100. There are now a number of companies that guarantee if you have any cash value at age 100 the policy goes to age 110 and beyond without any additional premium. Since you do not want, need or get back the cash value when you die, why would you possibly fund for a more expensive cash value equal to the Whole life policy death benefit at age 100. It is not complicated to figure out, using a $1 million policy, that the premium will be lower on a Universal Life policy that requires $1 of cash value to continue past age 100 than on a Whole Life policy that requires up to $1 million of cash value at age 100 to continue.

A strange situation has also developed recently. Many of the previously highly rated Mutual Whole Life insurance companies have had their ratings reduced while some of the companies offering Universal Life policies are now among the highest rated companies in the industry.

Stop listening to everyone's opinion and preconceptions. Go to the bottom line. Where the savings are.

FAT/THIN POLICIES

I believe in giving insurance companies the least amount of money for the most amount of insurance. Years ago some insurance man probably explained the uses for your policy's cash values in an emergency. He probably further stated that you could borrow against the cash value to put your children through school or for your own retirement.

I buy policies for my clients strictly for death purposes. The cash value is of little importance other than to keep the policy in force. The insurance company will not give you back the cash value at your death so it is meaningless. Therefore I try to squeeze all the cash value out of the policy which results in a lower premium. I call this a thin policy versus a fat policy with a larger unnecessary cash value. In this manner, using a thin policy, you can SAVE UP TO 30% ON YOUR PREMIUM OR INCREASE THE DEATH BENEFIT UP TO 30% for the same premium.

CHURNING

There are unscrupulous insurance people, managers and even insurance companies who advocate Churning—the replacing of old insurance policies with new ones—to generate new commissions and new business on the books. But the law says that if the new policy isn't in the best interests of the client, then it is an illegal practice. Nonetheless Churning has been going on for many many years and is practiced by ignorant, uneducated and sometimes crooked salesmen who make their living in this manner. There has been quite a bit of publicity about insurance companies participating in this terrible scheme and it is abhorrent for the industry and a terrible disservice to the public. Worst of all it casts a large net and the resulting media coverage makes the entire industry suspect for crimes of the few.

On the other hand there are times that a replacement of an old policy for a new one is in the best interest of the client. In those cases I would consider it malpractice if the replacement was *not* recommended.

Many insurance companies have stated for years that it is rarely in the best interest of the client to make any replacement. This is self serving and as bad a practice as churning. Can you imagine your reaction to a stockbroker who said it was never in your best interest to change any stock regardless of the change in circumstances? However many of the media have picked up these misstatements and continue to propagate the industry's stand on all replacement. It makes it more difficult for the professional salesman who is doing the right thing by his client when the client becomes confused by the inaccurate information from the media where one brush tars all.

USING AN IRREVOCABLE TRUST

Another aspect of the alternative-to-investment plans discussed in the concepts in this book has to do with the use of an Irrevocable Trust. This is a crucial part of the structuring of these concepts but is often misunderstood, out of lack of education, or misrepresented by naysayers.

One of the key elements of the value of my methods has to do with the fact of the estate and tax free nature of life insurance. Life insurance proceeds come to the named beneficiary of the policy income tax free. Congress has passed laws that protect these funds from income taxes. This makes them unique and uniquely valuable in asset management and estate planning. Very few investments are income tax free.

To make the benefits estate tax free, however, the policy must exist outside the estate of the person who is insured. If it resides within their estate, the proceeds will be subject to estate taxes as they pass from the owner to the beneficiaries. For that reason, we utilize an Irrevocable Trust.

An Irrevocable Trust is an actual legal entity separate from the person who establishes it. Property put into the Trust is no longer owned by the grantor, it exists outside the estate and is therefore not subject to estate taxes as it passes on to its trustees and beneficiaries.

By utilizing an Irrevocable Trust to purchase the life insurance policy, the proceeds from that policy will come to the heirs both income AND estate tax free. The way it works is that the person or couple seeking to purchase the insurance sets up the trust and gifts the money for the insurance premium to the trust. If the amount of money needed to fund the premium exceeds the individual lifetime tax free gift exemption of $600 thousand or the combined amount for a couple of $1.2 million or the annual allowable $10 thousands, gift taxes will be assessed on the amounts in excess. However, in almost all cases, it can be shown that the gift taxes will still be way less than the eventual estate taxes would be if the plan were not undertaken.

Once the money has been gifted to the trust, the trust purchases the life insurance policy on the lives of the couple or individual naming the Trust as beneficiary. In this way, the insurance proceeds are protected and the heirs receive them income and estate tax free.

One drawback of the Irrevocable Trust is that property placed into it can not be removed from it. This is why it is called an *Irrevocable Trust*; it cannot be revoked. It is for this reason that I caution people not to undertake these plans with anything but excess, extra, unneeded funds. If there is any concern that the money might be needed during your lifetime, you should not undertake these plans. However, you could, in that instance, simply gift the policy to the children and that way, if the money is needed during your lifetime, you can work it out with them.

People sometimes erroneously think that a Revocable Trust, or what is popularly called a Living Trust, will accomplish the same goal as an Irrevocable Trust. But this is simply not the case. The primary purpose of a Living Trust is to avoid probate costs and publicity, a wholly different matter from estate tax costs, and to arrange to shelter the $600 thousand tax exemption that each spouse in a marriage is allowed. If one of a couple dies and their $600 thousand exemption goes directly to the other, it becomes part of the remaining spouse's estate. Now when that spouse dies, only one $600 thousand portion can pass on the heirs tax free. If, however, the original $600 thousand went to an Irrevocable Trust or the children directly instead of into the remaining spouse's estate, it would remain tax free when it inevitably passed on to the heirs.

The differences between a Revocable Trust and Irrevocable Trust are significant. Most important, a Revocable Trust is revocable and the government does not view the assets placed within it to have been removed from your estate. A Revocable Trust can ONLY shelter up to the $1.2 million of combined tax exemptions from estate taxes. No matter how much more of a person's or couple's assets are placed into the trust, it won't protect more than $600 thousand–$1.2 million. Everything in excess of the $1.2 million will be subject to the exact same estate taxes as if it were not placed into the Revocable Trust! This is an extremely critical fact to know when undertaking your asset and estate planning!

ONLY an Irrevocable Trust removes property from your estate and allows it to pass to your heirs estate tax free.

So now you are likely, and rightly, thinking that you could place ANY asset into an Irrevocable Trust for the benefit of your heirs and avoid the estate taxes on that asset's value. Lawyers look at their clients at this point and say, "Well, if you want to avoid paying estate taxes, we can place your stocks or real estate into an Irrevocable Trust and you will derive the same benefit as you would from the life insurance. In this way, they too can pass to your heirs estate tax free."

Your lawyer is right, you CAN put your stocks or bonds or real estate into an Irrevocable Trust and therefore remove it from your estate. He is WRONG though, and, in my opinion, almost to a point of malpractice, to let you think that the same end will be accomplished. **IT WILL NOT**.

If you put shares of a stock worth $1 million dollars into an Irrevocable Trust for the good of your heirs, you will indeed have transferred $1 million out of your estate. You may or may not have to pay gift taxes to do this, but that is irrelevant to this discussion as you would or would not have had to pay the same gift taxes on a cash transfer of $1 million to the trust for the purchase of life insurance.

At your death, the $1 million worth of stock would indeed come to your heirs estate tax free. **HOWEVER, at whatever point that your heirs sell that stock, if it has gained in value, THERE WILL BE CAPITAL GAINS TAXES TO PAY**. The cost basis is the cost that was paid by the original owner. If the asset had been transferred at death it would have received a stepped-up basis and there would be no capital gains tax but there will be estate tax. The $1 million transfer only avoids the estate taxes; some gift taxes are paid or the exemptions are used. The profit or capital gain earned by that stock is fully taxable under law. So your heirs are left with a valuable asset that loses up to 1/3 of its value when they sell it. And of what real value is that? As soon as they sell the stock, or bond, or piece of real estate, capital gains taxes will deplete the gain by up to about 33%. The only way to avoid that is to have a stock, bond or piece of real estate that doesn't increase in value which actually defeats the purpose of transferring the asset out of your estate. Does that make sense to anyone except a few very confused and unknowledgeable attorneys, accountants and financial planners?

Again it is, or should be clear, that as an alternative to investments, the properly structured purchase of life insurance accomplishes goals that nothing else can. There is simply no way for any investment to perform as life insurance does for the good of your family and your estate.

CASH VALUES

I want to take a brief look at the manner is which cash values accrue to an insurance policy and the impact they have upon you. This is not a highly critical area of concern in most of the plans I recommend for my clients. For the purposes of using life insurance as an alternative to investing, I generally do not structure policies to accrue the largest cash values. However, it is a factor of insurance policies which people know just enough about to have it be of concern. Also, in the new 'fully guaranteed' policies and concepts I am presenting, the build up of cash values plays a hugely significant role in providing unprecedented returns.

All life insurance policies used for the purposes described in this book have an equity. This is called cash value. There are usually two columns on your initial proposal. Most of the times they are called accumulated value and cash value or surrender value.

The difference between the two columns is the initial administrative costs including commissions charged against the cash value of the policy. These expenses are usually amortized over a 10–20 year period depending on the individual insurance company. You will notice from that point on, after the amortization is complete that both columns are the same for the rest of the life of the policy.

In the case of a one-pay policy, the cash value will usually equal and exceed the initial premium by the fourth to tenth year depending on the company.

In the past, insurance agents told you that this cash value could be used in case of emergency, to put your children through school, or even for your own retirement by utilizing a loan against the policy. This is why you paid larger premiums to create larger cash values as described previously under the section on fat/thin policies.

My purpose now is to use these policies to optimize the death benefit and minimize the cash value. This is why I have recommended thin policies, saving up to 30%, with the lowest premiums possible since the cash value is not important for this purpose.

I am only interested in maximizing the death benefit at the lowest cost possible.

Cash values are available and can be used in a variety of ways including loans however it is not recommended in the overall concepts included in this book since any loan against the policy would deplete the death benefit.

Naturally, if you pay a greater premium this will create larger cash values thus providing extra margin that can be used to absorb any negative change of the original assumptions. If there is excess cash value and it grows because of positive impacts on the original assumptions then the death benefit may ultimately grow as described in Concept 21, The Most Incredible Policy of them All.

As a general rule, I do not recommend that my clients purchase policies which carry excessive cash values. Doing so only needlessly drives up the price and I believe most people would rather pay less and retain their funds, even knowing that they might have to come back at a later day and pay more into the policy if the assumptions change against them.

Nonetheless, you should be aware of how cash values work in a policy before making any decision about which premium option to utilize in making your purchase of a life insurance policy.

INSURANCE FOR THE UNINSURABLE

It is a tragedy I encounter all too often. Some people begin thinking about their estate planning and family legacies when they are too old or too ill to be insurable anymore.

It is human nature, I guess, to put off thinking about mortality and death until the topic is virtually unavoidable. But unfortunately, by that point, it is usually too late and they may be uninsurable.

Many people despair when the truth of this becomes known to them. Suddenly they see all too clearly what they often would not look at before: that the legacy of their lifetimes faces decimation and their heirs will not derive the benefits they had worked so hard and so long to provide. It is a sad realization, indeed. But despair is not necessary. There are still ways to accomplish the asset management goals of the uninsurable.

VERIFY

The very first thing you need to do is verify that you are indeed uninsurable. It can sometimes happen that what one insurance company turns down another will approve. Furthermore, advances in medicine may make a condition that five years ago caused you to be labeled "uninsurable" insurable now. But even if you get the same dire prognosis, "Uninsurable," there are still options available to you. My firm has always taken one exam and sent it to five or ten companies. This not only gives a greater possibility of securing coverage but it also pits one company against the other for the maximum leverage and it also provides diversification.

SURROGATES

Obviously, if one partner in a marriage is uninsurable the first place to look would be to the other. You could no longer benefit from a Last-to-Die policy, but at least coverage would be available that would meet your asset management goals.

If both partners are uninsurable, they should then look around at the other members of the extended family. Perhaps the elderly couple have younger siblings who are still insurable and a policy could be purchased on them. Now it would work that when the couple dies their children would suffer the depletion of the estate from estate taxes but, when the uncle and aunt died, they would regain it. This means that they could still expect to recoup the loss within the same generation. In all other regards, the plan works the same as any other. The funds for the policy are transferred from the couple's estate into an Irrevocable Trust and any gift taxes owed as a result of transfer are paid. The Trust then purchases a policy on the lives of the aunt and uncle, or whomever is available to serve as a surrogate whether it is aunt, uncle or both; cousin, godparent, or godparents. Of course, the selection of the surrogate should take into consideration the return the selection will earn and the time it might take for the heirs to recoup the loss. For example, a Last-to-Die policy on the heirs' 60-year-old Aunt and Uncle would pay a better return than a Male Only policy on their 70-year-old Godfather. But, in all likelihood, they will have to wait longer to receive that return. The options and impacts will have to be fully presented to the couple in order for them to make an informed decision that best fulfills their goals. Nonetheless, using a surrogate insured, the losses suffered can be fully recovered within the same generation and the heirs can ultimately receive the entire estate their parents had intended for them.

GENERATION SKIPPING

Even if there is no one to use as a surrogate, the losses suffered by the estate can still be recovered. However, you may now have to skip one generation to do so.

Though the parents are uninsurable, it is pretty safe to assume that their children are not. Using the same techniques as previously discussed, the parents can transfer funds to an Irrevocable Trust, paying any necessary gift taxes, and the Trust can now use the funds to purchase insurance on the lives of the children for the sake of grandchildren! One great benefit of doing this is that the children, at their younger ages, will receive a huge return for the insurance purchase. Now the portion of the estate lost to taxes is recovered for the grandchildren at significantly less cost. Whereas a policy on the 60-year-old Aunt and Uncle, had they been available, would have netted an approximate 10–1 return, a policy on the children for the sake of the grandchildren can net as much as a 16–1 to 50–1 return! So, if the parents needed to recoup $3 million for their heirs, it would cost $300 thousand using a last-to-die, one-pay policy on the Aunt and Uncle but only $60 thousand to $100 thousand if using a Last-to-Die, One-Pay policy on the lives of their son and daughter-in-law. If the couple's children will still inherit enough, despite the tax loss, to support them nicely throughout their lifetimes, the couple might want to consider utilizing this generation skipping method even if a surrogate is available just to take advantage of the great returns available at younger ages.

Moreover, if the couple could afford the entire $300 thousand premium which would have been needed to purchase the $3 million on the lives of the Aunt and Uncle, they might want to consider going ahead and applying that same amount to a policy taken out on the lives of their children. At a 30–1 return, the $300 thousand would net $9 million. At a 40–1 return it would net $12 million. And, at a 50–1 return it would provide a highly optimized $15 million! Now the couple has not simply recouped a $3 million tax loss, they have truly employed the power of life insurance as an Investment Alternative to create great wealth for their grandchildren and posterity.

Thinking creatively, with a deep comprehension of the opportunities and alternatives available, there is almost no financial situation which can not be enhanced and resolved by the inclusion of life insurance in a diversified financial portfolio.

BENEFIT YOURSELF, BENEFIT AMERICA

Every now and again, I meet with a prospect who says to me, "Though I see the merit and potentials of your plan, I have to tell you that I love my country, appreciate the opportunities it has afforded and do not want to undertake an action that will cheat it of its due." While I applaud the integrity and patriotism of people like this, their knowledge and logic leaves a little to be desired.

Please remember, **ALMOST ALL OF THE ESTATE PLANNING CONCEPTS INCLUDED IN THIS BOOK DO NOT TAKE A SINGLE DIME FROM UNCLE SAM'S POCKET**! In most every instance, the full estate taxes due on an estate are paid. The only difference is that your family recoups the loss of those taxes through the receipt of a life insurance death benefit equal to the cost of the tax. Maybe they even gain a little extra beyond that. Maybe they even gain a LOT. But the bottom line is that the government gets every single dollar it has claimed as its due. I greatly resent the media stories which lump life insurance with complicated estate plans drawn up by aggressive attorneys under the title of tax avoidance.

Furthermore, as your family uses its increased wealth, it puts more money into circulation. Your children invest, earn interest and pay taxes on that interest. They expand businesses, hire more people, make more money and all along the way the government is receiving more taxes. Taxes on the workers' salaries. Taxes on the sale of merchandise. Taxes on the increased business profits. If your children spend the money, they pay sales taxes. If they put it into savings, it is loaned out to others who use it to develop or expand business which pay and generate taxes. If they give some of it to charity it helps reduce the burden on the government to support those charitable endeavors.

Far from being 'cheated' of his due, Uncle Sam reaps the benefits of these plans over and over again.

It has long been considered fair to decry the rich, to abhor them for

311

their attempts and abilities to get around paying their fair share, to suggest that they avoid paying what others less fortunate get stuck with. The plans contained in this book make a mockery of such thinking.

I believe in my country and I believe that the concepts I have created for wealth creation and preservation are of great benefit to it. By helping to keep money circulating through our society, a form of "trickle down" economics DOES occur. How can anyone dispute it? With more funds to invest, more jobs are created. With more jobs created, more people have work. With more people working, more taxes are being paid AND more money is being spent on consumer goods. As consumers spend more, manufacturers sell more and then make more of the goods that are being bought. As more goods are being manufactured, more people are needed to work and the whole cycle begins anew bringing more and ever greater wealth to our nation. And at every step of the way, the benefits enjoyed by Americans of a healthier, more vital America are generating more and more revenues for the United States government and the governments of the individual states.

Being a patriot does not mean you have to be a fool. It does not mean you have to sacrifice your family's well-being for the good of your nation. You CAN provide for both.

We have now seen in every detail and every way how the plans I propose that you use as an alternative to some of your investments can reap greater benefits for your family and loved ones. I think it only fitting that we end by considering how they can reap great benefits for the family of Americans in this land we call home.

Now, you judge. You have seen how the programs work for you, you have been taught every detail of what makes them work and been made aware of both the benefits and potential drawbacks in a manner I have tried to keep simple and clear, and you have been shown how the programs work for the good of America. Tell me now, are they really, "Too good to be true?" or just "Too good to be passed up?"

PART SIX

Not Just Theory— Fact

We have reviewed the concepts and studied the simple principles of arithmetic that make them work. I have shown you what I *would* do in various financial and estate situations and what you *can* do in yours. We have examined the ways and means by which these concepts can be made to work for you, discussed your options and the factors which must be weighed in selecting the ones that will best accomplish your goals and best complement your specific needs, limitations and desires. Now I would like to share with you an actual case which I recently put together for a client so that you can see the reality of these programs in action. Utilizing several different methods simultaneously to achieve a conglomeration of goals, this case in particular demonstrates the power, flexibility and simple mathematical beauty of all the generalized approaches I have presented. More importantly, it is my hope that sharing this case with you will help move these concepts out of the realm of the theoretical and into the real world where you can better conceive of the many ways they can help you to achieve the same ends.

Now the facts. Obviously, I have deleted the name of the family for whom I developed the plan. Yet the case is real, as is the optimization which has been achieved. No longer mere theory, you can now see exactly how these methods work when people allow them to. I have also further changed some of the facts and ages as well as family situations to protect the confidentiality of the client. Furthermore, they have consented to this treatment.

Interestingly, the case was developed on behalf of an entire family dynasty and many of the family members were accountants. Yet they saw through the fog of their own profession's techniques to the reality

313

of the power of the life insurance concepts which you have now had a chance to study and learn. Their open-mindedness will reap them great reward and I hope you will take a page from their book, and mine, and similarly cut through the clutter of concepts out there to embrace the bottom line of financial optimization and estate tax planning. If the numbers are too large for you, or seem overwhelming, customize them to your own situation by halving them or subtracting zeroes. They all pro rata exactly the same at any level.

I received a call from a prospect who had seen one of my ads, read my book *Die Rich and Tax Free* and watched my three hour video seminar *Make Millions, Save Millions*.

After digesting my concepts and coming to realize the value of life insurance in offsetting the large estate taxes his family would have to pay, he called me for a proposal. He wanted to use life insurance to diversify his family's financial portfolio and maximize their assets. He told me the family was worth over $600 million and already had purchased $25 million of insurance. They were paying an annual premium of $260,000 and since they had already used all of their available exemptions, they were paying annual gift taxes of approximately $130,000.

I asked, considering the size of their estate, why they had bought only $25 million. He said that was what they had been sold and they did not realize they could buy more. I explained that, in fact, the maximum policy amount allowable on one individual is $200 million and that they needed that amount of coverage to at least begin to offset the $330 million of estate taxes their family's $600 million estate was facing. Actually they needed more based on their current assets and those assets' assumed future growth.

After we had spoken twice, they agreed to be examined and I explained that, although we were going to approach several different insurance companies in order to get the best rates, they would only need one examination which would go to all the prospective companies. Meanwhile, an analysis of their existing insurance showed that they could purchase the same $25 million of coverage they currently had for $80 thousand less a year than they were paying. That's about a full 1/3 savings! Furthermore, the same $260 thousand they were paying could actually produce $37.5 million instead of $25 million. This represented a 50% increase of $12.5 million at no additional cost which would protect the next $25 million of their assets from estate taxes.

It is rather remarkable to realize that you can remove $25 million from your estate at an annual gift tax cost of only $130 thousand. By transferring the $260 thousand annual premium to your children or an Irrevocable Trust and paying the gift tax of $130 thousand you have removed the $25 million policy from your estate and made it completely estate tax free. Normally your heirs would have to pay over $13 million of estate taxes on $25 million. It is even more remarkable to realize that you can create and transfer out of your estate $37.5 million for the same $130 thousand annual gift tax.

I was then informed that one of the principals had a $20 million IRA. It was obvious from the size of their estate that they would not need the IRA for their future retirement income. If we optimized this asset and offset the horrific taxes due on an IRA at death, it would not impact or compromise their lifestyle. I showed them how, at death, the IRA would be exposed to a 15% excise success tax, income tax and estate tax totaling $16 million and leaving the family approximately $4 million from this $20 million asset.

I suggested they distribute the IRA now and pay the approximate $8 million of income tax. There would be no 15% excise tax thanks to a new law which exempts all IRA distributions from the usual excise tax from January 1,1997 through December 31, 2000. The $12 million which remained from the $20 million IRA after the $8 million of income tax was paid could then provide $8 million to purchase a one-pay, last-to-die policy yielding $64 million income and estate tax free based on their ages and current assumptions and $4 million to pay the gift taxes. Now, instead of $4 million after all taxes, the IRA would produce $64 million. Left in its present form, the IRA would have to increase to $310 million to equal the same $64 million after excise, income and estate taxes were assessed. What chance do you really think the IRA has to increase from $20 million to $310 million during their lifetime? And why would they wait and hope when they could have the same $64 million result immediately by purchasing the life insurance policy?

The patriarch of this family and his wife are in their late 80's and are not really insurable. However they are still worth over $50 million and enjoy substantial income way beyond what their lifestyle requires. They were particularly interested in leaving as much as possible to their 8 grandchildren equally; they knew that their children were well taken care of and they wished to optimize what they left to the grandchildren.

I suggested they transfer $10 million to a Generation Skipping Trust for the benefit of the 8 grandchildren. They had already used all of their exemptions and therefore would have to pay double taxes of federal estate and generation skipping amounting to approximately another $11 million totaling $21 million. The generation skipping trust would purchase $100 million of last-to-die insurance on their children, the grandchildren's parents. In this manner the 8 grandchildren would each receive $12.5 million tax free upon the deaths of their parents. And the net after tax cost to the grandparents was really only $10 million since the $21 million would have been halved by estate taxes as it passed to their heirs. Yet, making the outlay of $21 million, $10 million to the trust and $11 million to taxes, in no way negatively impacted the lifestyle of the grandparents as they still had $29 million to generate sufficient income to support them. Meanwhile, this $21 million alone provided a further diversification of the overall portfolio while creating four times what the net estate would have been after all taxes.

I also showed them one final amazing approach that could be the ultimate maximum optimization method for continuing the family dynasty.

If the grandparents took the same $10 million that was transferred to the Generation Skipping Trust and the Trustee purchased insurance on the grandchildren's lives, the return would be approximately 50 to 1 based on their various ages and current assumptions and utilizing last-to-die policies. This would create an incredible $500 million. One half billion dollars created by utilizing funds from the grandparents which they did not need during the rest of their lives and which wouldn't really affect their children's estates since they were already more than comfortable.

One final point. There is a way described in another section of this book that could have guaranteed the return of the policies purchased on the grandchildren's lives and, based on current assumptions, if the grandchildren lived long enough would have created $1 billion. $1 billion tax free created from a $21 Million transfer that would have only been worth $11 million if left to languish in an estate that did not need it.

From having $25 million of insurance for which they were paying $80 thousand more a year than necessary and which would only protect the first $50 million of this family's financial dynasty, they were now in a position to create $37.5 million from the original insurance purchase, $64 million from the optimization of the IRA and $100 million to $500 million—up to a potential $1 billion—for the benefit of their posterity and all without damaging their lifestyle in any way.

If the grandparents had been in good health, it would have been possible at their ages, in the 80's, to create $10 million to $17 million **TAX FREE** for each $10 million transferred to the children instead of the current situation which will turn each $10 million into $4.5 million after taxes. This is being accomplished for our other older clients and on a **GUARANTEED BASIS**.

Even at $600 million, insurance can more than double the family's assets utilizing the Investment Alternative.

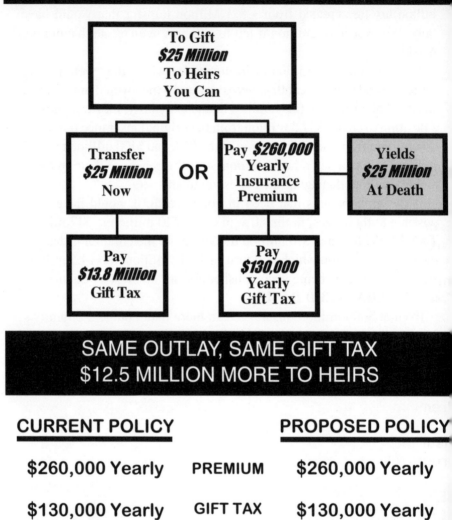

TAKE $25 MILLION OUT OF YOUR ESTATE
PAY $13.8 MILLION GIFT TAX
OR ONLY $130,000 YEARLY

To Gift
$25 Million
To Heirs
You Can

Transfer
$25 Million
Now

OR

Pay *$260,000*
Yearly
Insurance
Premium

Yields
$25 Million
At Death

Pay
$13.8 Million
Gift Tax

Pay
$130,000
Yearly
Gift Tax

SAME OUTLAY, SAME GIFT TAX
$12.5 MILLION MORE TO HEIRS

CURRENT POLICY		PROPOSED POLICY
$260,000 Yearly	PREMIUM	$260,000 Yearly
$130,000 Yearly	GIFT TAX	$130,000 Yearly
$25 Million	POLICY PAYS	$37.5 Million

SIMPLE MATHEMATICS TAKE YOU TO
THE BEST BOTTOM LINE RESULT

All figures are based on current assumptions. Charts are for illustrative purposes only.
This illustration used a last-to-die insurance policy for a male and female both age 60.
©1997 THE INVESTMENT ALTERNATIVE - Barry Kaye Associates

	Current	**INVESTMENT ALTERNATIVE METHOD**	Return Needed To Equal Investment Alternative
IRA	$20 Million	$20 Million	$310 Million
15% Excise Tax	[$3 Million]	$0*	[$46 Million]
Income Tax	[$8 Million]	[$8 Million]	[$124 Million]
Estate Or Gift Tax	[$5 Million]	[$4 Million]	[$76 Million]
Insurance Premium	$0	[$8 Million]	$0
Insurance Proceeds	$0	$64 Million	$0
NET TO HEIRS	$4 Million	$64 Million	$64 Million

$4 MILLION BECOMES $64 MILLION AFTER TAX

All figures are based on current assumptions. Charts are for illustrative purposes only.
*3 year exemption effective Jan 1, 1997 unless you die.
©1997 THE INVESTMENT ALTERNATIVE - Barry Kaye Associates

$21 MILLION TO NET $100 MILLION VERSUS $495 MILLION TO NET $100 MILLION

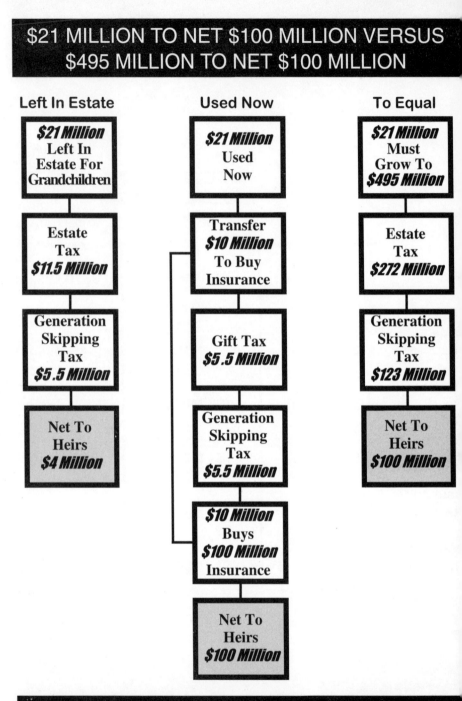

Left In Estate

$21 Million Left In Estate For Grandchildren

Estate Tax **$11.5 Million**

Generation Skipping Tax **$5.5 Million**

Net To Heirs **$4 Million**

Used Now

$21 Million Used Now

Transfer **$10 Million** To Buy Insurance

Gift Tax **$5.5 Million**

Generation Skipping Tax **$5.5 Million**

$10 Million Buys **$100 Million** Insurance

Net To Heirs **$100 Million**

To Equal

$21 Million Must Grow To **$495 Million**

Estate Tax **$272 Million**

Generation Skipping Tax **$123 Million**

Net To Heirs **$100 Million**

$4 MILLION OR $100 MILLION THE CHOICE IS UP TO YOU

All figures are based on current assumptions. Charts are for illustrative purposes only.
This illustration used a last-to-die insurance policy for a male and female both age 60.
©1997 THE INVESTMENT ALTERNATIVE - Barry Kaye Associates

$10 MILLION WORTH $4.5 MILLION AFTER TAX CAN BE WORTH UP TO $17 MILLION

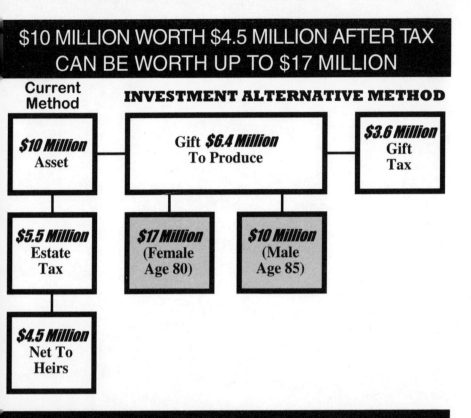

Current Method

INVESTMENT ALTERNATIVE METHOD

$10 Million Asset	Gift **$6.4 Million** To Produce	**$3.6 Million** Gift Tax
$5.5 Million Estate Tax	**$17 Million** (Female Age 80)	**$10 Million** (Male Age 85)
$4.5 Million Net To Heirs		

YOU TOO CAN ACHIEVE THESE SAME INCREDIBLE RESULTS

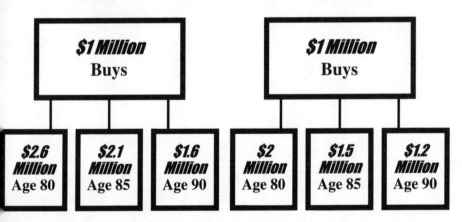

FEMALE			MALE		
$1 Million Buys			**$1 Million** Buys		
$2.6 Million Age 80	**$2.1 Million** Age 85	**$1.6 Million** Age 90	**$2 Million** Age 80	**$1.5 Million** Age 85	**$1.2 Million** Age 90

All figures are based on current assumptions. Charts are for illustrative purposes only.
This illustration used individual insurance policies based on ages shown above.

PART SEVEN

Charts and Tables

On the following pages you will find an abundance of tables that will give you information relative to your own mortality and federal estate taxation. You will also find charts that will help you customize the concepts you have read about to your own financial and estate situation. The information on these charts will help you determine your estate tax exposure, the return you can receive from your insurance purchase, the premiums based on one pay and life pay, individual male, and female and last-to-die policies. Using this information, you should be able to begin formulating the best approach to suit your needs.

The policy premium charts should be extremely helpful in not only showing you your costs at any age from 30 to possibly 90, but giving you a further understanding of how a policy actually works and the true meaning of 'based on current assumptions.' Using these charts will eliminate any later surprises and prevent misunderstanding in the event of an agent forgetting to give you the full information. In some cases it will also be a reminder to clients who forgot what they were shown when they originally bought their policy.

You can extrapolate your own age from the charts. All premiums are based on $1 million. You can pro rata up or down to the amount you wish to buy for the approximate premium. Each chart shows the premium based on current assumptions of interest and mortality. Any change in the interest or mortality can effect the premium, cash value, or death benefit. I am not overly concerned with the mortality tables since most people are living longer, due to the advances in medicine, but the rates can change . Interest can go up or down reflecting the changes in these rates based on the economy. At the time of this printing most companies rates are running between 6% and 7% with a guaranteed interest rate of approximately 4%.

I have used some of the lowest priced, highest rated insurance companies, when possible, to give you an approximate idea of the premiums. I have shown the premium at the current mortality and interest rate; the rate if interest goes down 1% and if interest goes up 1%. The next to last column shows the premium based on the GUARAN-TEED rate (the worst possible scenario). Since I have never seen this situation since the new type policies started in the late 70's, and the rate is incorrect from the beginning since NO POLICY has ever started with the lowest guaranteed interest and the highest guaranteed mortality, I have included one last necessary column. It shows the death benefit at age 100 (it increases to this amount over the years), based on current assumptions if you pay the over-funded guaranteed premium.

While you can pay the flexible premium based on any of the rates on the charts, most people choose to pay the lowest possible current premium. In certain cases, for incredible tax free returns as described earlier in the book, you may want to pay the guaranteed rate. For any advice on the implementation of these rates, and existing rates at the time of reading this book call 800–662–5433.

$1,000,000 Death Benefit based on

Male Age 30

Insurance Company	Current Mortality Current Interest	Current Mortality Current Interest +1%	Current Mortality Current Interest -1%	Guaranteed Mortality Guaranteed Interest	Death Benefit at age 100 based on guaranteed premium at current interest and mortality
E	40,513	30,525	56,105	200,714	19,894,838
A	45,227	35,486	59,612	401,522	19,929,372
D	53,916	41,507	72,811	231,651	11,745,985

Male Age 35

Insurance Company	Current Mortality Current Interest	Current Mortality Current Interest +1%	Current Mortality Current Interest -1%	Guaranteed Mortality Guaranteed Interest	Death Benefit at age 100 based on guaranteed premium at current interest and mortality
E	52,167	39,749	70,890	237,180	16,899,472
A	58,647	46,446	76,171	439,615	17,199,759
B	63,290	50,558	93,448	144,562	10,412,717
D	68,413	53,488	90,389	272,649	10,233,326

©1997 The Investment Alternative - Barry Kaye Associates

325

One Payment Premium for
$1,000,000 Death Benefit based on

Male Age 40

Insurance Company	Current Mortality Current Interest	Current Mortality Current Interest +1%	Current Mortality Current Interest -1%	Guaranteed Mortality Guaranteed Interest	Death Benefit at age 100 based on guaranteed premium at current interest and mortality
E	68,610	53,347	90,823	280,301	14,313,990
A	78,687	63,505	99,841	521,700	14,495,957
B	84,233	68,361	119,926	182,667	9,243,567
D	91,507	73,502	117,010	321,356	8,775,488

Male Age 45

Insurance Company	Current Mortality Current Interest	Current Mortality Current Interest +1%	Current Mortality Current Interest -1%	Guaranteed Mortality Guaranteed Interest	Death Benefit at age 100 based on guaranteed premium at current interest and mortality
E	90,048	71,625	115,954	330,236	12,078,643
A	102,985	84,490	128,029	545,371	12,642,664
D	104,501	84,773	131,696	498,863	8,984,994
B	112,759	93,295	154,277	230,686	8,169,688

$1,000,000 Death Benefit based on

Male Age 50

Insurance Company	Current Mortality Current Interest	Current Mortality Current Interest +1%	Current Mortality Current Interest -1%	Guaranteed Mortality Guaranteed Interest	Death Benefit at age 100 based on guaranteed premium at current interest and mortality
E	117,749	95,940	147,395	387,301	10,142,291
A	133,122	111,043	162,194	595,186	10,745,727
D	134,337	119,910	164,302	581,057	7,835,394
B	149,019	125,659	196,294	289,831	7,216,815

Male Age 55

Insurance Company	Current Mortality Current Interest	Current Mortality Current Interest +1%	Current Mortality Current Interest -1%	Guaranteed Mortality Guaranteed Interest	Death Benefit at age 100 based on guaranteed premium at current interest and mortality
E	152,507	127,258	185,707	451,405	8,474,736
A	170,501	144,714	203,524	694,499	7,914,675
D	170,506	145,490	202,795	676,289	6,845,428
B	201,745	174,425	253,993	362,293	6,227,090

© 1997 The Investment Alternative - Barry Kaye Associates

One Payment Premium for
$1,000,000 Death Benefit based on

Male Age 60

Insurance Company	Current Mortality Current Interest	Current Mortality Current Interest +1%	Current Mortality Current Interest -1%	Guaranteed Mortality Guaranteed Interest	Death Benefit at age 100 based on guaranteed premium at current interest and mortality
E	193,422	165,130	229,481	520,978	7,022,650
A	214,251	185,092	250,637	719,641	7,914,675
D	217,206	189,956	251,056	793,208	5,986,043
C	224,367	192,719	264,517	532,836	5,036,816
B	260,371	229,500	316,392	446,974	5,399,600

Male Age 65

Insurance Company	Current Mortality Current Interest	Current Mortality Current Interest +1%	Current Mortality Current Interest -1%	Guaranteed Mortality Guaranteed Interest	Death Benefit at age 100 based on guaranteed premium at current interest and mortality
E	243,315	212,794	281,053	594,131	5,751,500
D	266,197	238,098	300,162	921,000	5,255,073
A	267,331	235,492	306,060	799,191	6,500,693
C	276,343	242,642	317,800	592,119	4,349,293
B	325,908	295,224	386,805	541,945	4,606,719

$1,000,000 Death Benefit based on

Male Age 70

Insurance Company	Current Mortality Current Interest	Current Mortality Current Interest +1%	Current Mortality Current Interest -1%	Guaranteed Mortality Guaranteed Interest	Death Benefit at age 100 based on guaranteed premium at current interest and mortality
E	313,343	281,828	351,039	667,278	4,623,099
D	326,133	298,555	358,592	1,083,587	4,641,562
A	332,813	299,415	372,387	850,683	5,252,886
C	340,771	306,310	381,855	751,949	3,986,609
B	420,106	385,080	476,703	646,193	3,796,367

Male Age 75

Insurance Company	Current Mortality Current Interest	Current Mortality Current Interest +1%	Current Mortality Current Interest -1%	Guaranteed Mortality Guaranteed Interest	Death Benefit at age 100 based on guaranteed premium at current interest and mortality
A	404,897	371,680	443,234	942,153	4,298,651
E	405,169	373,478	441,746	736,780	3,644,100
C	417,399	384,201	455,782	957,447	3,646,565
D	433,500	433,500	441,849	1,248,366	3,906,522
B	499,628	465,966	550,669	729,080	3,059,128

One Payment Premium for
$1,000,000 Death Benefit based on

Male Age 80

Insurance Company	Current Mortality Current Interest	Current Mortality Current Interest +1%	Current Mortality Current Interest -1%	Guaranteed Mortality Guaranteed Interest	Death Benefit at age 100 based on guaranteed premium at current interest and mortality
A	464,817	434,020	499,474	991,404	3,404,553
E	545,161	512,244	581,883	797,204	2,790,160
B	573,469	543,819	615,180	802,817	2,411,182
C	587,365	552,879	625,524	990,291	2,912,126
D	736,900	736,900	736,900	1,253,533	2,788,461

Male Age 85

Insurance Company	Current Mortality Current Interest	Current Mortality Current Interest +1%	Current Mortality Current Interest -1%	Guaranteed Mortality Guaranteed Interest	Death Benefit at age 100 based on guaranteed premium at current interest and mortality
C	667,945	636,530	702,119	887,084	2,090,381

Male Age 89

Insurance Company	Current Mortality Current Interest	Current Mortality Current Interest +1%	Current Mortality Current Interest -1%	Guaranteed Mortality Guaranteed Interest	Death Benefit at age 100 based on guaranteed premium at current interest and mortality
D	1,623,200	1,623,200	1,623,200	1,623,200	1,747,779

$1,000,000 Death Benefit based on

Male Age 30

Insurance Company	Current Mortality Current Interest	Current Mortality Current Interest +1%	Current Mortality Current Interest -1%	Guaranteed Mortality Guaranteed Interest	Death Benefit at age 100 based on guaranteed premium at current interest and mortality
E	3,060	3,060	3,383	9,554	13,779,712
A	3,123	2,691	3,708	9,664	13,638,899
G	3,382	3,360	4,005	9,370	16,417,778
B	3,410	2,675	4,142	10,306	16,514,794
H	3,437	2,890	4,196	9,955	11,769,752
D	3,488	3,007	4,147	9,676	7,953,133
C	3,492	2,958	4,221	10,482	10,295,650

Male Age 35

Insurance Company	Current Mortality Current Interest	Current Mortality Current Interest +1%	Current Mortality Current Interest -1%	Guaranteed Mortality Guaranteed Interest	Death Benefit at age 100 based on guaranteed premium at current interest and mortality
E	3,620	3,085	4,336	11,804	12,194,004
A	4,092	3,558	4,793	11,936	11,302,729
B	4,143	3,585	5,376	12,724	14,338,950
G	4,262	3,840	5,030	11,736	14,587,924
H	4,435	3,765	5,331	12,312	10,578,192
C	4,490	3,857	5,326	12,961	9,422,148
D	4,495	3,920	5,252	11,927	7,242,370

Life Payment Premium for $1,000,000 Death Benefit based on

Male Age 40

Insurance Company	Current Mortality Current Interest	Current Mortality Current Interest +1%	Current Mortality Current Interest -1%	Guaranteed Mortality Guaranteed Interest	Death Benefit at age 100 based on guaranteed premium at current interest and mortality
E	4,834	4,260	5,668	14,743	10,827,043
B	5,454	4,967	7,086	15,944	12,486,996
A	5,557	4,905	6,389	14,905	9,742,606
G	5,668	5,160	6,589	14,892	12,891,310
C	5,857	5,122	6,799	16,196	8,669,385
H	5,938	5,142	6,968	15,396	9,477,586
D	6,163	5,496	7,012	14,886	6,541,102

Male Age 45

Insurance Company	Current Mortality Current Interest	Current Mortality Current Interest +1%	Current Mortality Current Interest -1%	Guaranteed Mortality Guaranteed Interest	Death Benefit at age 100 based on guaranteed premium at current interest and mortality
E	6,480	6,060	7,440	18,594	9,674,128
G	7,355	6,482	8,444	19,063	11,586,407
D	7,407	6,610	8,384	18,756	5,788,299
A	7,534	6,751	8,506	18,794	8,301,963
C	7,716	6,879	8,759	20,441	8,019,873
H	7,722	6,792	8,892	19,442	8,647,891
B	7,779	6,962	9,407	20,216	10,944,449

$1,000,000 Death Benefit based on

Male Age 50

Insurance Company	Current Mortality Current Interest	Current Mortality Current Interest +1%	Current Mortality Current Interest -1%	Guaranteed Mortality Guaranteed Interest	Death Benefit at age 100 based on guaranteed premium at current interest and mortality
E	8,734	8,559	9,809	23,718	8,713,657
D	9,865	8,984	10,918	23,897	5,469,295
G	9,903	8,862	11,166	24,720	10,408,458
A	9,931	9,006	11,051	23,969	7,657,578
C	10,166	9,230	11,304	26,105	7,499,096
H	10,319	9,267	11,609	24,839	7,879,073
B	10,634	9,688	12,451	25,943	9,728,078

Male Age 55

Insurance Company	Current Mortality Current Interest	Current Mortality Current Interest +1%	Current Mortality Current Interest -1%	Guaranteed Mortality Guaranteed Interest	Death Benefit at age 100 based on guaranteed premium at current interest and mortality
E	11,775	11,360	12,958	30,662	7,938,389
D	13,076	12,127	14,182	30,594	5,179,669
A	13,149	12,065	14,426	30,981	6,812,369
H	13,406	12,255	14,792	32,177	7,287,407
C	13,434	12,409	14,651	33,804	7,087,909
G	13,720	12,506	15,153	32,486	9,391,813
B	15,520	14,152	17,057	33,835	8,596,754

©1997 The Investment Alternative - Barry Kaye Associates

Life Payment Premium for
$1,000,000 Death Benefit based on

Male Age 60

Insurance Company	Current Mortality Current Interest	Current Mortality Current Interest +1%	Current Mortality Current Interest -1%	Guaranteed Mortality Guaranteed Interest	Death Benefit at age 100 based on guaranteed premium at current interest and mortality
E	15,710	15,560	16,975	40,146	7,293,481
H	17,343	16,131	18,779	42,252	6,765,650
A	17,502	16,251	18,942	40,557	6,037,806
D	17,667	16,679	18,789	39,333	4,877,796
C	17,796	16,698	19,068	24,270	2,749,503
G	19,115	17,731	20,708	43,275	8,550,848
B	23,470	19,623	22,622	44,740	7,818,073

Male Age 65

Insurance Company	Current Mortality Current Interest	Current Mortality Current Interest +1%	Current Mortality Current Interest -1%	Guaranteed Mortality Guaranteed Interest	Death Benefit at age 100 based on guaranteed premium at current interest and mortality
E	22,059	22,059	22,419	53,324	6,714,600
H	22,903	22,836	24,285	56,357	6,286,995
D	23,155	22,207	24,214	50,437	4,551,394
A	23,595	22,192	25,175	53,859	5,767,636
C	23,630	22,488	24,924	31,320	2,476,590
G	28,909	24,392	27,609	58,494	7,887,226
B	32,430	27,500	29,960	59,996	7,189,941

$1,000,000 Death Benefit based on

Male Age 70

Insurance Company	Current Mortality Current Interest	Current Mortality Current Interest +1%	Current Mortality Current Interest -1%	Guaranteed Mortality Guaranteed Interest	Death Benefit at age 100 based on guaranteed premium at current interest and mortality
D	30,978	30,184	31,858	65,304	4,164,211
A	32,294	30,789	33,959	72,404	5,055,407
C	32,440	32,440	33,541	41,730	2,238,399
E	33,060	33,060	33,060	71,705	6,096,849
H	34,375	34,375	35,053	76,267	5,800,585
G	35,423	33,896	37,111	80,205	7,325,100
B	52,780	35,374	39,172	81,782	6,514,366

Male Age 75

Insurance Company	Current Mortality Current Interest	Current Mortality Current Interest +1%	Current Mortality Current Interest -1%	Guaranteed Mortality Guaranteed Interest	Death Benefit at age 100 based on guaranteed premium at current interest and mortality
D	44,670	44,094	45,298	85,174	3,629,717
A	45,013	43,456	46,711	98,500	4,789,826
E	48,060	48,060	48,819	97,483	5,494,252
C	49,220	49,220	49,220	57,710	2,026,399
G	51,113	49,729	52,620	111,936	6,666,232
H	52,542	52,542	52,542	104,698	5,390,341
B	76,550	46,128	49,868	109,447	5,771,664

Life Payment Premium for $1,000,000 Death Benefit based on

Male Age 80

Insurance Company	Current Mortality Current Interest	Current Mortality Current Interest +1%	Current Mortality Current Interest -1%	Guaranteed Mortality Guaranteed Interest	Death Benefit at age 100 based on guaranteed premium at current interest and mortality
I	49,560	49,560	49,560	49,560	1,000,000
A	63,422	61,992	65,170	133,597	4,892,434
D	73,690	73,690	73,690	111,556	2,861,948
G	73,846	72,685	75,101	128,494	5,019,513
E	77,588	76,277	78,984	132,219	4,722,606
C	90,580	90,580	90,580	90,940	1,125,406
B	110,450	56,941	60,544	146,268	4,915,395

Male Age 85

Insurance Company	Current Mortality Current Interest	Current Mortality Current Interest +1%	Current Mortality Current Interest -1%	Guaranteed Mortality Guaranteed Interest	Death Benefit at age 100 based on guaranteed premium at current interest and mortality
I	64,680	64,680	64,680	64,680	1,000,000
D	112,040	112,040	112,040	164,611	2,677,265
C	125,230	125,230	125,230	125,230	1,189,854

Male Age 90

Insurance Company	Current Mortality Current Interest	Current Mortality Current Interest +1%	Current Mortality Current Interest -1%	Guaranteed Mortality Guaranteed Interest	Death Benefit at age 100 based on guaranteed premium at current interest and mortality
D	84,480	84,480	84,480	84,480	1,000,000

$1,000,000 Death Benefit based on

Female Age 30

Insurance Company	Current Mortality Current Interest	Current Mortality Current Interest +1%	Current Mortality Current Interest -1%	Guaranteed Mortality Guaranteed Interest	Death Benefit at age 100 based on guaranteed premium at current interest and mortality
A	31,760	24,977	42,027	373,301	18,254,571
E	31,992	24,165	44,826	179,046	18,175,498
B	42,197	34,027	62,758	266,579	16,747,572
D	46,138	35,416	62,706	201,166	10,447,594

Female Age 35

Insurance Company	Current Mortality Current Interest	Current Mortality Current Interest +1%	Current Mortality Current Interest -1%	Guaranteed Mortality Guaranteed Interest	Death Benefit at age 100 based on guaranteed premium at current interest and mortality
E	40,960	30,916	56,420	211,514	15,415,199
A	41,209	32,650	53,825	410,080	15,664,093
B	54,324	44,036	79,025	326,422	14,383,371
D	58,860	45,902	78,229	236,698	9,073,603

One Payment Premium for
$1,000,000 Death Benefit based on

Female Age 40

Insurance Company	Current Mortality Current Interest	Current Mortality Current Interest +1%	Current Mortality Current Interest -1%	Guaranteed Mortality Guaranteed Interest	Death Benefit at age 100 based on guaranteed premium at current interest and mortality
A	53,767	43,054	69,127	485,044	13,204,893
E	54,457	42,009	72,942	249,707	12,993,178
B	69,286	56,521	98,571	399,599	12,385,357
D	77,870	62,176	100,465	278,308	7,778,595

Female Age 45

Insurance Company	Current Mortality Current Interest	Current Mortality Current Interest +1%	Current Mortality Current Interest -1%	Guaranteed Mortality Guaranteed Interest	Death Benefit at age 100 based on guaranteed premium at current interest and mortality
A	68,770	55,548	87,215	525,594	11,305,463
E	73,021	57,757	94,870	293,456	10,878,470
D	78,501	64,055	98,790	424,615	8,515,606
B	92,513	76,795	126,778	492,228	10,554,811

338

$1,000,000 Death Benefit based on

Female Age 50

Insurance Company	Current Mortality Current Interest	Current Mortality Current Interest +1%	Current Mortality Current Interest -1%	Guaranteed Mortality Guaranteed Interest	Death Benefit at age 100 based on guaranteed premium at current interest and mortality
A	88,249	72,120	110,115	538,542	9,711,693
E	96,680	78,301	122,062	343,502	9,084,496
D	98,800	82,090	121,272	490,852	7,396,934
B	122,806	103,792	162,164	604,287	8,959,437

Female Age 55

Insurance Company	Current Mortality Current Interest	Current Mortality Current Interest +1%	Current Mortality Current Interest -1%	Guaranteed Mortality Guaranteed Interest	Death Benefit at age 100 based on guaranteed premium at current interest and mortality
A	114,532	95,147	140,033	600,856	8,193,240
E	123,981	102,377	152,827	400,197	7,590,061
D	124,843	106,018	149,315	577,438	6,527,454
B	163,677	141,075	207,977	741,567	7,576,627

©1997 The Investment Alternative - Barry Kaye Associates

One Payment Premium for
$1,000,000 Death Benefit based on

Female Age 60

Insurance Company	Current Mortality Current Interest	Current Mortality Current Interest +1%	Current Mortality Current Interest -1%	Guaranteed Mortality Guaranteed Interest	Death Benefit at age 100 based on guaranteed premium at current interest and mortality
A	149,417	126,607	178,508	693,171	6,926,126
E	159,218	134,429	191,213	463,839	6,305,498
D	160,107	139,371	186,207	692,762	5,823,037
C	180,180	151,272	217,591	369,402	3,684,759
B	209,869	183,792	258,335	898,507	6,431,638

Female Age 65

Insurance Company	Current Mortality Current Interest	Current Mortality Current Interest +1%	Current Mortality Current Interest -1%	Guaranteed Mortality Guaranteed Interest	Death Benefit at age 100 based on guaranteed premium at current interest and mortality
A	191,437	165,526	223,504	753,126	5,846,332
E	197,978	170,617	232,194	535,044	5,234,280
D	198,900	177,080	225,570	826,644	5,201,864
C	225,228	193,598	264,809	451,425	3,390,422
B	264,187	235,022	315,556	1,985,628	5,458,811

$1,000,000 Death Benefit based on

Female Age 70

Insurance Company	Current Mortality Current Interest	Current Mortality Current Interest +1%	Current Mortality Current Interest -1%	Guaranteed Mortality Guaranteed Interest	Death Benefit at age 100 based on guaranteed premium at current interest and mortality
A	239,901	211,841	273,639	840,066	4,921,122
D	242,386	220,367	268,540	987,033	4,646,027
E	248,292	219,403	283,265	610,470	4,284,807
C	282,699	249,354	323,020	605,243	3,369,446
B	345,079	313,795	396,705	1,308,101	4,504,066

Female Age 75

Insurance Company	Current Mortality Current Interest	Current Mortality Current Interest +1%	Current Mortality Current Interest -1%	Guaranteed Mortality Guaranteed Interest	Death Benefit at age 100 based on guaranteed premium at current interest and mortality
D	295,488	274,071	320,174	1,130,612	3,955,274
A	302,173	273,413	335,726	906,771	4,027,102
E	338,137	308,497	372,653	689,000	3,434,766
C	357,642	324,567	396,299	739,893	3,014,184

©1997 The Investment Alternative - Barry Kaye Associates

One Payment Premium for $1,000,000 Death Benefit based on

Female Age 80

Insurance Company	Current Mortality Current Interest	Current Mortality Current Interest +1%	Current Mortality Current Interest -1%	Guaranteed Mortality Guaranteed Interest	Death Benefit at age 100 based on guaranteed premium at current interest and mortality
A	358,585	331,486	389,301	903,161	3,169,921
E	464,986	433,249	500,680	762,211	2,705,271
D	490,000	490,000	490,000	1,143,190	2,836,793
B	512,325	483,986	525,545	1,698,508	2,897,606
C	539,196	503,371	579,130	959,019	2,794,249

Female Age 85

Insurance Company	Current Mortality Current Interest	Current Mortality Current Interest +1%	Current Mortality Current Interest -1%	Guaranteed Mortality Guaranteed Interest	Death Benefit at age 100 based on guaranteed premium at current interest and mortality
C	638,360	605,264	674,508	1,003,232	2,289,614
D	809,200	809,200	809,200	1,032,086	1,893,301

Female Age 89

Insurance Company	Current Mortality Current Interest	Current Mortality Current Interest +1%	Current Mortality Current Interest -1%	Guaranteed Mortality Guaranteed Interest	Death Benefit at age 100 based on guaranteed premium at current interest and mortality
D	1,354,900	1,354,900	1,354,900	1,354,900	1,504,841

$1,000,000 Death Benefit based on

Female Age 30

Insurance Company	Current Mortality Current Interest	Current Mortality Current Interest +1%	Current Mortality Current Interest -1%	Guaranteed Mortality Guaranteed Interest	Death Benefit at age 100 based on guaranteed premium at current interest and mortality
A	2,225	2,112	2,661	8,407	14,266,228
E	2,660	2,660	2,683	8,309	12,240,458
H	2,684	2,627	3,284	8,651	10,460,424
C	2,941	2,459	3,539	9,105	9,020,707
D	2,965	2,553	3,540	8,419	7,066,612
G	3,120	3,120	3,120	8,056	14,821,812
B	3,340	2,259	3,395	9,006	14,433,864

Female Age 35

Insurance Company	Current Mortality Current Interest	Current Mortality Current Interest +1%	Current Mortality Current Interest -1%	Guaranteed Mortality Guaranteed Interest	Death Benefit at age 100 based on guaranteed premium at current interest and mortality
E	2,820	2,660	3,415	10,201	10,758,203
A	2,878	2,486	3,413	10,319	33,746,435
G	3,240	3,240	3,645	10,037	12,971,683
H	3,457	3,389	4,169	10,633	9,300,576
C	3,740	3,179	4,440	11,188	8,190,699
D	3,835	3,342	4,496	10,314	6,364,299
B	3,980	3,022	4,397	11,050	12,386,585

Life Payment Premium for
$1,000,000 Death Benefit based on

Female Age 40

Insurance Company	Current Mortality Current Interest	Current Mortality Current Interest +1%	Current Mortality Current Interest -1%	Guaranteed Mortality Guaranteed Interest	Death Benefit at age 100 based on guaranteed premium at current interest and mortality
E	3,795	3,560	4,488	12,627	9,406,995
A	3,826	3,334	4,476	12,770	10,901,829
G	4,080	4,080	4,668	12,621	11,436,022
H	4,578	4,527	5,401	13,175	8,256,686
B	4,710	4,020	5,669	13,656	10,748,585
C	4,820	4,180	5,628	12,860	7,462,758
D	5,179	4,603	5,928	12,739	5,692,370

Female Age 45

Insurance Company	Current Mortality Current Interest	Current Mortality Current Interest +1%	Current Mortality Current Interest -1%	Guaranteed Mortality Guaranteed Interest	Death Benefit at age 100 based on guaranteed premium at current interest and mortality
A	5,046	4,431	5,833	15,887	9,254,214
E	5,183	4,562	5,981	15,712	8,222,868
G	5,417	5,280	6,236	15,932	9,930,179
D	5,447	4,904	6,123	15,997	5,423,130
H	5,927	5,875	6,873	16,412	7,414,647
C	6,238	5,515	7,163	17,267	6,823,607
B	6,260	5,541	7,445	17,110	9,264,579

$1,000,000 Death Benefit based on

Female Age 50

Insurance Company	Current Mortality Current Interest	Current Mortality Current Interest +1%	Current Mortality Current Interest -1%	Guaranteed Mortality Guaranteed Interest	Death Benefit at age 100 based on guaranteed premium at current interest and mortality
A	6,787	6,028	7,729	19,934	7,881,269
D	7,033	6,419	7,776	20,085	5,056,873
E	7,038	6,314	7,943	19,718	7,243,417
G	7,097	6,840	8,042	20,283	8,759,862
H	7,788	7,735	8,855	20,624	6,672,695
C	8,065	7,232	9,099	21,694	6,296,255
B	8,430	7,655	9,808	21,639	8,044,482

Female Age 55

Insurance Company	Current Mortality Current Interest	Current Mortality Current Interest +1%	Current Mortality Current Interest -1%	Guaranteed Mortality Guaranteed Interest	Death Benefit at age 100 based on guaranteed premium at current interest and mortality
D	9,195	8,532	9,975	25,756	4,778,975
A	9,224	8,296	10,340	25,286	6,764,419
E	9,322	8,480	10,341	25,016	6,494,035
G	9,812	9,000	10,899	26,145	7,720,028
H	10,069	9,974	11,251	26,209	6,071,301
C	10,425	9,472	11,574	27,557	5,863,529
B	11,850	10,704	13,062	27,751	7,026,839

©1997 The Investment Alternative - Barry Kaye Associates

Life Payment Premium for
$1,000,000 Death Benefit based on

Female Age 60

Insurance Company	Current Mortality Current Interest	Current Mortality Current Interest +1%	Current Mortality Current Interest -1%	Guaranteed Mortality Guaranteed Interest	Death Benefit at age 100 based on guaranteed premium at current interest and mortality
D	12,366	11,689	13,145	33,642	4,541,566
E	12,513	11,561	13,631	32,212	5,859,238
A	12,787	11,667	14,095	32,557	5,842,404
C	13,599	12,524	14,857	19,210	2,290,045
G	14,059	12,974	15,309	34,237	6,878,798
H	14,298	14,298	14,298	33,821	2,820,702
B	16,190	14,622	17,170	35,967	6,282,043

Female Age 65

Insurance Company	Current Mortality Current Interest	Current Mortality Current Interest +1%	Current Mortality Current Interest -1%	Guaranteed Mortality Guaranteed Interest	Death Benefit at age 100 based on guaranteed premium at current interest and mortality
D	16,277	15,628	17,011	44,022	4,295,848
E	16,422	15,379	17,617	42,428	5,405,543
A	17,794	16,470	19,301	42,878	5,573,331
C	18,128	16,958	19,461	24,740	2,056,050
G	18,730	17,448	20,160	45,893	6,376,824
H	20,678	20,678	20,678	44,682	5,142,583
B	23,210	19,608	22,291	47,837	5,783,286

$1,000,000 Death Benefit based on

Female Age 70

Insurance Company	Current Mortality Current Interest	Current Mortality Current Interest +1%	Current Mortality Current Interest -1%	Guaranteed Mortality Guaranteed Interest	Death Benefit at age 100 based on guaranteed premium at current interest and mortality
D	21,341	20,762	21,986	57,367	3,976,672
E	22,255	22,059	23,439	56,978	4,973,412
G	24,169	22,920	25,618	63,017	5,905,064
A	24,662	23,135	26,359	57,578	4,936,097
C	24,887	23,674	26,237	32,910	1,849,574
H	31,265	31,265	31,265	60,276	4,679,694
B	35,870	62,516	29,784	65,344	5,240,585

Female Age 75

Insurance Company	Current Mortality Current Interest	Current Mortality Current Interest +1%	Current Mortality Current Interest -1%	Guaranteed Mortality Guaranteed Interest	Death Benefit at age 100 based on guaranteed premium at current interest and mortality
D	28,744	28,265	29,269	73,373	3,485,366
E	34,953	34,059	36,000	78,870	4,482,948
H	47,831	47,831	47,831	84,040	4,406,143
G	35,277	34,061	36,583	89,405	5,432,359
A	35,283	33,950	37,133	79,696	4,805,353
C	38,170	38,170	38,170	46,070	1,664,234
B	59,950	40,147	37,024	89,574	4,722,109

Life Payment Premium for $1,000,000 Death Benefit based on

Female Age 80

Insurance Company	Current Mortality Current Interest	Current Mortality Current Interest +1%	Current Mortality Current Interest -1%	Guaranteed Mortality Guaranteed Interest	Death Benefit at age 100 based on guaranteed premium at current interest and mortality
I	37,440	37,440	37,440	37,440	1,000,000
G	41,729	40,780	42,727	128,493	5,092,235
H	47,831	47,831	47,831	84,040	4,406,143
D	49,000	49,000	49,000	94,896	2,752,310
A	51,299	49,752	53,279	111,930	4,182,687
E	59,037	57,825	60,326	110,772	4,037,369
C	76,590	76,590	76,590	76,950	1,000,000
B	90,720	51,602	48,505	123,737	4,135,441

Female Age 85

Insurance Company	Current Mortality Current Interest	Current Mortality Current Interest +1%	Current Mortality Current Interest -1%	Guaranteed Mortality Guaranteed Interest	Death Benefit at age 100 based on guaranteed premium at current interest and mortality
I	47,400	47,400	47,400	47,400	1,000,000
D	80,920	80,920	80,920	143,033	2,554,761
C	112,200	112,200	112,200	112,200	1,146,400

Female Age 90

Insurance Company	Current Mortality Current Interest	Current Mortality Current Interest +1%	Current Mortality Current Interest -1%	Guaranteed Mortality Guaranteed Interest	Death Benefit at age 100 based on guaranteed premium at current interest and mortality
I	61,320	61,320	61,320	61,320	1,000,000

$1,000,000 Death Benefit based on

Last To Die Age 30

Insurance Company	Current Mortality Current Interest	Current Mortality Current Interest +1%	Current Mortality Current Interest -1%	Guaranteed Mortality Guaranteed Interest	Death Benefit at age 100 based on guaranteed premium at current interest and mortality
A	16,397	11,568	24,418	141,440	40,376,938
B	19,506	14,268	27,749	158,397	12,992,850
D	20,140	12,940	32,106	224,651	12,884,782

Last To Die Age 35

Insurance Company	Current Mortality Current Interest	Current Mortality Current Interest +1%	Current Mortality Current Interest -1%	Guaranteed Mortality Guaranteed Interest	Death Benefit at age 100 based on guaranteed premium at current interest and mortality
A	22,772	16,380	32,987	171,604	33,746,435
D	26,923	17,945	41,243	270,025	11,359,593
B	27,058	20,164	37,511	201,855	11,164,679
E	27,470	19,226	40,326	166,281	12,153,893
C	30,284	20,711	46,047	328,698	8,267,968

One Payment Premium for
$1,000,000 Death Benefit based on

Last To Die Age 40

Insurance Company	Current Mortality Current Interest	Current Mortality Current Interest +1%	Current Mortality Current Interest -1%	Guaranteed Mortality Guaranteed Interest	Death Benefit at age 100 based on guaranteed premium at current interest and mortality
A	30,532	22,185	43,387	206,260	28,068,952
E	35,552	25,410	50,782	199,864	10,460,807
D	35,836	24,778	52,780	323,756	10,009,862
B	37,746	28,761	50,866	258,672	9,746,329
C	39,338	27,783	57,684	371,711	7,786,834

Last To Die Age 45

Insurance Company	Current Mortality Current Interest	Current Mortality Current Interest +1%	Current Mortality Current Interest -1%	Guaranteed Mortality Guaranteed Interest	Death Benefit at age 100 based on guaranteed premium at current interest and mortality
A	41,514	30,695	57,559	247,670	23,305,709
E	47,052	34,631	65,832	240,494	8,983,900
D	49,900	35,918	70,454	386,659	8,620,236
C	52,093	38,073	73,440	531,963	7,088,513
B	52,636	41,104	68,858	330,778	8,466,806

$1,000,000 Death Benefit based on

Last To Die Age 50

Insurance Company	Current Mortality Current Interest	Current Mortality Current Interest +1%	Current Mortality Current Interest -1%	Guaranteed Mortality Guaranteed Interest	Death Benefit at age 100 based on guaranteed premium at current interest and mortality
A	57,526	43,609	77,357	297,523	19,315,405
E	62,593	47,133	85,771	288,498	7,696,125
D	66,415	49,682	90,141	459,266	7,532,194
C	70,198	52,415	96,236	595,381	6,612,269
B	73,031	58,540	92,694	421,970	7,318,799

Last To Die Age 55

Insurance Company	Current Mortality Current Interest	Current Mortality Current Interest +1%	Current Mortality Current Interest -1%	Guaranteed Mortality Guaranteed Interest	Death Benefit at age 100 based on guaranteed premium at current interest and mortality
F	78,764	60,008	104,862	n/a	n/a
A	79,541	61,960	103,634	355,917	15,957,602
E	84,593	64,983	111,825	345,530	6,573,555
D	87,754	67,997	114,621	541,098	6,546,073
C	89,032	68,449	118,155	982,469	6,720,149
B	101,105	83,268	124,450	536,735	6,284,409

©1997 The Investment Alternative - Barry Kaye Associates

One Payment Premium for
$1,000,000 Death Benefit based on

Last To Die Age 60

Insurance Company	Current Mortality Current Interest	Current Mortality Current Interest +1%	Current Mortality Current Interest -1%	Guaranteed Mortality Guaranteed Interest	Death Benefit at age 100 based on guaranteed premium at current interest and mortality
F	109,586	86,574	140,299	n/a	n/a
A	109,635	87,914	138,274	422,764	13,105,874
E	114,400	90,892	145,765	412,072	5,585,154
D	114,897	92,246	114,564	630,491	5,645,960
C	118,853	94,657	151,749	463,111	3,465,740
B	132,148	111,669	158,322	679,886	4,044,723

Last To Die Age 65

Insurance Company	Current Mortality Current Interest	Current Mortality Current Interest +1%	Current Mortality Current Interest -1%	Guaranteed Mortality Guaranteed Interest	Death Benefit at age 100 based on guaranteed premium at current interest and mortality
D	148,742	123,614	180,464	723,122	4,813,748
E	150,467	123,188	185,519	488,013	4,716,177
A	151,429	125,219	184,688	499,293	10,691,195
C	153,191	125,607	189,304	298,894	2,604,811
B	176,230	153,341	204,407	854,635	4,605,444

$1,000,000 Death Benefit based on

Last To Die Age 70

Insurance Company	Current Mortality Current Interest	Current Mortality Current Interest +1%	Current Mortality Current Interest -1%	Guaranteed Mortality Guaranteed Interest	Death Benefit at age 100 based on guaranteed premium at current interest and mortality
F	177,893	209,541	248,553	n/a	n/a
D	191,039	164,244	223,661	806,689	3,999,998
C	198,567	168,089	236,824	368,764	2,252,583
E	200,903	170,289	238,782	574,395	3,931,610
A	205,308	174,852	242,586	583,200	8,650,342
B	211,608	188,501	239,225	475,745	3,124,744

Last To Die Age 75

Insurance Company	Current Mortality Current Interest	Current Mortality Current Interest +1%	Current Mortality Current Interest -1%	Guaranteed Mortality Guaranteed Interest	Death Benefit at age 100 based on guaranteed premium at current interest and mortality
D	237,152	210,616	268,384	862,638	3,230,427
C	257,666	225,320	296,794	484,820	2,230,997
E	264,254	231,545	303,256	666,719	3,232,416
A	288,512	252,351	331,281	668,103	6,738,871
B	315,946	287,176	349,184	1,292,767	3,246,086

One Payment Premium for
$1,000,000 Death Benefit based on

Last To Die Age 80

Insurance Company	Current Mortality Current Interest	Current Mortality Current Interest +1%	Current Mortality Current Interest -1%	Guaranteed Mortality Guaranteed Interest	Death Benefit at age 100 based on guaranteed premium at current interest and mortality
D	280,306	257,255	306,936	867,498	2,472,736
E	347,193	314,069	385,250	757,574	2,601,355
C	402,842	371,602	438,472	786,360	2,212,615
A	407,844	366,062	455,607	743,816	5,006,572
B	438,989	470,454	474,270	1,540,098	2,637,962

Last To Die Age 85

Insurance Company	Current Mortality Current Interest	Current Mortality Current Interest +1%	Current Mortality Current Interest -1%	Guaranteed Mortality Guaranteed Interest	Death Benefit at age 100 based on guaranteed premium at current interest and mortality
D	360,884	338,229	385,963	786,691	1,672,185

$1,000,000 Death Benefit based on

Last To Die Age 30

Insurance Company	Current Mortality Current Interest	Current Mortality Current Interest +1%	Current Mortality Current Interest -1%	Guaranteed Mortality Guaranteed Interest	Death Benefit at age 100 based on guaranteed premium at current interest and mortality
F	981	370	1,598	n/a	n/a
A	1,138	949	1,498	6,175	11,915,801
D	1,267	950	1,767	8,358	7,885,601
B	1,297	1,061	1,632	5,425	11,059,992
C	1,387	1,039	1,094	6,866	8,035,584
H	1,525	1,126	2,096	7,267	8,172,039
G	1,880	1,880	1,927	5,718	10,920,856

Last To Die Age 35

Insurance Company	Current Mortality Current Interest	Current Mortality Current Interest +1%	Current Mortality Current Interest -1%	Guaranteed Mortality Guaranteed Interest	Death Benefit at age 100 based on guaranteed premium at current interest and mortality
F	1,266	683	1,973	n/a	n/a
A	1,588	1,355	2,038	7,724	10,247,184
D	1,709	1,290	2,296	10,039	6,950,930
B	1,812	1,508	2,227	6,889	9,565,632
C	1,902	1,471	2,518	8,699	7,463,747
H	2,042	1,542	2,714	8,809	7,300,150
G	2,400	2,400	2,622	7,248	9,507,192
E	3,090	3,090	3,090	7,534	8,101,298

©1997 The Investment Alternative - Barry Kaye Associates

Life Payment Premium for $1,000,000 Death Benefit based on

Last To Die Age 40

Insurance Company	Current Mortality Current Interest	Current Mortality Current Interest +1%	Current Mortality Current Interest -1%	Guaranteed Mortality Guaranteed Interest	Death Benefit at age 100 based on guaranteed premium at current interest and mortality
F	1,807	1,178	2,622	n/a	n/a
A	2,145	1,858	2,709	9,642	8,860,432
D	2,330	1,784	2,987	12,054	6,126,521
C	2,492	1,985	3,193	10,617	7,077,518
B	2,554	2,168	3,060	8,805	8,301,464
H	2,727	2,126	3,528	10,889	6,551,206
G	2,840	2,840	3,571	9,212	8,323,334
E	3,090	3,090	3,090	9,405	7,229,952

Last To Die Age 45

Insurance Company	Current Mortality Current Interest	Current Mortality Current Interest +1%	Current Mortality Current Interest -1%	Guaranteed Mortality Guaranteed Interest	Death Benefit at age 100 based on guaranteed premium at current interest and mortality
F	2,629	1,824	3,472	n/a	n/a
A	2,948	2,609	3,645	12,135	7,704,226
D	3,262	2,619	4,082	14,471	5,298,671
C	3,344	2,746	4,139	13,636	6,656,624
E	3,489	3,489	4,045	11,861	6,469,093
B	3,610	3,132	4,214	11,332	7,227,870
H	3,642	3,126	4,573	13,527	5,914,960
G	3,963	3,320	4,854	11,773	7,524,451

$1,000,000 Death Benefit based on

Last To Die Age 50

Insurance Company	Current Mortality Current Interest	Current Mortality Current Interest +1%	Current Mortality Current Interest -1%	Guaranteed Mortality Guaranteed Interest	Death Benefit at age 100 based on guaranteed premium at current interest and mortality
F	3,742	2,817	4,648	n/a	n/a
A	4,147	3,771	4,998	15,457	6,744,247
E	4,414	4,089	5,370	15,087	5,822,281
D	4,439	3,680	5,375	17,405	4,655,531
C	4,587	3,831	5,555	17,507	6,273,007
H	4,792	4,792	5,864	17,048	5,401,905
B	5,101	4,526	5,801	14,714	6,320,269
G	5,314	4,433	6,404	15,164	6,548,872

Last To Die Age 55

Insurance Company	Current Mortality Current Interest	Current Mortality Current Interest +1%	Current Mortality Current Interest -1%	Guaranteed Mortality Guaranteed Interest	Death Benefit at age 100 based on guaranteed premium at current interest and mortality
F	5,185	4,075	6,194	n/a	n/a
A	5,862	5,485	6,883	19,894	5,953,460
C	5,930	5,078	6,990	21,829	6,058,112
E	6,090	5,589	7,204	19,448	5,278,488
D	6,112	5,164	7,096	21,120	4,109,904
H	6,715	6,715	7,554	21,832	4,971,751
G	7,152	6,079	8,439	19,776	5,911,397
B	7,215	6,553	7,994	19,316	5,549,722

Life Payment Premium for $1,000,000 Death Benefit based on

Last To Die Age 60

Insurance Company	Current Mortality Current Interest	Current Mortality Current Interest +1%	Current Mortality Current Interest -1%	Guaranteed Mortality Guaranteed Interest	Death Benefit at age 100 based on guaranteed premium at current interest and mortality
F	7,551	6,288	8,691	n/a	n/a
C	8,165	7,200	9,328	28,977	5,810,616
D	8,239	7,241	9,398	26,043	3,667,526
A	8,344	8,042	9,549	25,895	5,294,809
E	8,794	8,090	9,762	25,437	4,816,964
H	9,566	9,566	10,014	28,324	4,599,787
B	9,746	9,050	10,540	25,708	4,971,364
G	9,902	8,610	11,405	26,174	5,346,827

Last To Die Age 65

Insurance Company	Current Mortality Current Interest	Current Mortality Current Interest +1%	Current Mortality Current Interest -1%	Guaranteed Mortality Guaranteed Interest	Death Benefit at age 100 based on guaranteed premium at current interest and mortality
F	10,890	9,478	12,263	n/a	n/a
C	10,967	9,889	12,229	15,690	1,716,061
D	11,259	10,159	12,503	33,347	3,377,716
E	11,652	11,090	13,082	33,850	4,463,789
A	12,076	11,986	13,474	34,297	4,747,245
H	12,387	12,387	13,469	37,437	4,278,594
B	13,719	13,021	14,492	34,811	4,463,597
G	13,903	12,560	15,603	35,358	4,855,604

$1,000,000 Death Benefit based on

Last To Die Age 70

Insurance Company	Current Mortality Current Interest	Current Mortality Current Interest +1%	Current Mortality Current Interest -1%	Guaranteed Mortality Guaranteed Interest	Death Benefit at age 100 based on guaranteed premium at current interest and mortality
C	15,490	15,490	16,578	20,730	1,392,336
D	16,139	14,399	16,868	44,762	3,221,827
H	17,032	15,580	18,806	49,896	3,982,919
B	17,404	16,789	18,071	48,086	4,175,745
A	17,843	17,843	19,064	46,197	4,287,045
E	18,090	18,090	18,090	46,089	4,140,633
G	19,757	18,560	21,608	48,501	4,421,092

Last To Die Age 75

Insurance Company	Current Mortality Current Interest	Current Mortality Current Interest +1%	Current Mortality Current Interest -1%	Guaranteed Mortality Guaranteed Interest	Death Benefit at age 100 based on guaranteed premium at current interest and mortality
D	21,311	20,149	22,570	60,745	3,062,355
H	24,275	22,492	26,216	67,692	3,721,421
G	26,661	24,880	28,586	67,448	4,086,092
E	27,090	27,090	27,090	64,126	3,844,490
B	29,448	28,629	30,310	67,431	3,774,286

Life Payment Premium for $1,000,000 Death Benefit based on

Last To Die Age 80

Insurance Company	Current Mortality Current Interest	Current Mortality Current Interest +1%	Current Mortality Current Interest -1%	Guaranteed Mortality Guaranteed Interest	Death Benefit at age 100 based on guaranteed premium at current interest and mortality
D	28,691	27,689	29,760	81,850	2,794,676
G	34,087	32,501	35,769	96,209	3,711,951
H	35,563	33,607	37,651	93,250	3,420,628
E	38,090	38,090	38,090	90,417	3,491,912
A	44,543	41,823	47,144	88,039	3,268,625
B	48,439	47,456	49,450	96,039	3,366,705
C	56,160	56,160	56,160	61,740	1,540,029

Last To Die Age 85

Insurance Company	Current Mortality Current Interest	Current Mortality Current Interest +1%	Current Mortality Current Interest -1%	Guaranteed Mortality Guaranteed Interest	Death Benefit at age 100 based on guaranteed premium at current interest and mortality
D	45,085	43,801	46,425	103,243	2,200,605
H	52,150	50,075	54,331	129,327	3,030,006

Federal Estate Tax Table

Asset	Tax	Asset	Tax
$ 1,000,000	$ 153,000	$ 11,000,000	$ 5,480,000
1,100,000	194,000	12,000,000	6,148,000
1,200,000	235,000	13,000,000	6,748,000
1,300,000	277,000	14,000,000	7,348,000
1,400,000	320,000	15,000,000	7,948,000
1,500,000	363,000	16,000,000	8,548,000
1,600,000	408,000	17,000,000	9,148,000
1,700,000	453,000	18,000,000	9,748,000
1,800,000	498,000	19,000,000	10,348,000
1,900,000	543,000	20,000,000	10,948,000
2,000,000	588,000	21,000,000	11,548,000
2,100,000	637,000	22,000,100	12,100,000
2,200,000	686,000	23,000,000	12,650,000
2,300,000	735,000	24,000,000	13,200,000
2,400,000	784,000	25,000,000	13,750,000
2,500,000	833,000	26,000,000	14,300,000
2,600,000	886,000	27,000,000	14,850,000
2,700,000	939,000	28,000,000	15,400,000
2,800,000	992,000	29,000,000	15,950,000
2,900,000	1,045,000	30,000,000	16,500,000
3,000,000	1,098,000	31,000,000	17,050,000
3,100,000	1,153,000	32,000,000	17,600,000
3,200,000	1,208,000	33,000,000	18,150,000
3,300,000	1,263,000	34,000,000	18,700,000
3,400,000	1,318,000	35,000,000	19,250,000
3,500,000	1,373,000	36,000,000	19,800,000
3,600,000	1,428,000	37,000,000	20,350,000
3,700,000	1,483,000	38,000,000	20,900,000
3,800,000	1,538,000	39,000,000	21,450,000
3,900,000	1,593,000	40,000,000	22,000,000
4,000,000	1,648,000	45,000,000	24,750,000
4,500,000	1,923,000	50,000,000	27,500,000
5,000,000	2,198,000	55,000,000	30,250,000
5,500,000	2,473,000	60,000,000	33,000,000
6,000,000	2,748,000	65,000,000	35,750,000
6,500,000	3,023,000	70,000,000	38,500,000
7,000,000	3,298,000	75,000,000	41,250,000
7,500,000	3,573,000	80,000,000	44,000,000
8,000,000	3,848,000	85,000,000	46,750,000
8,500,000	4,123,000	90,000,000	49,500,000
9,000,000	4,398,000	95,000,000	52,250,000
9,500,000	4,673,000	100,000,000	55,000,000
10,000,000	4,948,000	105,000,000	57,750,000

1980 Commissioners Standard
Ordinary Mortality Table

Life Expectancy in Years

Age	Male	Female	Age	Male	Female	Age	Male	Femal
0	70.83	75.83	34	39.54	43.91	67	12.76	15.83
1	70.13	75.04	35	38.61	42.98	68	12.14	15.10
2	69.20	74.11	36	37.69	42.05	69	11.54	14.38
3	68.27	73.17	37	36.78	41.12	70	10.96	13.67
4	67.34	72.23	38	35.87	40.20	71	10.39	12.97
5	66.40	71.28	39	34.96	39.28	72	9.84	12.26
6	65.46	70.34	40	34.05	38.36	73	9.30	11.60
7	64.52	69.39	41	33.16	37.46	74	8.79	10.95
8	63.57	68.44	42	32.26	36.55	75	8.31	10.32
9	62.62	67.48	43	31.38	35.66	76	7.84	9.71
10	61.66	66.53	44	30.50	34.77	77	7.40	9.12
11	60.71	65.58	45	29.62	33.88	78	6.97	8.55
12	58.75	64.62	46	28.76	33.00	79	6.57	8.01
13	58.80	63.67	47	27.90	32.12	80	6.18	7.48
14	57.86	62.71	48	27.04	31.25	81	5.80	6.98
15	56.93	61.76	49	26.20	30.39	82	5.44	6.49
16	56.00	60.82	50	25.36	29.53	83	5.09	6.03
17	55.09	59.87	51	24.52	28.67	84	4.77	5.59
18	54.18	58.93	52	23.70	27.82	85	4.46	5.18
19	53.27	57.98	53	22.89	26.98	86	4.18	4.80
20	52.37	57.04	54	22.08	26.14	87	3.91	4.43
21	51.47	56.10	55	21.29	25.31	88	3.66	4.09
22	50.57	55.16	56	20.51	24.49	89	3.41	3.77
23	49.66	54.22	57	19.74	23.67	90	3.18	3.45
24	48.75	53.28	58	18.99	22.86	91	2.94	3.15
25	47.84	52.34	59	18.24	22.05	92	2.70	2.85
26	46.93	51.40	60	17.51	21.25	93	2.44	2.55
27	46.01	50.46	61	16.79	20.44	94	2.17	2.24
28	45.09	49.52	62	16.08	19.65	95	1.87	1.91
29	44.16	48.59	63	15.38	18.86	96	1.54	1.56
30	43.24	47.65	64	14.70	18.08	97	1.20	1.21
31	42.31	46.71	65	14.04	17.32	98	0.84	0.84
32	41.38	45.78	66	13.39	16.57	99	0.50	0.50
33	40.46	44.84						

Deaths Per Thousand At Various Ages
1980 Commissioners Standard
Ordinary Mortality Table

Number Expected to Die Each Year

Age	Males Per 1,000	Females Per 1,000	Age	Males Per 1,000	Females Per 1,000	Age	Males Per 1,000	Females Per 1,000
0	4.18	2.89	34	2.00	1.58	67	30.44	17.43
1	1.07	.87	35	2.11	1.65	68	33.19	18.84
2	.99	.81	36	2.24	1.76	69	36.17	20.36
3	.98	.79	37	2.40	1.89	70	39.51	22.11
4	.95	.77	38	2.58	2.04	71	43.30	24.23
5	.90	.76	39	2.79	2.22	72	47.65	26.87
6	.85	.73	40	3.02	2.42	73	52.64	30.11
7	.80	.72	41	3.29	2.64	74	58.19	33.93
8	.76	.70	42	3.56	2.87	75	64.19	38.24
9	.74	.69	43	3.87	3.09	76	70.53	42.97
10	.73	.68	44	4.96	3.32	77	77.12	48.04
11	.77	.69	45	4.55	3.56	78	83.90	53.45
12	.85	.72	46	4.92	3.80	79	91.05	59.35
13	.99	.75	47	5.32	4.05	80	98.84	65.99
14	1.15	.80	48	5.74	4.33	81	107.48	73.60
15	1.33	.85	49	6.21	4.63	82	117.25	82.40
16	1.51	.90	50	6.71	4.96	83	128.26	92.53
17	1.67	.95	51	7.30	5.31	84	140.25	103.81
18	1.78	.98	52	7.96	5.70	85	152.95	116.10
19	1.86	1.02	53	8.71	6.15	86	166.09	129.29
20	1.90	1.05	54	9.56	6.61	87	179.55	143.32
21	1.91	1.07	55	10.47	7.09	88	193.27	158.18
22	1.89	1.09	56	11.46	7.57	89	207.29	173.94
23	1.86	1.11	57	12.49	8.03	90	221.77	190.75
24	1.82	1.14	58	13.59	8.47	91	236.98	208.87
25	1.77	1.16	59	14.77	8.94	92	253.45	228.81
26	1.73	1.19	60	16.08	9.47	93	272.11	251.51
27	1.71	1.22	61	17.54	10.13	94	295.90	279.31
28	1.70	1.26	62	19.19	10.96	95	329.96	317.32
29	1.71	1.30	63	21.06	12.02	96	384.55	375.74
30	1.73	1.35	64	23.14	13.25	97	480.20	474.97
31	1.78	1.40	65	25.42	14.59	98	657.98	655.85
32	1.83	1.45	66	27.85	16.00	99	1000.00	1000.00
33	1.91	1.50						

The Chance Of Dying Before Age 65[1]

From a group of 1,000 persons your age, the chart below illustrates the number who will still be alive at age 65. The third column indicates the probability that you will not be aliv at age 65.

From 1,000 Males			From 1,000 Females		
Age at Last Birthday	Number Still Alive at 65	Chance of Not Being Alive	Age at Last Birthday	Number Still Alive at 65	Chance of Not Being Alive
30	755	25%	30	832	17%
31	757	24%	31	833	17%
32	759	24%	32	834	17%
33	761	24%	33	835	17%
34	763	24%:	34	836	16%
35	764	24%	35	837	16%
36	766	23%	36	834	16%
37	767	23%	37	841	16%
38	769	23%	38	843	16%
39	772	23%	39	845	16%
40	773	23%	40	847	15%
41	775	23%	41	850	15%
42	778	22%	42	853	15%
43	780	22%	43	855	15%
44	784	22%	44	858	14%
45	787	21%	45	860	14%
46	791	21%	46	863	14%
47	795	21%	47	867	13%
48	800	20%	48	871	13%
49	805	20%	49	875	13%
50	810	19%	50	879	12%
51	816	18%	51	882	12%
52	823	18%	52	886	11%
53	829	17%	53	892	11%
54	835	17%	54	898	10%
55	843	16%	55	904	10%
56	854	15%	56	911	9%
57	864	14%	57	918	8%
58	876	12%	58	926	7%
59	888	11%	59	935	7%
60	903	10%	60	944	6%
61	918	8%	61	953	5%
62	935	7%	62	963	4%
63	954	5%	63	973	3%
64	976	2%	64	986	1%

1 Based on Commissioners 1980 Standard Ordinary Mortality Table.

1986 Life Expectancy Table
Life Expectancy in Years[1]

Age	Male	Female	Age	Male	Female	Age	Male	Female
0	71.3	78.3	30	43.7	49.7	60	18.0	22.5
1	71.1	78.0	31	42.7	48.8	61	17.3	21.7
2	70.2	77.0	32	41.8	47.8	62	16.7	20.9
3	69.2	76.1	33	40.9	46.8	63	16.0	20.1
4	68.2	75.1	34	40.0	45.9	64	15.3	19.4
5	67.3	74.1	35	39.1	44.9	65	14.7	18.6
6	66.3	73.1	36	38.2	44.0	66	14.1	17.9
7	65.3	72.2	37	37.3	43.0	67	13.4	17.1
8	64.3	71.2	38	36.4	42.1	68	12.8	16.4
9	63.3	70.2	39	35.5	41.1	69	12.2	15.7
10	62.4	69.2	40	34.5	40.2	70	11.7	15.0
11	61.4	68.2	41	33.6	39.2	71	11.1	14.3
12	60.4	67.2	42	32.8	38.3	72	10.6	13.7
13	59.4	66.2	43	31.9	37.3	73	10.1	13.0
14	59.4	65.2	44	31.0	36.4	74	9.6	12.4
15	57.5	64.3	45	30.1	35.5	75	9.1	11.7
16	56.5	63.3	46	29.2	34.6	76	8.6	11.1
17	55.6	62.3	47	28.4	33.7	77	8.2	10.5
18	54.6	61.3	48	27.5	32.8	78	7.7	9.9
19	53.7	60.4	49	26.6	31.8	79	7.3	9.4
20	52.8	59.4	50	25.8	31.0	80	6.9	8.8
21	51.9	58.4	51	25.0	30.1	81	6.5	8.3
22	51.0	57.5	52	24.1	29.2	82	6.1	7.8
23	50.1	56.5	53	23.3	28.3	83	5.8	7.3
24	49.2	55.5	54	22.5	27.5	84	5.5	6.8
25	48.2	54.6	55	21.8	26.6	85	5.2	6.4
26	47.3	53.6	56	21.0	25.8			
27	46.4	52.6	57	20.2	24.9			
28	45.5	51.7	58	19.5	24.1			
29	44.6	50.7	59	18.8	23.3			

[1] **Latest table available in 1990 from Department of Health and Human Services. Based on expectancies during 1986.**

SPIA $1,000,000 Annuity - Life

Male

Age	Annual Annuity Income	Tax Exclusion Ratio	Non Taxable Income	After 40% Federal Income Tax	Net Return
70	$ 110,093	58.6%	$ 64,510	$ 91,861	9.1%
75	131,783	63.2	83,287	112,384	11.2
80	163,754	67.9	111,189	142,728	14.2
85	209,859	74.5	156,345	188,454	18.8
89	259,611	80.2	208,208	239,050	23.9

Female

Age	Annual Annuity Income	Tax Exclusion Ratio	Non Taxable Income	After 40% Federal Income Tax	Net Return
70	$ 96,284	67.0%	$ 64,510	$ 83,575	8.3%
75	113,625	73.3	83,287	101,490	10.1
80	140,743	78.9	111,046	128,865	12.8
85	183,586	85.1	156,232	172,644	17.2
89	233,674	89.2	208,437	223,579	22.3

Joint (100% To Survivor)

Age	Annual Annuity Income	Tax Exclusion Ratio	Non Taxable Income	After 40% Federal Income Tax	Net Return
70	$ 84,510	58.9%	$ 49,776	$ 70,616	7.0%
75	96,692	64.6	62,463	83,000	8.3
80	115,184	70.6	81,320	101,639	10.1
85	143,034	76.8	109,850	129,761	12.9
89	174,178	82.0	142,826	161,637	16.1

Net returns based upon life expectancy.

Call 1-800-343-7424 for current rates.

BOCA

Based On Current Assumptions

All figures are based on current assumptions of mortality and interest; any change could affect the cash value, death benefit or outlay as indicated on the proposal.

BOCT

Based On Current Taxes

All figures are based on current income taxes. Any change in the income tax laws will impact this program, producing higher or lower after tax yield.

BOLE

Based On Life Expectancy

All figures are based on current life expectancy. This term denotes a period for which the annuitant will be taxed on the interest alone. After such period the annuitant will be taxed on the entire income.

FAT - POLICY-THIN

The Most Insurance For The Least Money

Give the insurance company the least amount of money for the most insurance. Only if you are sophisticated and understand you have left no margin for interest drop. Any rise in interest can make a thin policy fat and a fat policy obese.

All figures are based on current assumptions. Charts are for illustrative purposes only.

INDEX